Exploding The Creativity Myth

RELATED TITLES

The Poetry Toolkit, Rhian Williams
Writing Your Self, John Killick and Myra Schneider

Exploding The Creativity Myth

The computational foundations
of linguistic creativity

TONY VEALE

B L O O M S B U R Y
LONDON · NEW DELHI · NEW YORK · SYDNEY

Bloomsbury Academic
An imprint of Bloomsbury Publishing Plc

50 Bedford Square	175 Fifth Avenue
London	New York
WC1B 3DP	NY 10010
UK	USA

www.bloomsbury.com

First published 2012

British Library Cataloguing-in-Publication Data
A catalogue record for this book is available from the British Library.

ISBN: HB: 978-1-4411-6637-1
PB: 978-1-4411-8172-5

Library of Congress Cataloging-in-Publication Data
Veale, Tony, 1967–
Exploding the creativity myth : the computational foundations
of linguistic creativity / Tony Veale.
p. cm.
Includes bibliographical references and index.
ISBN 978-1-4411-6637-1 (alk. paper) – ISBN 978-1-4411-8172-5 (pbk. : alk. paper) –
ISBN 978-1-4411-5516-0 (ebook pdf : alk. paper) – ISBN 978-1-4411-8868-7
(ebook epub : alk. paper) 1. Creativity (Linguistics) 2. Generative grammar.
3. Grammar, Comparative and general–Coordinate constructions. I. Title.

P37.5.C74V43 2012
401'.9–dc23

2012005160

Typeset by Deanta Global Publishing Services, Chennai, India
Printed and bound in India

For Hyesook

Contents

Preface

Creativity touches almost every aspect of our daily lives. Linguistic creativity is especially pervasive, both in our communication with other people and in the constant stream of media to which we are continuously exposed. This pervasiveness has lead to creativity being studied in a multitude of forms and in a wide array of disciplines by scholars and practitioners alike. Thus, creativity has been studied not just by psychologists, neuroscientists, linguists and cognitive scientists, but by critics, historians and even management theorists, while creators themselves, whether writers, artists, musicians or entrepreneurs, frequently offer us their own field-tested insights into the creative process. But even in this all-embracing swirl of disciplines and viewpoints, the perspective we apply in this book – the algorithmic perspective of Computer Science – can stick out as something of a gatecrasher to the party.

This is a natural reaction, since we are far more likely to associate computation and algorithms with the rigid, pre-programmed behaviour of machines than with the adaptive, freewheeling behaviour of real human beings. Yet, as I show in this book, the computational perspective is very much suited to the study of creativity. For this to be so, we must simply assume it is possible to meaningfully generalize over specific instances of creativity to arrive at a schematic understanding of what happens when and in which order, and of what resources are used in which stages of the process. This is an assumption that is made in almost every practical study of creativity; just think of all those books and self-help manuals that attempt to explain creativity with anecdotes, or that aim to improve your creative potential by generalizing over case-studies. But this is more or less what we mean when we talk of an algorithmic process: a well-defined sequence of tasks and sub-tasks that allows us to achieve a complex goal in a somewhat orderly fashion. There may well be a great many algorithms that lead to creative results in different contexts, and we should not caricature the computational perspective by assuming that there is a single grand algorithm that reduces the whole of human creativity to a few simple functions and procedures. Rather, we may have to explore many specific forms of creativity before we can arrive at any substantial high-level understanding of the phenomenon. By focusing on novel variation at the level of words and phrases, this book represents just one expedition of the many that will be needed to fully explore linguistic creativity in algorithmic terms. I hope readers will find the journey to be both rewarding and fun.

Because creativity is so often used to produce surprising results, there is a natural tendency to expect the workings of creativity to be equally surprising and perhaps even mysterious. But we must dispel the myths if we are to see creativity with a clear eye. The real surprise, if we can call it a surprise, is that the algorithmic mechanisms of creativity all follow from a common-sense understanding of how best to maximize the utility of our frequently incomplete knowledge of a topic or domain. This knowledge, in turn, is surprising only in its lack of mystery: as we'll see in this book, linguistic creativity does not rely on privileged sources of knowledge that must be acquired through intense scholarship, but on the kind of mundane, everyday knowledge – of clichés, stereotypes and conventions – that we all possess in abundance and which we all take for granted. We use this familiar knowledge to create familiar surprises for an audience, to concoct novel uses of language that depart from the familiar yet which are understandable only in relation to the familiar. We use linguistic creativity to re-invent and re-imagine the familiar, so that everything old can be made new again.

This constant churn of re-invention in language is nowhere more apparent than on the World Wide Web (WWW). With the aid of a web-browser, we can explore the old and the new and every shade of variation in between. We all rely on intuitions about what is familiar and what is novel to guide us in our explorations of the world, but when our intuitions concern language, a good linguist will seek empirical evidence for these intuitions in a corpus. A corpus is a representative (and usually quite large) body of text from which we can derive quantifiable observations about the likelihood and frequency of different kinds of linguistic phenomena. As a vast and continuously growing body of text and other media, the web certainly meets some of the requirements of a corpus, though it is far from ideal. Nonetheless, in an exploration such as ours, the positives do out-weigh the negatives, not least because readers can easily test the observations in this book for themselves, by firing up their favourite search-engine and then following their own noses on the web.

However, as I show in this book, it is not just humans that can learn about language by browsing the web. Search engines like Google, Yahoo and Bing are designed for human users, but they can also be used by computers to acquire targeted texts for their own purposes, on a much larger scale and in a much shorter time frame. We'll see here how computers can acquire from the web the familiar knowledge of language and the world that we humans take for granted, so that we in turn can gain a broader appreciation of the foundational role of the familiar in the creative.

Novelty only ever makes sense in relation to the familiar, and as will become clear in the chapters to follow, many familiar influences have inevitably left their mark on the substance of this book. In particular, the algorithmic view of creativity presented here has been shaped and enriched by many conversations and debates with colleagues and friends in the field, such as Simon Colton, Kurt Feyaerts, Geert Brône, Charles Forceville, Patrick Hanks, Bipin Indurkhya, Marc and Tim DeMey, Bob French, John Barnden, Mark Keane, Diarmuid O'Donoghue, Pablo Gervás, Amílcar Cardoso, Francisco Pereira, Geraint Wiggins, Graeme Ritchie, Tim Fernando, Josef van Genabith and my students Guofu Li and Yanfen Hao. My editor at Bloomsbury, Gurdeep Mattu, has also been a constant source of encouragement and sound advice. I am indebted to them all for their insightful comments and suggestions, which have helped to make the book much clearer in purpose and sharper in execution than it would otherwise have been. Finally, I am grateful to the readers of this book for joining me on this computationally-minded exploration of creative language; I hope that in the process you will gain a new appreciation for the familiar and often disdained elements of language – from clichés to stereotypes to dead metaphors – and see in these habitual forms the means to re-invent the familiar for yourself.

October 2011
KAIST, Daejeon, Korea

1

Creation myths

Separating poetic fiction from prosaic fact

Creativity is a topic that delights in mystery and which invites myth-making at every turn. Our popular conception of creativity is not shaped by any formal definition, but by hand-me-down metaphors and historical anecdotes. It's easy to see why: creativity exists in the interstices between our definitions, where it can circumvent rules and overcome constraints. As soon as we think we've hemmed it in with a tight, rule-based definition, creativity is already hard at work on an escape plan. Our myths and metaphors may be the only constructs that are stretchy enough to keep pace with this restless, genre-bending phenomenon. Yet we must handle these appealing 'creation' myths with caution, for their purpose is not so much the illumination of creativity as the enhancement of our appreciation of it, by emphasizing effect over cause, perception over process and mystery over method. We thus begin our exploration of linguistic creativity by roasting a few popular chestnuts, to find some facts behind the convenient fiction.

Elementary myths

Like the pointy-hatted wizards of children's storybooks, hidden from the world in high towers, modern-day stage magicians have every reason to jealously guard the secrets of their trade. Naturally they possess a strong commercial motive for this secrecy, for a loose-lipped magician can easily put himself, and his colleagues, out of a job. Yet the best magicians have a more profound reason to maintain their silence: magic evokes wonder through illusion, and illusion requires an equal measure of curiosity and ignorance if it is to succeed. All of a magician's virtuosity and training are for naught if their trickery fails to generate wonder.[1] Unless one has a professional interest in the craft, there is no bargain to be had in trading an outsider's wonder for an insider's knowledge.

Creative thinking can generate as much wonder and awe in an audience as a magician's best illusions. It too can be diminished by explanations that emphasize what seems obvious and simple *after* the fact. In trivializing the creative process, such post-hoc explanations can make soft-focus myths seem far more preferable to hard facts, as even Sherlock Holmes learns to his cost in the tale of *The Red-Headed League*.[2] In this short story by Arthur Conan Doyle, the great detective is engaged by Mr Jabez Wilson to investigate the titular league. On first meeting, Holmes performs his usual cold-reading of his new client, to note that 'Beyond the obvious facts that he has at some time done manual labour, that he takes snuff, that he is a Freemason, that he has been in China, and that he has done a considerable amount of writing lately, I can deduce nothing else'. This is false modesty, naturally, for Wilson is suitably amazed (Watson, for his part, knows better by now). But Holmes then makes the mistake of explaining his conclusions, noting for instance that the tattoo of a pink-scaled fish on Wilson's wrist is very much in the Chinese fashion. 'Well, I never!', replies Wilson,[3] 'I thought at first that you had done something clever, but I see now that there was nothing in it, after all'. Holmes ruefully sums up this lesson with the motto 'Omne ignotum pro magnifico', remarking to Watson that 'I make a mistake in explaining . . . and my poor little reputation, such as it is, will suffer shipwreck if I am so candid'. Why seek to provide a factual explanation of the creative act, when what an audience really wants is wonder and illusion?[4]

Jabez Wilson is hardly qualified to judge the merits of Holmes' technique, and Holmes is being kind when he later describes his client as 'not over-bright'.[5] Yet Wilson's response echoes popular sentiments about our appreciation of creative insights. Our most enduring myths suggest that truly creative thinkers should distinguish themselves as very different and unusual kinds of people, with very different ways of thinking about the world. But as demonstrated in the work of creativity theorists such as Margaret Boden[6] and Keith Sawyer,[7] scholars must look past the myths and metaphors to see the mechanisms that lie behind the popular rationalizations. Sawyer, for instance, identifies a wide range of popular misconceptions that only serve to keep creativity at arm's length, from the mystifying belief that creativity emerges from the unconscious to the romantic notion that children are inherently more creative than adults. Our metaphors of creativity are even more numerous and deeply entrenched in our everyday language. To list just the most popular ones, we like to think of creative people as rule-breakers, groundbreakers, pathfinders, trailblazers and revolutionaries, as child-like and eccentric as they are gifted. These people do not employ linear thought processes, but exploit quick-witted mental agility to pursue a non-linear path to a solution. They do not ploddingly converge on a solution by following rules, but divergently juggle a host of possibilities at once. Last, and definitely least, these people grasp the big picture, see the woods for the trees, think outside the box and colour outside the lines. Some metaphors have more substance than others, but all are perhaps more useful than the historical anecdotes that have assumed mythic status in the study of creativity. In spite of the most appealing legends, one does not need to be an opium fiend, an absent-minded streaker, an infantile vulgarian or an ear-lopping manic-depressive to be creative; neither does one need to be anti-social, unconventional, a high-functioning autistic or an alcoholic. Yet these are the kind of hooks on which – aided by the narrative demands of TV dramas and Hollywood biopics – we so often hang our appreciation of the creative individual.

Of course, if Holmes does suffer reputational damage for a willingness to reveal his methods, he is himself partly to blame, for his explanations are not as revealing as he likes to think. Wilson is right to conclude that there is no real magic in how Holmes arrives at his impressive conclusions, but he is wrong to claim that there is 'nothing in it', just as he is wrong to suggest that it isn't clever. While Holmes' inferences are far from miraculous, they certainly deserve to be called 'clever'. As the detective is always at pains to point out – especially to the long-suffering Dr Watson – his is a technique that anyone can emulate, with the proper dedication and attention to detail. Yet for all that, Holmes offers a most unhelpful account of his reasoning. Despite what he tells Wilson, he does not simply pay attention to the details of a scene to truly see where others merely look. It is more accurate to say that he sifts the mass of available sense data to determine the most telling details from which the most informative inferences can be drawn. What his explanation fails to make clear is how he determines which details are salient and which are not. When Holmes lists the few specific details that lead him to his conclusions about his new client, he makes it seem that the only details are the salient details, and so it seems that every detail is a salient detail. He does not list, or even hint at, the preponderance of other details from which no useful inference could be drawn. It only seems 'there is nothing in it, after all' because Holmes fails to communicate the most demanding part of the trick.

If Holmes is seen as a *producer* of creative inferences, and Wilson and Watson are seen as admiring *consumers*, then Holmes does a very poor job indeed of explaining the producer's perspective, for this is very different to that of the end consumer. A producer starts from the beginning – a blank page, an empty canvas or an unresolved situation – and must reach an as-yet unseen end through a process of creative sense-making. A consumer has the luxury of starting from this now-achieved end, while also possessing a clear view of the beginning. So what seems like a straight line to a naïve consumer like Jabez Wilson can seem more like an arboreal tangle of branch-points, dead-ends, retreats and re-starts to a producer. Were the consumer to truly put himself in the position of the producer, and set aside the benefit of hindsight, a very different view would present itself. As Watson tells us midway through *The Red-Headed League*, 'I had heard what he [Holmes] had heard, I had seen what he had seen, and yet from his words it was evident that he saw clearly not only what had happened and what was about to happen, while to me the whole business was still confused and grotesque'. The real story of creativity then, the story that the enduring myths and metaphors so conveniently overlook, is the story of how creative individuals navigate this frustrating thicket of potentially overwhelming choices. It is this story that will chiefly exercise us here in this book.

Despite his inability to replicate Holmes' results, Watson offers more insight into the detective's methods than Holmes himself can provide. Holmes, he tells us, makes such great leaps of deduction by chaining small-scale insights into a compelling large-scale interpretation: 'It is so long a chain, and yet every link rings true',[8] Watson notes admiringly. Holmes is so practiced at building these impressively long chains of deductions that 'his brilliant reasoning power would rise to the level of intuition, until those who were unacquainted with his methods would look askance at him as on a man whose knowledge was not that of other mortals'. This is an intriguing description, since in the popular imagination the notions of intuition and reason are generally defined in sharp opposition to one another. Intuition is driven by feelings, hunches and gut instincts and is for the most part an ineffable phenomenon. When we invoke intuition as a rationale for anything, we wield it as a black box whose inner workings are largely beyond our understanding or our scrutiny. Reason, in contrast, is driven by rules, laws and logical models of cause and effect, and reasoned arguments stand or fall on our ability to openly scrutinize their internal consistency. Artists and poets rely on intuition to communicate profound feelings and to explore an emotional truth that lies beyond the realm of objective facts. Scientists and mathematicians can also exploit intuition, but only as a means of speculation; the results of intuition cannot stand on their own in science, but must be buttressed with logical proofs or empirical demonstrations. In spite of such deep differences, the good doctor offers a means of reconciling these two competing modes of thought. Holmes is so practiced and assured at using logical reasoning to build complex chains of cause and effect precisely because the process has become internalized and automatized, so that it can operate without the need for constant, conscious control.

If we cast intuition in the central role in our account of creativity, our account becomes little more than a vague hunch about how other vague hunches might achieve creative ends. Yet if we cast logic in this role, we lose sight of what makes creativity so special, or at any rate *feel* so special. Sensations and emotions undoubtedly have as much a part to play in our understanding of creativity as in our appreciation of creativity. By reconciling these complementary forms of thought – opaque hunches and transparent deductions – we can allow that intuition plays a significant role in the creative process without conceding the ability to explicate this process in logical terms. Watson's belief that 'brilliant reasoning power' can be based on chain-building logical deduction yet still – with sufficient skill and automatization – 'rise to the level of intuition' is thus an appealing means of shifting the focus from intuition to reason, while casting aside all of the myth-making baggage that intuition brings with it. Moreover, Dr Watson's diagnosis also allows for the possibility of creative computers in the not-too-distant future. We'll see hints of what those computers might look like throughout this book.

Old chestnuts and new speak

Whether it is used to solve a crime or simply to impress Watson, Holmes uses his logical technique for essentially creative ends. By linking small but telling details into a coherent big-picture perspective, Holmes creates sense and imposes meaning where previously there was confusion and misunderstanding. His reputation for intellectual wizardry is built on the twin pillars of discipline and automatization: Holmes applies his methods rigorously in a largely automatic manner that is not slowed or interrupted by the dictates of self-conscious, rule-following thought. In the words of contemporary psychologist Mihály Csíkszentmihályi,[9] Holmes achieves a *state of flow*, immersing himself in a challenge without self-conscious concern for how it is to be resolved.

Automatization can lend our actions the assuredness and speed of second nature, yet it does not always lead to creative ends. In the realm of language, for instance, it is possible to write fluently and prolifically while operating entirely on automatic pilot, to produce texts that appear to promise much more than they deliver. In a state of flow, a challenging task can be accomplished with an almost joyful feeling of effortlessness, yet a creative result must nonetheless bear the fruits, if not the signs, of effort. However one measures 'effort' in creative writing, whether real or simply perceived, the reader expects to see ample evidence of the writer's conscious engagement with the text. Automatization can lend us speed and even fluidity, but it must serve the larger goal of successful communication if it is to produce creative results in language.

Automatic language is often unthinking language, and a sign that words have been chosen more for how well they influence our view of the writer than for how they influence our appreciation of the writer's meaning. This question of whether lazy language promotes lazy thinking, and vice versa, is one that greatly exercised the writer and political thinker George Orwell. In a famously polemical essay from 1946 titled *Politics and The English Language*,[10] Orwell notes that '[language] becomes ugly and inaccurate because our thoughts are foolish, but the slovenliness of our language makes it easier for us to have foolish thoughts'. English, for Orwell, was a language in decline, especially in political circles, but it was a decline that Orwell believed could be halted and even reversed. His well-meaning and entertaining essay presents a prescription – and a few proscriptions – for achieving this reversal, but not without burnishing a few ill-founded myths in the process. Orwell's essay is at its best when it *shows* us how to write, and at its worst when it *tells* us how not to write. He rails against the use of verbal padding and pretentious synonyms for commonplace words, and waves a banner for little England with his plea that we disdain the false grandeur of foreign imports in favour of the 'homely' Anglo-Saxon word-stock. Orwell's distaste for fashionable metaphors is even more caustic, reflecting his suspicion that metaphors like 'toe the line' and 'ring the changes' are popular precisely because they are fashionable, and not because they have proven themselves as effective carriers of meaning. Canute-like, Orwell hopes to rid the English language of the baleful tides of fashion, as though he believed language could be frozen in a golden age, and not allowed to evolve to suit the needs and tastes of its users.

What seems to irk Orwell most about these currents of linguistic fashion is that they rob English of its *Englishness*. In promoting the use of plain, unshowy Anglo-Saxon language that carries its meaning clearly, Orwell's protectionist instincts extend even to language that is ostensibly creative, albeit at a minor level. He notes that finding the right word in the right context can be difficult, as any writer can attest, and suggests that lazy writers who are unequal to the task are sometimes more inclined to invent foreign-sounding new words – like 'de-regionalize, impermissible, extramarital, non-fragmentary' – than to 'think up the English words that will cover one's meaning'. Yet it would be wrong to suggest that Orwell has set his face against linguistic creativity. It is more accurate to say that Orwell has disdain for showy language that sacrifices clarity to fashion, but that he sees no inherent tension between plain language and creative language. Indeed, for Orwell, creative language is plain language that is made to order, more like a fresh loaf of bread or a homemade stew than a pretentious ready-made meal that comes in a can. In contrast, uncreative language is larded with stale metaphors that have lost not just their freshness, but also their power to evoke vivid imagery in the mind of the reader. Orwell's claims regarding metaphor are supported by some of the most appealing and memorable examples in the essay, where he shows how potent images can be wrung from the apt juxtaposition of the even most mundane objects. Yet it is in his discussion of metaphor that the essential incoherence of his arguments about language becomes most apparent.

Orwell divides metaphors into three distinct-seeming categories – *living*, *dying* and *dead* – though the boundaries between these categories are not as sharp as he seems to believe. A living metaphor is a bespoke construction that is freshly minted by a speaker for a particular communicative purpose. A dead metaphor, in contrast, is a fossilized pairing of words and meanings that has become accepted as part of the normal fabric of a language. Such metaphors have earned their own place in the dictionary, and speakers may not even be aware of their frequent uses of dead metaphors. If the 'leg' of a table, the 'neck' of a bottle and the 'body' of a wine are all dead metaphors, then everyday language can be seen as a graveyard for the linguistic creativity of previous generations of writers. As one might expect, Orwell encourages the creation of fresh, bespoke metaphors wherever possible and is even tolerant of dead metaphors, though given their pervasiveness in language he could hardly do otherwise. It is to the immense rump of stale and dying metaphors that lie between these two extremes, neither fresh nor entirely dead, that Orwell most directs his ire.

Politics and the English Language sparkles with metaphors and similes that are fresh and vivid, such as when Orwell frets that 'prose consists less and less of words chosen for the sake of their meaning, and more and more of phrases tacked together like the sections of a prefabricated henhouse'. The image of a 'prefabricated henhouse' seems wonderfully old-world to a modern reader, and certainly quainter than it would have seemed in 1946. If writing today, Orwell might instead use the metaphor of a superstore flat-pack for some self-assembly coffee table, and rail against the IKEAification of language. But it takes effort to concoct your own metaphors, just as it takes effort to build your own coffee tables or, more realistically, to bake your own bread. Only the most zealous amongst us would have the time and energy to make everything ourselves, even in language, and we all rely on the occasional re-use of other people's metaphors. But these re-used metaphors are already in the process of becoming stale, and like a fish plucked from the sea or a flower picked from the garden are already dying. Of course, the area marked out by metaphors that are fresh and alive on one hand, and dead and buried on the other, is vast: Orwell describes it as 'a huge dump of worn-out metaphors which have lost all evocative power and are merely used because they save people the trouble of inventing phrases for themselves'. By the time a new metaphor becomes fashionable, it has already been allocated a place in Orwell's junkyard of old clunkers.

Choosing an apt metaphor is not like buying fruits and vegetables in the grocery store, and we can't simply prod and squeeze a metaphor to test for over-ripeness, as we would a melon. If you don't grow it yourself, how can you be sure of its freshness? Orwell has the answer: 'Never use a metaphor, simile, or other figure of speech which you are used to seeing in print'. The printed media contain a wealth of commonly occurring dead metaphors, which we can scarcely avoid re-using, so Orwell is really advising against the re-use of metaphors that are still living but which are over-used and stale. But how are living metaphors ever to become dead metaphors if they are not first worked to death? Metaphors rarely suffer a quick death, but age slowly in a process of familiarization and conventionalization that the psychologists Dedre Gentner and Brian Bowdle[11] have memorably named *the career of metaphor*. As we'll see later, metaphors take on new characteristics as they age, and the way they are processed in the brain most likely changes too, as they become more familiar.

Languages grow and evolve by acquiring new words and new wordsenses, and so the English we speak today is very different from the English that was spoken in Shakespeare's time. Rather like a garden whose soil is continuously nourished by the re-absorption of dead plants, language is immeasurably enriched by the constant absorption of newly conventionalized senses from once-fresh metaphors. When linguists and lexicographers and even casual dictionary users employ 'sense' to refer to the established, enumerable meanings of a word, they are using a dead metaphor that shares a common lineage with 'common sense' and our 'sense' of touch, sight, smell and so on. For the purposes of this book and others like it, we can all be glad that this once-living metaphor had the decency to die and leave its body to linguistic science. Though Orwell's essay is aimed at all readers who care about English, he seems content to assume that the job of working a metaphor to death is best left to others; we can benefit from the added richness after the metaphor has died, but on no account should we dirty our hands with this unseemly job ourselves.

Orwell believed that English was a sick language that needed to be made healthy again, but his essay conflates the symptoms of this disease with its cause. Yes, lazy writers over-use fashionable metaphors, reach for readymade canned phrases rather than taking the time to concoct their own, and choose words for how they make themselves sound rather than how well they communicate their meanings. But the converse is not also true: re-use is not always lazy or bad, and if done properly it can even be creative. Neither is a desire to save time and mental energy a bad thing, either for the writer or the reader. Creative writers often harness constructive ambiguity for their own ends, to create texts that reward repeat visitors and which yield something new with each successive reading. The most effective means of communicating a complex idea may involve the re-purposing of familiar metaphors and tired figures of speech – as when Christopher Hitchens said of the late reverend Jerry Falwell: 'If you gave Falwell an enema, he'd be buried in a matchbox'[12] – rather than the novel construction of entirely new metaphors and conceits. Lazy writers use clichés as though they were something to be proud of, yet clichés are not in themselves shameful, and an appropriate cliché can effectively frame the received wisdom that a creative writer wishes to subsequently undermine or subvert.

Orwell is scathing about over-familiar language because he also conflates semantic meaning with pragmatic intent. Writers use familiar phrases to evoke familiar meanings, yet these meanings can still be stretched to achieve creative ends. A recent legal case argued before the U.S. Supreme court demonstrates this point nicely, by showing that conventional metaphors can have very unconventional ramifications. In a case resolved in March 2011,[13] AT&T had argued that since corporations are viewed as legal persons under US law, AT&T is also entitled to the personal privacy protections that the law extends to real persons. The nub of AT&T's argument is a linguistic one: 'personal' is the adjectival form of 'person', hence AT&T is as entitled to 'personal' rights – as entrenched in familiar phrases like 'personal privacy' – as it is to 'person' rights (AT&T was seeking protection against 'disclosure of law enforcement information on the grounds that it would constitute an unwarranted invasion of personal privacy'). The court unanimously rejected this argument, and it did so on linguistic grounds. In a unanimous decision that recognizes the dangers of making blanket statements about language, Chief Justice Roberts wrote: 'We disagree. Adjectives typically reflect the meaning of corresponding nouns, but not always. Sometimes they acquire distinct meanings of their own'.[14] In rebutting AT&T's *person/personal* link with the counter-examples *corn/corny*, *crank/cranky* and *crab/crabbed*, the court was adopting a subtly un-Orwellian stance: re-use enriches a language by turning the novel and creative into the familiar and conventional, so one cannot presume the existence of a 'grammatical imperative' between words that are related in form yet which are free to grow along their own creative trajectories. As if to remind the plaintiffs that familiar language should not always be taken at face value, Justice Roberts concludes the court's decision with an ironic clip across the ear: 'We trust AT&T will not take it personally'.

Goodthinkful languagecrimes

The themes of Orwell's essay echo throughout each of the chapters of this book, sometimes in resonance with Orwell's views, but more often in jarring dissonance. For instance, the next chapter, *Enigma Variations*, explores the creative benefits of engaging directly with clichés and other over-familiar figures of speech. These much-derided linguistic forms are just another resource in the writer's arsenal, one that the thoughtful writer should not be afraid to use merely because they are so often abused by others. It is because we expect so little from clichés, and hold their conventionalized insights in such low regard, that the cliché and the worn-out figure of speech are the ideal vehicles for creative variation. For the myth that clichés embody the antithesis of creative thinking is itself a cliché, one that leads Orwell to a truly sense-defying diagnosis when he argues for a closed-mind approach to good writing: you can 'shirk' the responsibility to write well, he says, 'by simply throwing your mind open and letting the ready-made phrases come crowding in'. In Chapter 3, *Shock and Awe*, we argue that a creative writer is better served by an open-minded approach to the expressive possibilities of language, and so the more phrases that crowd in, the better. Clichés may have expected meanings, but good writers can choose to use them in ways that creatively exploit the expectations of the audience. In fact, this power of selectivity is the chief advantage that the creative producer wields over the consumer of the creative act, and in Chapter 3 we show how a producer can squeeze maximal surprise value from this simple act of selection.

In language, that which is timeworn is time-tested. A great deal of what we know (or think we know) about the world is acquired through language, so while individuals can afford to be snooty about timeworn figures of speech, communities cannot. Chapter 4, *Round Up The Usual Suspects*, explores the value of proverbial similes and other familiar figures of speech as inter-generational repositories of cultural knowledge. Far from being the dumping ground of language, as Orwell would have it, these forms collectively preserve and perpetuate a great deal of conventional wisdom that can be exploited in fresh new metaphors. Chapter 4 considers the wealth of stereotypical knowledge that can be harvested from similes on the World Wide Web, and shows how this knowledge can be put to work, on a computer no less, in producing new metaphors.

Orwell appears deeply suspicious about the ability (and inclination) of speakers to package ideas into neat, reusable chunks of words and meanings. He worries that a flood of ready-made phrases into our unguarded minds 'will construct your sentences for you – even think your thoughts for you', but as argued above, this presumes that writers exercise no power of selection over the diversity of options at their disposal. Were we to apply these suspicions to all levels of language, our speech would be denuded of all but the simplest words, and Orwell's huge dump would overflow not just with idioms, but with multi-morpheme words, compound nouns, phrasal verbs and all the other reusable chunks of language we take for granted. Chapter 5, *Pimp My Ride*, explores the means by which creative writers introduce new chunks into a language. All linguistic creativity uses language, but the most enduring creativity adds to language too.

Dictionaries, style manuals and old-fashioned grammarians strive to be definitive about language, but the only definitive statement that can be made about creative language is that one cannot be definitive, at least in any non-trivial and non-circular way. As George Bernard Shaw put it, 'the only golden rule is that there is no golden rule'.[15] Each of Orwell's pronouncements about good writing is thus easily falsified by a simple consideration: How might a creative writer subvert this injunction in meaningful ways? Take, for instance, Orwell's principled stance against disingenuous language. He argues that 'The great enemy of clear language is insincerity. When there is a gap between one's real and one's declared aims, one turns as it were instinctively to long words and exhausted idioms, like a cuttlefish spurting out ink'. Orwell does not explicitly consider creative language here, but he does it no favours by using propagandist language ('the great enemy') to denounce one of the most playful aspects of creative interaction. Creative speakers often use superficially insincere forms to more effectively communicate a meaning that is deeply felt and sincerely held. After all, most metaphors are demonstrably false in a literal sense, and exploit a gap between one's apparent and one's real meaning, while irony also requires a speaker to create a discernible gap between a statement's real and declared aim. In both cases, however, the sincerity gap is carefully calibrated so as to be recognizable to a discerning listener. In the words of researcher Sam Glucksberg,[16] the insincerity here is real, but it is a 'pragmatic insincerity' that aids rather than hinders communication. Chapter 6, *Six Ridiculous Things Before Breakfast*, explores the ways in which creative writers exploit insincerity and absurdity to get their meanings across in the sharpest ways possible.

A more productive way to view Orwell's 'huge dump of worn-out metaphors' is to see it instead as a vast flea market of second-hand language. Most things for sale in a flea market are so old and tatty that we could never give them as gifts, and this informs Orwell's intuition that the use of second-hand language is fundamentally disrespectful to an audience. Yet there are real bargains to be had in such markets, for shrewd buyers who are choosy about what they buy and inventive in how they subsequently use it. In our final chapter, *Think Like an Investor*, we examine the true second-hand value of all those timeworn and ready-made phrases. Building on Robert Sternberg and Todd Lubart's *investment theory of creativity*,[17] we explore the range of creative options that exist for writers who invest in second-hand language, from value investors to who re-invest in old-fashioned values to short-sellers who profit from the inadequacies of conventional wisdom. eBay exploited the World Wide Web to become the global flea market of choice, and we conclude Chapter 7 by showing how computers can likewise be used to wring maximal creative value from the language of the Web.

I want to believe

Arthur Conan Doyle, creator of the world's greatest detective, and Harry Houdini,[18] the greatest magician of the golden age, were contemporaries and one-time friends. Each in his own way was caught up in the wave of enthusiasm for all things mystical and spiritualistic that swept through the early decades of the twentieth century. Each had a similar deeply-felt reason for wanting to believe that the spirits of the dead could be summoned to walk and talk among the living: Conan Doyle had lost his son Kingsley during the Great War, while Houdini was adrift after the loss of his mother. Yet Conan Doyle, whose creation demonstrated the powers of reason and deduction to dispel any mystery and see through any fraud, was an avid and unshakeable believer in spiritualism and spiritualists, while Houdini, the show-man who specialized in miraculous, death-defying escapes, was equally unshaken in his belief that spiritualists were purveyors of trickery and illusion.

In fact, Conan Doyle was convinced that Houdini was himself a spiritualistic medium, who used supernatural powers to perform his feats of stage magic. 'Why go around the world seeking a demonstration of the occult when you are giving one all the time?',[19] he wrote in one of his many letters to Houdini. If the mediums that Conan Doyle had recommended had failed to impress Houdini, then it was because the magician was sub-consciously causing them to fail with his own superior powers. Doyle believed that Houdini used a 'dematerializing and reconstructing force' to escape from his various shackles, hand-cuffs, milk-cans and water tanks, which allowed him to pass through 'the molecules of that solid object toward which it is directed'.[20] How could the creator of Sherlock Holmes believe such nonsense? Perhaps he equated his own mental acuity with that of Holmes, so that his failure to see through the trickery of mediums was merely proof that there was no logical explanation, and that supernatural deeds were indeed afoot? Conan Doyle appealed to reason, not to belief, when he wrote to Houdini that 'my reason tells me that you have this wonderful power, for there is no alternative'.[21] Yet this was the same reason that allowed him to believe not just in fairies, but in photographic evidence for fairies, of a kind that would not convince Jabez Wilson, never mind Sherlock Holmes.

George Orwell closed his mind to the most productive techniques of creative language, for fear that their abuse would allow a 'catalogue of swindles and perversions' to be perpetrated upon the unsuspecting reader. In his dystopian novel *Nineteen Eighty Four*,[22] Orwell shows how the techniques of linguistic creativity can be used to cover up the foulest persecutions. For instance, the creatively named 'Miniluv', or 'Ministry of Love', instills love of the state apparatus through torture, while 'Minipax', or 'Ministry of Peace', preserves public order by maintaining a state of perpetual war. Yet the insincere inventiveness that Orwell condemns in *Nineteen Eighty Four* provides what are perhaps the most creative and enjoyable parts of a justly celebrated novel. Arthur Conan Doyle, in contrast, opened his mind to the most far-fetched interpretations of creative trickery, and became prey in turn to the swindles and perversions of unscrupulous mediums. Orwell and Conan Doyle thus represent extreme points in the understanding of creativity: The former was over-cautious and given to proscription, the latter was over-trusting and given to mystification. In many ways, Harry Houdini[23] offers a better touchstone for linguistic creativity than either one of these professional writers.

Though Houdini concealed his methods as diligently as any professional magician, he made no secret of the fact that he was a skilled performer of clever illusions, and not a true magician in the occult sense. He saw his trade as requiring a mix of 'mechanical perfection'[24] and theatrical 'self-exploitation'. The latter is the theatrical equivalent of Glucksberg's 'pragmatic insincerity', in which magicians use the trappings of magic to inspire wonder in an audience, but calibrate their performance so that the end result is appreciated as an ingenious trick rather than a supernatural feat. We know we've been hoodwinked, as we are supposed to know, and so we ask '*how* did he do it?' rather than '*why* can he do it?'. While Houdini's tricks relied on his remarkable athletic ability, combined with an expert knowledge of the locksmith's trade, his most astounded admirers still wanted to believe in more. His wife Bess knew better, noting 'it was Houdini himself that was the secret'.[25] Conan Doyle and his contemporaries believed in the supernatural – even in the face of protestations from informed practitioners – because they wanted to believe, and perhaps even needed to believe, and not because logical reason dictated that they believe. Yet in the end, whether on stage or in language, creativity relies on a mix of very human qualities that are not so mysterious after all: playfulness, risk-taking, discipline, deft unselfconscious execution, and above all, a willingness to exploit and leverage the expectations of an audience. These are the themes that we pursue in the rest of this book, as we attempt, Houdini-like, to wriggle free from the myths and misconceptions that constrain our understanding of linguistic creativity.

2

Enigma variations

Why it pays for words to occasionally take leave of their senses

An inventive turn of phrase can lend colour and intensity to the monochrome conventionality of everyday language. These occasional flashes of linguistic Technicolor appeal not just to the ear but to the eye – the mind's eye, that is – by placing words in surprising combinations and novel contexts to convey more resonant images than conventional language alone can muster. Yet, as we'll see in this chapter, a mastery of creative sense-making requires, first and foremost, a mastery of everyday language, with all its conventions and hackneyed turns of phrase. We thus begin our exploration of creative language by wholeheartedly embracing the value of novel variation on a familiar theme. Even in the most creative language, there is no place like home.

Oh, we're off to see the Wizard

The creators of Technicolor could not have asked for a better showcase for their invention than 1939s *The Wizard of Oz*. This film, a cinematic treatment of L. Frank Baum's classic children's novel,[1] demonstrated the wonders of the new technology by integrating it side-by-side with the monochromatic world it was created to supplant. While Technicolor was used to depict the most fantastical and dream-like elements of the story, plain old black-and-white was used for the drab world of rural Kansas, where Dorothy Gale, the heroine, begins her exciting journey. But the story really takes off when Dorothy is knocked unconscious and dreamily awakens in Oz, where Technicolor brings the world of munchkins and witches and flying monkeys to vivid, colour-saturated life. Everything in Oz seems new and fresh and even a little dangerous. Yet, at the same time, it all seems strangely familiar. When Dorothy finally awakes from her Technicolor dream to find herself back in sepia-toned Kansas, she groggily casts an eye over the familiar faces of her friends and exclaims 'you, and you, and you, and you were there'. The audience happily concludes that Dorothy's creative adventures were just a flight of fancy, but one nonetheless grounded in a world of very familiar ideas and experiences.

The cinematic creativity of *The Wizard of Oz* suggests a simple but helpful analogy for the workings of creativity in language. We can think of the monochromatic world of rural Kansas as the world of conventional language, populated by hard-working, plain-speaking people with straightforward and uncomplicated values. In contrast, the colourful world of Oz represents a creative departure from the norm, a flight of the imagination that reassembles our familiar experiences of the workaday world in a way that is fresh and striking, yet not so new and unusual that it cannot be fully understood or appreciated. Ludwig Wittgenstein, the enigmatic twentieth-century philosopher of language, argued that philosophers constantly get themselves into terminological muddles by using words like 'truth' or 'knowledge' (or 'creativity') outside of the workaday contexts in which their meanings are grounded.[2] As Wittgenstein memorably put it, 'philosophical problems arise when language *goes on holiday*'.[3] Befuddled philosophers don't do this deliberately, but whenever we engage in linguistic creativity, this is exactly what we do: we knowingly take our words on vacation, yanking them out of their everyday contexts to plonk them down in new and exotic settings. In these far off worlds, our words are more relaxed and more playful in what they convey, and show sides of themselves we do not normally see.

The meaning of words when '*on holiday*' must share many commonalities with the meaning of words 'at home', much like the characters in Oz share many similarities with the characters back in Kansas. Otherwise, we could not relate their meanings and identify the holiday version as a more colourful and creative variation of the workaday version (and philosophers would not get themselves into such referential tangles). So, for instance, when fashion designer Karl Lagerfeld describes his sunglasses as '*a Burqa for my eyes*',[4] we know that the word 'Burqa' is definitely on holiday, and that its vacation meaning must be related to its everyday meaning in some easily recoverable way. In this case, the similarities are both deep and superficial: Lagerfeld's perpetual sunglasses, like the conventional Burqa, are black, and hide what they cover from outside view. Both shield their wearers from the unwanted gaze of others. Sunglasses cover a small part of the human body, while burqas cover the whole face, yet because the eyes are so revealing about a person, each preserves the privacy of the individual. Figure 2.1 offers a simplified view of the salient conceptual landscape before it is reshaped in Lagerfeld's comparison.

In his *Poetics*,[5] Aristotle argued for a taxonomic approach to metaphor production and comprehension. The name or label for one idea, he said, can be applied to another, more distant idea, if each is organized under a common abstraction. We thus understand the metaphor by identifying this generalization and seeing the two ideas as interchangeable specializations with their own distinct associations. In the Aristotelian view, since sunglasses and burqas are both *wearable* objects, the pair are potentially interchangeable. The conceptual organization that arises after Lagerfeld's metaphor is shown in Figure 2.2.

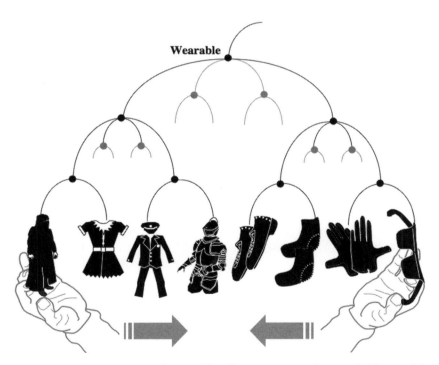

FIGURE 2.1 *The category of wearable objects, imagined as a child's 'mobile'. Lagerfeld's comparison effectively moves two superficially different objects closer together.*

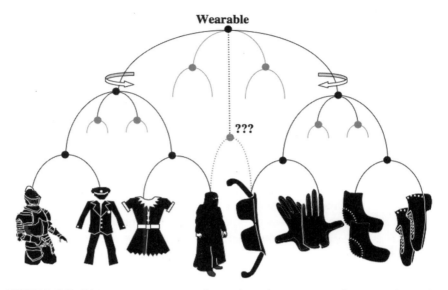

FIGURE 2.2 *Objects in mirror are closer than they appear. When two dissimilar objects reveal deep similarities, we may propose a new explanatory category to house them both.*

English doesn't provide us with a simple way for saying '*dark things that you wear to protect your privacy*', or with a word for denoting this mental category of things, but it does provide words for a range of its most evocative members, such as 'veil', 'burqa' and 'sunglasses'. Lagerfeld effectively uses the name of one such member to denote the category as a whole. In the process, *Burqa* and *Sunglasses* come to be seen as members of the same implied category, one defined by the specific features they have in common. These shared features are key to the success of the metaphor, for we cannot meaningfully describe X as Y just because they share a common generalization. As Cicero tells us in Book III of his *De Oratore*, a treatise in which the Roman orator fuses rhetorical technique with moral philosophy, 'a metaphor is . . . contracted into a single word . . . put into a position not belonging to it as if it were it's own place, and if it is recognizable it gives pleasure, but if it contains no similarity it is rejected'.[6]

A pleasurable metaphor exploits the fact that Y has obvious qualities that are also present in X, but in a less obvious way. In a relationship that has been memorably characterized as *salience imbalance* by the psychologist Andrew Ortony,[7] the comparison to Y helps to make these qualities more apparent in X. When words go on holiday in creative metaphors and similes, they go where they can make a salient contribution to our sense of another concept.

No matter how exotic the new locale, it is a working holiday that our words enjoy whenever we dispatch them on flights of metaphorical fancy.

Lagerfeld is following in the footsteps of Aristotle and Cicero, as are we all, when he takes 'burqa' on holiday, leaving it to us as listeners to appreciate its relaxed meaning in its new setting and its new category. For the most part we do this naturally, without ever being told how. Our secondary goal in this book is to explore the linguistic cues that let us know when, and why, our words and phrases have taken leave of their workaday senses.

Because of the wonderful things he does

There are no wizards in the real world, or no genuinely magical ones at any rate. Dorothy also seems to have brought this subconscious nugget of back-water wisdom with her to Oz, for when her dog Toto pulls back the curtain, the wizard of Oz is revealed to be a fake. 'Pay no attention to that man behind the curtain' he bellows in vain, as all the apparent manifestations of his pre-sumed powers are shown to be the simple products of pulleys and levers, a box of cheap carnival tricks operated by a crystal-gazing charlatan. Lacking the power to offer real solutions to his supplicants' problems, the wizard instead palms them off with purely symbolic trinkets: a diploma for the scarecrow who wanted a brain, a ticking watch for the tin man who wanted a heart, and a medal of valour for the lion who wanted courage.

Looking for the roots of creativity can seem like a journey into the strong-hold of a powerful and mysterious wizard. It is a journey that is bound to dis-appoint. Rather than genuine magic, we are likely to find a collection of ropes and pulleys that, when operated in the right sequence, produce creativity-like effects. Like Dorothy and her friends, we may feel cheated by the discovery, and imagine that the real magic lies elsewhere. Or we might feel that the creativity resides in some deeper and inaccessible part of the person who pulls on the levers and tugs on the ropes, rather than in these simple mecha-nisms themselves. Our search for concrete answers is just as likely to yield symbolic IOUs. Not a watch, or a diploma, but terminology and jargon and metaphors and myths that are intended to serve as placeholders for the real feeling of understanding that never arrives. We have been culturally trained to view creativity as a mysterious process, a force of nature or even a divine gift that is both a blessing and a curse for those it touches. Artists are supposed to suffer for their art, following their passions to the detriment of their health and social well-being. We encourage and are encouraged by the myth that crea-tive geniuses necessarily flirt with madness, and if we don't seem especially creative ourselves, we can comfort ourselves that it is because we are *too* sane and well-balanced.

There are many reasons to be suspicious of these cultural myths and metaphors of creativity, not least because we are all creative when it comes to language. Everyone is linguistically creative to a different degree, perhaps, at least in ways that are socially prized by our peers. But you don't need to be mad to make an inspired wisecrack, or starve in a garret to construct a good joke, or spend a lifetime in self-imposed exile to formulate a witty rejoinder. Rather, these examples of linguistic creativity are an organic part of everyday language use. Only a small number of speakers go on to become professional poets, authors or comedians, and an even smaller number receive any kind of widespread appreciation for their efforts. Yet we are all inspired amateurs when it comes to language, and we are all capable of seasoning our speech with occasional witticisms, puns, word blends, comic metaphors, colourful similes and cheeky analogies. No one goes to galleries or museums to see classic witticisms hanging framed on the walls, but some witty epigrams can be as conceptually subversive and challenging as the kind of idea-driven art installations that one often finds in museums of modern art.

A well-turned phrase can often appear magical, and elegant authors are sometimes said to 'write like an angel'. But there is more trickery and technique than genuine magic in linguistic creativity. Though he affected an air of what the Italians call *Sprezzatura*, the appearance of doing everything with a natural grace and nonchalance, Oscar Wilde worked hard at his craft, polishing and reworking his witticisms until each became a delightful linguistic confection. Each seems as light as a soufflé yet each is dense with meaning. Wilde preferred to have this hard work go unnoticed,[8] so that his pearls of humorous wisdom took on the natural lustre of the real thing rather than the artificial shine of the man-made 'cultured' alternative. If given the choice, who wouldn't prefer to be considered a sublime talent for whom everything comes naturally, rather than a disciplined craftsman who has to work hard and occasionally even break a sweat? (In this vein, consider Wilde's judgement on the dubious virtue of plain speaking: 'the man who would call a spade a spade should be compelled to use one'). Wilde's witticisms have justifiably stood the test of time, but consume too many of them in one sitting and you may feel like you've eaten a whole box of éclairs. Moreover, when consumed *en masse*, we begin to see the unifying conceptual and linguistic patterns that lie behind each distinctively phrased aphorism. The patterns can charitably be considered the application of a Wildean technique, or uncharitably dismissed as superficial trickery. In either case, the curtain is pulled back and an array of levers and pulleys is partially revealed. Wilde was a talented man who developed that talent through the disciplined application of technique and hard work. Like the Great Oz, or Harry Houdini, he burnished his image through theatrical self-invention, but was no less creative for being less than a wizard.

If I only had a brain

When philosopher Daniel Dennett proposed a new theory of consciousness in his 1991 book *Consciousness Explained*,[9] sceptical wags re-christened his efforts *Consciousness Explained Away*.[10] Dennett's challenge was to provide a persuasive explanation of how physical brains can give rise to consciousness by appealing to the workings of lower-level processes that are not themselves conscious. At some level in the hierarchy of mental processes a qualitative transformation must occur, and consciousness must simply emerge out of *un*consciousness. Creativity poses an analogous philosophical conundrum, and exposes our potential solutions to the same damning critique, insofar as any formal attempt to explain creativity in terms of the combined workings of specific, lower-level *un*-creative mechanisms might just as easily be dismissed as *Creativity Explained Away*. No matter how specific such an explanation might be, it will inevitably demand the same leap of faith: that the creative devil will somehow emerge from the non-creative details. In fact, the more specific the account, the less wiggle-room it can offer for this transformation to occur. Accounts that are so unambiguous that they hint at algorithmic realization on a computer will additionally require a leap of faith that only the most zealous advocates of *Artificial Intelligence* (AI) are willing to entertain.

An algorithm is any ordered sequence of detailed instructions for achieving a specific, well-defined goal, and the word 'algorithm' can be applied to any such sequence of instructions, from a recipe for *Eggs Benedict* to the best way to balance your chequebook. An algorithm can be as simple as the one we learn for doing long division in primary school, or as powerful as the *PageRank* algorithm that Google uses to order its search results so that the most authoritative sites (as measured by the number of other sites that lend credence to them by explicitly linking to them, among other factors[11]) are pushed to the top of the list. The execution of a mere algorithm is widely held to be the very antithesis of acting creatively, since algorithms typically allow no freedom of choice as to how, or in what order, their component instructions should be obeyed. This view is not so very modern as it sounds, and can be traced back to Lady Ada Lovelace, daughter of the poet Byron and notionally one of the world's first computer programmers. Lovelace was a computing enthusiast before computers were a practical reality, having designed algorithms for an early mechanical computer that was, unfortunately, never built in her lifetime, Charles Babbage's *Analytical Engine*. Yet Lovelace was also one of the first to articulate a strong creative prejudice against algorithms: 'The Analytical Engine', she said, 'has no pretensions whatever to originate anything. It can do whatever we know how to order it to perform'.[12]

Lady Lovelace's objection to the very possibility of an algorithm exhibiting creativity continues to reverberate in the sentiments of contemporary thinkers. The psychologist Teresa Amabile, who has extensively studied human creativity in an industrial setting, puts it most bluntly: for her, an algorithm can only be applied to a problem when the 'solution is clear and straightforward',[13] while creativity is generally reserved for those tasks that lack 'a clear and readily identifiable path to a solution'.[14] So algorithms are fine for robotic vacuum cleaners that follow a preordained path around your house, but don't expect them to get creative when they come upon your sleeping cat. However, while computers are algorithmic machines, and a large program like Microsoft Word is certainly an algorithmic system, there is no such thing as the Microsoft Word 'algorithm'. Rather, Word is a large accretion of many different algorithms for achieving many different goals. Word is an often unpredictable piece of software that has undergone continuous development by a myriad developers for decades. It is not a single algorithm in the Amabile sense, but a whole army of algorithms, with its own arcane chain of command and rules of engagement.

The stereotypical algorithm is neat and orderly, with a logical purpose that is readily grasped by the domain specialists who apply it. In this neatness there is no scope for whimsical behaviour and no possibility of doing the unexpected or the unplanned. Most simple algorithms that can be applied by a human exhibit these stereotypical traits, but when the stereotype is used to suggest that computers cannot be original, it becomes a straw man. What is true of simple programs may not be true of large unruly programs that grow in scope and complexity as they interact with the world and acquire their own knowledge from the web. These complex programs are certainly algorithmic, but they are not 'algorithms' in the sense employed by Lovelace or Amabile. Their complexity makes their behaviour in context difficult to predict, and in this difficulty lies their ability to surprise us. Most people think of creativity as a distinctly human trait, which is why we find it hard to cede the possibility of creative behaviour to a machine. Yet, as we gradually accept these increasingly complex and stereotype-defying programs as intelligent and unpredictable in their own non-human way, we may also begin to acknowledge a nascent form of non-human creativity in the originality of their behaviour.

If I only had a heart

For those who grant the possibility of an intelligent computer, most often it is a distinctively cold and alien intelligence that is ceded, one that is utterly lacking in human warmth and empathy. Some may find comfort in this lack of emotional intelligence as computers gradually chip away at our intellectual sense of selves, from beating human world champions at progressively harder games of intelligence to finding proofs that have eluded our sharpest mathematical minds. Computers may have the smarts, but humans still have the hearts.

This debate about emotion is both profound and simplistic, profound because it goes to the core of what makes us human, and simplistic because it rapidly descends into self-serving *Star Trek* clichés about superior human qualities. As so dramatically played out week after week on the U.S.S. Enterprise, these ineffable qualities make humans superior to computers,[15] androids, Vulcans, or to anything at all that prizes logic and calculation over empathy and intuition. The *Star Trek* worldview has even found its way into serious academic discourse, as typified by *The Emperor's New Mind*, the 1989 book in which the physicist Roger Penrose sets out his anti-AI stall and argues that it is quantum mechanics, and not mechanical quantification, that provides the key to human intelligence.[16] Penrose's book opens with a fictional prologue in which mankind has, in the future, built a full-blown artificially-intelligent computer named *The Ultronic*. A young man named Adam (a not-too-subtle nod to the divine origins of man, perhaps?) gets to ask the first question of this supreme mechanical intellect: '*how does it feel to be a computer?*'. The *Ultronic* is Penrose's Tin Man, and Adam his Dorothy, though a name like *The Ultronic* is surely the sci-fi equivalent of a black hat and a dastardly moustache, so this unfeeling computer is just as surely poised for a fall. While Penrose stops short of having the *Ultronic* spout steam from its ears while babbling 'does not compute', Adam's question hits its mark in a way that allows the human audience to howl with superiority-tinged laughter.

The cliché of the logical computer that excels in the intellectual realm but stumbles badly in the emotional realm is an entertaining if dated sci-fi trope. Many computer scientists are actually very interested in affective emotional computing,[17] and conduct research into allowing computers to better understand the moods of their users so that they may ultimately serve them better. This work has several interesting dimensions, from recognizing the mood of a user in real-time as he/she bangs the keyboard in frustration or fires off an email in anger, to recognizing the sentiment of an incoming email or an on-line product review. This latter dimension is a linguistic one, and does not require cameras or biometric sensors to evaluate. Rather, the sentiment of a text can simply be considered as a function of the sentiment of the emotive words and phrases that it contains.[18] In many cases, the goal is to assess the gross sentiment of a text – is it broadly positive or negative overall? – rather than to arrive at a nuanced understanding of its content. But research in sentiment analysis is also beginning to consider more creative carriers of affect in a text, such as humour, metaphor, sarcasm and irony (all topics we'll return to later). Computers need not always show a tin ear to the feelings of others, if those feelings are expressed – even creatively – in words.

If I only had the nerve

The Scarecrow and the Tin Man each lack a vital part of the human body, leading each to sadly conclude that they also lack the human qualities that correspond to those parts. The lion too is missing some vitals, though Baum departs from his anatomical metaphor to directly tell us that the lion is lacking in courage. *The Wonderful Wizard of Oz* is, after all, a children's book, and is no place for certain anatomical metaphors of an adult nature.

Linguistic creativity can be an especially risky form of creative endeavour, and humour, in particular, requires the courage to offend. When a young Muslim stand-up made her debut in late 2001, she opened her act with the line '*I'm Shazia Mirza. At least that's what it says on my pilot's licence*'.[19] To be humorously creative is to be brilliantly cruel, to use knowledge for the seemingly perverse ends of identifying and exploiting the logical weaknesses and prejudices of a topic or an opponent. Aristotle described wit as a kind of *educated insolence*,[20] in which a speaker is knowingly and creatively disrespectful. It takes nerve to stick your neck out, to laugh at power or to make fun of convention and those that adhere to it. Though cultural taboos make for easy targets, especially the big ones like *Religion*, *Sex* and *Death*, it takes bravery, or recklessness, to knowingly violate a taboo in a context that holds it sacred. Jokes about child abuse, rape or the Holocaust are much more likely to provoke a disgusted wince than a howl of laughter. Embassies have been burned and cartoonists have been forced into hiding because newspapers have published cartoons deemed offensive to the figureheads of certain religions. Less offensive jokes can also misfire, or even perilously backfire, since the most creative witticisms achieve concision at the cost of increased ambiguity. This is especially true of irony, which, at its most daring, is a linguistic high-wire act without a safety net. As we'll discuss in Chapter 6, speakers can employ a range of subtle cues to communicate their ironic intent to an audience, and thereby reduce the risk of being misunderstood. Nonetheless, irony remains a high-risk strategy for off-the-cuff creativity.

Gossip is intriguing and titillating, and sometimes shocking, because it tells us something we didn't already know. In contrast, creative language often shocks by reminding us of something we do already know, or could have worked out for ourselves. Formalists have the luxury of stipulating new labels for concepts, but creativity doesn't work by stipulation: a new way of saying something must yield its meaning in a self-evident manner, without explicit dictats from the writer. So creative speakers often use our prior knowledge of a topic to surprise and even shock us, by focusing on little used associations or valid but unconventional perspectives. The knowledge exploited in this way can be acquired from a formal education, but is just as likely to come from direct experience of the world, or from observation of how others use language to convey meaning. Creative insolence arises from how this knowledge is used. It can be used gratuitously, to suggest much more than the writer is willing to say openly, or it can be used contemptuously, to dismiss or subvert a jaded convention that may once have been fresh and creative but is now no more than a descriptive crutch.

Where troubles melt, like lemon drops

As discussed in the first chapter, creativity is a vague and amorphous concept whose boundaries are always shifting, from one culture to another and from one historical era to the next. As Keith Sawyer has pointed out, the word 'creativity' has not always meant what we assume it to mean today, and its meaning may continue to change in tandem with ongoing changes in society and technology.[21] It seems easier, and perhaps more helpful, to point to ingredients that are prized in many different forms of creativity than to try and hem all of creativity into a single all-encompassing definition. Thus, Beth Hennessy and Teresa Amabile note that a 'combination of novelty and appropriateness is found in most conceptual definitions of creativity',[22] which seems an eminently sensible response to the clear presence of novelty and appropriateness in the most obviously creative products. But ingredients alone do not separate a creative success from an abject failure; consider how little separates the world's best *crème brûlée* from the world's worst scrambled eggs. The real challenge lies not in identifying the key ingredients of creative behaviour, but in specifying precise thresholds and meaningful ratios for combining these ingredients, as well as a principled means of integration. Just how much novelty and appropriateness should a product possess, and how should they be realized, for it to be deemed creative? In turn, the means by which novelty and appropriateness are realized in a product raises a host of additional process-related issues, of which technique, finesse and concision are just a few.

We return to the means of integration in Chapter 5, when we explore the dominant integrative frameworks in linguistic creativity.

Even if we limit ourselves to issues of linguistic creativity, as we do in this book, the intersection of language and creativity leaves a vast territory to explore, and its boundaries are not always sharply drawn. This territory not only includes meanings that are given creative linguistic expression, but also includes creative insights that are expressed linguistically, which may be quite different things altogether. For instance, is John Lennon's observation '*Life is what happens to you while you're busy making other plans*' a true act of linguistic creativity, or does the creativity reside wholly in an insight about life which is then given a rather straightforward linguistic expression? A persuasive argument can be offered for either perspective; though not obviously figurative, Lennon's remark is pithy, witty and eminently quotable, and thus has many of the qualities we typically associate with creative language. But if we allow that linguistic creativity can cover any act of creative insight that is then given a convenient linguistic form, we are forced to incorporate a general theory of what it means to be creative into our specific perspective on linguistic creativity.

To avoid circular boundary disputes, our primary focus in this book is a sweet-spot in the space of creative language called *creative linguistic variation*. This sweet-spot contains all those expressions that are playful in their use of words, that stretch words or familiar phrases to fit novel (but apt) meanings, and which can be seen as pleasurable variations on a familiar convention, an entrenched stereotype, or an existing turn of phrase. We have thus exchanged one problem word, 'creative', for three slightly less troublesome words, 'pleasurable', 'variation' and 'novel'. Fortunately, this exchange does not require any semantic sleights of hand. Variation of a familiar form has long been a useful strategy for producing clever but understandable novelty. But novelty alone is not the purpose of creativity: one can generate random numbers with a set of dice, or a list of random words with a pin and a dictionary. Neither is *novelty + appropriateness* the whole story. A writer of fiction can name her characters by simply taking a pin to a telephone directory: one random jab for a first name, another for a surname, and in this way a novel but sensible character name is generated. A truly creative variation is a delicate balance of the novel and the familiar, of the appropriate and the inappropriate. If words seem to be in the wrong place, then they are in the wrong place at the *right* time. A creative variation is not just any novel combination of familiar elements, but a deliberate departure from a convention that is given a distinctive and knowing twist.

In essence, a linguistic variation is creative if it exploits knowledge of words (or phrases) and their meanings to shoehorn additional meaning and resonance into a tired form. Both the listener and the speaker must be party to the variation, for one must have the knowledge to know that the other intended (or can recover) the additional layer of meaning that is communicated. Remember Cicero's injunction that 'if it is recognizable it gives pleasure', otherwise 'it is rejected'. To be deemed clever, the effect of this additional meaning should be disproportionately larger than the effort needed to communicate it. For example, an early-riser is one who is '*up at the crack of dawn*', so a late-riser can be said to be '*up at the crack of* noon'. The variation here is simple – one time of day, 'noon', is substituted for another time of day, 'dawn' – and the description is more or less funny depending on the context in which it is used and the kind of person it is used to describe. Since '*up at the crack of dawn*' is a cliché, the familiar norm underlying the 'noon'-variation is easily recovered by a listener. With this norm comes the stereotype of the early-riser, a hard-working person who seizes the day with zest. The sharp contrast between 'dawn' and 'noon' suggests the received meaning of the variation should also undermine the norm; we thus construe it as a sarcastic description of a slacker who sleeps the day away, the very opposite of a hard-working early-riser. Likewise, the variation '*carpe* per *diem*' only makes sense if one is familiar with the saying '*carpe diem*' from the poet Horace,[23] and its common translation '*Seize the day*'. Only by considering the former as a playful variation on the latter do we see its inherent cynicism, and arrive at the intended meaning '*seize the expense account*'. The insertion of an innocuous-seeming 'per' changes the tone of the idiom completely, tainting the pure optimism of Horace and Walt Whitman (and Robin Williams in *Dead Poets Society*) with the grasping avarice of a Gordon Gekko.

The lexicographer Patrick Hanks describes variations such as these as *exploitations* of a recognizable *norm*. In his *Theory of Norms and Exploitations* (TNE),[24] Hanks outlines how a great many creative acts in language, including metaphors, can be understood as a controlled departure from a linguistic norm. Hanks' term 'exploitation' is especially apt here, since the speaker not only exploits the norm as a vehicle for a new meaning, but also exploits the listener's knowledge of this norm, as well as the listener's ability to reconstruct the speaker's newly-minted meaning. In her theory of *Optimal Innovation*, the humour theorist Rachel Giora champions a somewhat similar *something borrowed something new* view of linguistic creativity.[25] For Giora, an optimally innovative stimulus is one that induces a novel meaning (or 'response') in the recipient, while allowing for the recovery of a more typical response. She and her colleagues have collected persuasive evidence for the claim that listeners find these optimally-innovative stimuli (such as '*crack of noon*') more pleasurable than similar stimuli that are much more familiar (e.g. '*crack of dawn*') or much less familiar (e.g. '*break of noon*').

Hanks and Giora provide nicely complementary views on the workings of creative variation. For Hanks, exploitation is a means of revitalizing tired language, of stretching the meanings of familiar words and phrases to accommodate new but related situations. For Giora, we do this primarily because we find it pleasurable to be stimulated by novelty and variety. Familiarity can certainly breed contempt, not just for other people but for the over-used words and phrases whose habitual meanings encourage lazy, unthinking language use. But an exploitation can inject new life into an old saw, and make us think again about the relationship between words and their meanings. Whereas routine over-use can calcify these relationships, and make us feel that we as speakers have no say in how words get their meanings, innovative exploitations allow us all to put our own stamp on language, and to influence, in our own small way, the daily course of its development.

Simple variations

In the HBO drama *The Sopranos*, gangsters who become FBI informants earn the contempt of every right-thinking family member. The label 'Judas' is reserved for the most egregious of these turncoats, but *The Sopranos* gives us the following creative riff:

> What kind of person does that? It's like Judas or something. Eating that last supper with Jesus and the whole time he knows they're gonna crucify him. I mean, at least Judas didn't go into any apostle protection program. He hung himself. He knew what he did. (*The Sopranos*, episode 54, 'Rat Pack')

Though scripted by a talented screenwriter (Matthew Weiner, creator of *Mad Men*), the angry humour of these lines has a natural feel, and even the stand-out variation, '*apostle protection program*', seems spontaneous and uncontrived. We can tell immediately that the variation is a play on '*witness protection program*', an oft-whispered topic in *The Sopranos*, and a convenient cover-story for the disappearance of sundry villains that Tony, the mobster-in-chief, has surreptitiously done in. In any case, 'witness' is by far the most common word that can precede the pairing of 'protection' and 'program'. Looking to the web, most other words that can take this position convey a related perspective, such as 'informer' and even 'victim', but no other wording has a web-frequency that even comes close to that of 'witness *protection program*'. Intriguingly, the conflation of witnesses and apostles has a Biblical resonance: apostles are, after all, witnesses to a divine truth who go forth to bring this truth to others, while informants 'swear by almighty God' to tell the truth about a criminal conspiracy. So in a sense, apostles *are* evangelical witnesses of a sort, and the two ideas are largely interchangeable in a religious context. Indeed, if we again look to the web, we see that the conjunction '*apostles and witnesses*' has a web-count of over 70,000 hits. Since '*apostle protection program*' is sound on a semantic level, and purposeful but anachronistic on a pragmatic level, the variation seems both silly *and* clever, and prompts us to laugh at its silliness even as we admire its cleverness.

Some words, like the 'sleight' of '*sleight of hand*', or word combinations like 'protection program', are so distinctive that they are rarely found outside the confines of specific stock phrases. This distinctiveness makes these phrases an ideal basis for simple and recognizable creative variation. Take '*sleight of hand*', a phrase that literally denotes the kind of fleet-fingered prestidigitation practiced by magicians whenever they palm a coin or deal a card from the bottom of the deck. More generally, however, '*sleight of hand*' has come to mean any kind of deft trickery or skilful deception, as in the following headline from the *Guardian* newspaper in April 2010: '*David Cameron accused of sleight of hand over "magic" £12bn cuts*'. A magician's hands are his most important assets, but different kinds of non-magical trickery can exploit different parts of the body, metaphorical or otherwise. It can be jarring to hear '*sleight of hand*' used to describe acts of trickery that have nothing at all to do with manual dexterity, such as the verbal trickery of a politician or the nimble-footed trickery of a football star. Simple substitution, however, can be used to fold a more apt body-part into the familiar phrase, to yield a mildly creative and easily understood variation. Consider the following possibilities:

sleight of *hand*	(923,000 hits)	sleight of *mind*	(821,000 hits)
sleight of *foot*	(79,800 hits)	sleight of *wing*	(16,500 hits)
sleight of *word*	(482,000 hits)	sleight of *tongue*	(64,700 hits)
sleight of *mouth*	(27,300 hits)	sleight of *pen*	(60,900 hits)

The Google web-counts for each phrase (as of April 2010) are shown in parentheses. Unsurprisingly, 'sleight of *hand*' has a higher web-frequency than any variation that replaces 'hand' with another word, making this familiar phrase an easily recoverable home-base for understanding each variation. When it comes to making sense of creative variations, there is certainly no place like home. It's also worth noting that, at 644,000 hits, the common misspelling '*slight* of hand' has a lower web-frequency than not just the correct spelling, but the semantic variation 'sleight of *mind*' as well. This variation is commonly used to describe various kinds of mental deception or mind control, but has also come to denote the specific kind of stage magic performed by mentalists. Footballers and dancers can likewise be said to practice 'sleight of *foot*', though the phrase has also found gainful employment in describing magic tricks that, oddly, make use of the feet. The variation 'sleight of *word*' is usually reserved for those writers whose work requires them to torture words into becoming double-agents, duplicitously appearing to say one thing while actually suggesting quite another. Poets, philosophers and politicians are all frequently accused of playing shell games with language, of skilfully using words more for misdirection than for clarity. When the critic H. A. Maxson accuses the poet Robert Frost of a 'constant sleight of word – his seeming to say one thing firmly and absolutely but saying something very different, something vague and general and ungrounded',[26] his critique is itself a kind of creative variation on a variation, since we owe the variation 'sleight of *wing*' to Frost's poetic description of a thrush's grace in his poem *Come In*.[27]

Successive variations on the same familiar form make it easier to generate even more novel variations. For instance, '*sleight of mind*' makes it seem less of a stretch to coin '*sleight of brain*' (over 1,000 web-hits) and '*sleight of thought*' (about 200 web-hits), while '*sleight of tongue*' makes '*sleight of eye*' (over 2,000 web-hits) more plausible. In general, any new twist is grist for further elaboration in the variation mill, and if the change introduced by a novel variation is suggestive of yet another familiar expression, it may even be possible to merge both forms at the point of variation. When magician Harry Allen wrote his self-help guide to humorous stage patter for wannabe magicians, a combination of '*sleight of tongue*' (a double allusion to magic and language) and '*tongue in cheek*' (a double allusion to language and humour) provided the perfect title for his book, '*sleight of tongue in cheek*' (a multi-faceted allusion to magic, language and humour). Allen offers another title, '*sleight of foot in mouth*', for tongue-tied magicians with a sillier sense of humour. Other double-edged variations on '*sleight of hand*' are also possible. For those who would trick their bodies into ignoring pain, author Tess Lea offers the variation '*sleight of mind over matter*', while for those more interested in self-defence, a news release from the Russian Ministry of the Interior offers the variation '*sleight of hand-to-hand*' to describe how one citizen used some deft moves to disarm an armed robber.[28] Other variations that are, as yet, still looking for a good home include '*sleight of word of mouth*' (might this describe the way studios create buzz for new movies?) and the surprisingly overlooked '*sleight of brain over brawn*'.

Simple variations on a familiar phrase are easily understood in terms of the more familiar meaning, or the 'more salient response' in the words of Giora and her colleagues. Though often straightforward, this process of creative sense-making is not a deterministic one. The 'sleight of *[hand]*' variations above each allow for a spectrum of possible meanings, ranging from more literal 'stage magic' interpretations (using hands, mouths, tongues and so on to perform tricks for an audience) to looser interpretations suited to more general contexts of use, in which any kind of skilled misdirection or seeming deception is considered to be a kind of metaphorical wizardry. The intended meaning of each variation will vary from context to context and suggest different qualities whether one is talking of politics, poetry, sport or professional stagecraft. So the context of use, rather than any formal characteristic of the variation, is the final arbiter of what is actually meant. Indeed, some creative variations on a familiar phrase make no change at all to the original wording.

When Irving Berlin sang '*There may be trouble ahead, but . . . let's face the music and dance*',[29] he employed the familiar phrase '*face the music*' in two different senses at once. The first conveys the conventional meaning of '*face up to the negative consequences of one's actions*', while the second conveys a more upbeat message of '*enjoy the moment*' or even '*seize the day*'. The variation here arises not through formal modification of the phrase itself, but through the way it is embedded in a context that draws out the melodic meaning of the word 'music'. Berlin doesn't perform any word-switching in this lyric, but does perform some skilful *sense*-switching, by fusing the oddly idiomatic sense of 'music' with its more general meaning, that of a pleasurable tune. The simplest variations are often the most subtle, refusing to draw attention to themselves as they gently work their magic on us. More than any other, these are the truest sleights of word and tongue in our repertoire of linguistic trickery.

Enigmatic variations

Sleight of hand is not the showy, applause-winning part of stage magic, but the set of subtle skills that allow a magician to secretly manipulate his props. Though perhaps deserving of our most sincere applause, these sleights of hand are precisely the part of a magician's act that a professional least wants us to see. In contrast, the most ostentatious acts of magical skill are called 'flourishes', visual displays of technical virtuosity that are designed to grab our attention and make us gasp with envy. Each is important, but a good magic act relies on both skill-sets working together in harmony. Similarly, in linguistic creativity, a grand flourish is far more likely to grab our attention than an altogether more subtle sleight of hand. While an eye-catching flourish, such as a one-handed cut of the deck, is often just a superfluous gimmick, such flourishes are entertaining to behold, and provide a magician with an opportunity to show-off the technical mastery that otherwise goes unseen in the real workings of a trick. So it is in language, where creativity can be found in the low-key variation of a norm, or in an ostentatious flourish that stops us in our tracks and prompts us to look and wonder at its sense-making virtuosity.

Stupidity and pain are, from a humour perspective at least, the gifts that keep on giving, and so the state of being hung-over presents a great many opportunities for creative schadenfreude. Unsurprisingly, the adjectives most commonly used to describe a hangover significantly overlap with the words used to describe its main symptom, a headache, and include *throbbing, raging, blistering, thumping, cracking, splitting, excruciating, crippling, blinding, screaming, stonking, pounding, banging* and *crushing*. The adjectives convey, in rather direct terms, the perceived physical effects of the hangover on our heads, skulls and brains. Yet, though effective at evoking different kinds of pain, these adjectives lack novelty and mystery. In his autobiography *Hitch-22*, Christopher Hitchens recounts a tale of being dragged to a 'massage' parlour by the author Martin Amis in the 1970s, as part of the latter's research for a novel. Already sceptical, his enthusiasm for the expedition was further dented, he tells us, by a '*paint-bubbling hangover*'[30] born of the previous night's alcoholic excesses.

That a well-turned phrase can appear so effortless in form yet require such effort to understand only enhances the audience's appreciation for the writer's apparent ingenuity. Paint fumes can cause nauseating headaches, while 'painting the town red' is a common euphemism for a drinking binge, and cheap alcohol is often compared to paint-thinner, but these resonances are a mere bonus. The key to resolving a '*paint-bubbling hangover*' lies in identifying the more familiar phrase on which it enigmatically plays. Here is just one possibility. Hangovers, like severe headaches, are often described as *blistering*, perhaps because we imagine the throbbing inside our heads to be so powerful that it can actually raise blisters on the *outside* of our heads. Blisters are painful in themselves, but can also be symptoms of a deeper and more worrying affliction. Paint, like skin, can also develop blisters, especially if subjected to the intense heat of a paint-stripping[31] device. These blisters are raised by pockets of hot air, which causes the melted paint to bubble. A 'paint-bubbling' hangover is therefore a hangover that is so blisteringly intense that the equivalent intensity would cause dried paint to bubble and blister. When the curtain is finally pulled back, as Hitchens intended it to be, '*paint-bubbling hangover*' is seen to be a creative variation on the much more familiar '*blistering hangover*', one that paints a vivid mental image for a phrase and a meaning that have long lacked any visual potency.

These enigmas are not intended to remain enigmas, but are designed to be solved. Like the joke riddle in a Christmas cracker, or the free gift in a box of breakfast cereal, these linguistic puzzles often seem like cute little presents from the author. They are difficult to decode by design, but not so difficult that they frustrate the reader, or so cryptic that that they fail to convey their intended meanings. In *The Book of Tea*, Kakuzo Okakura observes that the real power of suggestion is not economy, where more is expressed with less, but engagement, so that the reader is invited to collude with the author in the construction of a creative meaning. Okakura puts it as follows: 'In leaving something unsaid, the beholder is given a chance to complete the idea and thus a great masterpiece irresistibly rivets your attention until you seem to become actually a part of it'.[32] Michael Chabon uses this technique on a smaller scale in his 1995 novel *Wonder Boys*, when he describes the preferred substances of his narrator as '*whiskey, cigarettes, and the various non-Newtonian drugs*'.[33] This enigmatic description evokes Albert Einstein's merging of space and time into a single relativistic notion, *Space-time*, which is often called 'non-Newtonian' because it argues, counter to Newton, that space is curved and the perception of time is relative. We can thus decode a '*non-Newtonian drug*' as a reference to the kind of mind-bending hallucino-genic drug, such as LSD, that can seriously alter the taker's perception of space and time. Chabon's phrasing casually suggests that the reader possesses the same intimate knowledge of controlled substances, allowing us to ground his metaphor in our own knowledge of this somewhat sordid topic. The effect, as Okakura puts it, is that we do seem to '*become actually a part of it*'.

Both '*paint-bubbling hangover*' and '*non-Newtonian drug*' appear enigmatic at first, yet are ultimately understood as creative variations of a more familiar expression. In the simplest bean-counting terms, '*blistering hangover*' finds over 2,000 hits on Google, while '*blistering headache*' finds over 10,000. The conjunction '*bubbling and blistering*' appears in over 3,000 web-documents, over 1,000 of which explicitly mention 'paint'. Similarly, the conjunction '*bubbles and blisters*' has more than 16,000 web-hits, suggesting that bubbles and blisters are conceptual soul mates in a painting context. This further suggests that 'blistering' can be replaced with 'bubbling' if 'paint' is also baked into the replacement as a modifier. Thus, '*paint-bubbling*' is born of '*blistering*' by way of '*paint blisters*' and '*paint bubbles*'. In the case of Chabon's '*non-Newtonian drugs*', '*space-bending drug*' appears in just a handful of web-documents, while '*time-bending drug*' is much more frequent with over 10,000 web-hits. This is not to suggest that Hitchens and Chabon use Google as a thesaurus (or as an anti-thesaurus, for that matter, to avoid overly frequent phrasing), or that writers like Chabon and Hitchens are knowingly algorithmic in their writing processes. Nonetheless, these raw numbers capture an essential truth about creative writing: even the most strikingly creative variations can only convey ideas that the reader already knows how to understand.

This is not to say, however, that creative communication is a deterministic process, for when an artist leaves something unsaid, an audience may fill the gap in unexpected ways. A puzzle may have more than one solution, and allow for more solutions than its creator could ever anticipate. Even in a tightly constrained cross-weave of linguistic expressions like a crossword, a solver can sometimes find alternate ways of plausibly answering some of the clues while still satisfying the inter-locking constraints of the puzzle grid. In such a case, where some of the answers diverge from the official solution, we would still consider the alternate solution to be valid. Indeed, we might even consider it more creative than the official solution, insofar as it represents a departure from the tightly scripted expectations of the author. Unlocking the meaning of an enigmatically original use of language has much in common with the solving of a crossword puzzle, but we should be careful to allow for the possibility that there is no single, definitive solution. An artist's primary goal in using creative forms may be to goad the consumer into a comparable act of intellectual engagement. When the Irish playwright Brendan Behan was asked by an interviewer to talk about the 'message' of his latest play, he angrily retorted 'what the hell do you think I am, a bloody postman?'.[34] There is more to creative language than the delivery of messages in a novel form, and it is often a convenient fiction to talk of these forms as having a definitive interpretation. Nonetheless, while we can accept some variability in how a message is received, and even accept that a creative writer does not always seek to communicate a specific message, it still falls to us to show how writers imbue words with meanings so that an audience can then unpack *something like* those meanings at the other end.

It's not too much of a leap to suppose that as writers try to put their ideas on paper, the most familiar expressions are usually the first ones to come to mind. Orwell cautions us to avoid the easy temptations of overly familiar phrasing, yet an opportunistic writer may recognize in this familiarity the seed of an *optimal innovation*, an imaginative new way of evoking the same idea that *exploits* the familiar form as a convenient stepping stone. When the Irish farmer-turned-poet Patrick Kavanagh wrote accusingly of his native land, *'O stony grey soil of Monaghan, You burgled my bank of youth!'*,[35] he used poetry to refashion a more searing indictment from the familiar metaphor *'you have stolen my youth'*. Expressions like Kavanagh's do not spring fully formed from the mind of the poet, like Athena from the forehead of Zeus, but must be worked and polished, often via a process of deliberate variation on less creative forms. The first words to a writer's mind need not be the ones that end up on the page, but they can serve as a vital bridge between what is written and what is evoked in the reader's mind.

Creative insolence

So, we can be creative with language by knowingly sending our words on holiday, to shake them out of their routine contexts where their meanings are habitual and virtually automatic, and to relocate them to new contexts that highlight and exploit selected aspects of these meanings. The word 'knowingly' is important here, as important as the word 'educated' in Aristotle's view of humour as *educated insolence*. The history of invention contains many happy accidents that have made their lucky discoverers rich and famous, but in linguistic creativity, luck alone doesn't cut it, unless the speaker is quick enough to recognize and take ownership of the serendipitous potential of a mistake. Our words are encumbered with a great many associations and expectations. It takes knowledge and insight to recognize that many of these associations can be downplayed, and others temporarily magnified, so that a word can be creatively used as a colourful means of denoting just a small shard of its habitual meaning. Recall Karl Lagerfeld's comparison of his sunglasses to a burqa. Though our understanding of the word 'burqa' is encumbered with a great many stereotypical associations about the role of women in Muslim societies, Lagerfeld's remark casts all of these aside, to temporarily accentuate the role of a burqa as a dark shield against prying eyes. Of course, listeners don't just forget that 'burqa' has all those awkward religious associations as well. Rather, they simply acknowledge that those associations are not part of the baggage that the word takes on holiday. Nonetheless, they *do* come to mind, perhaps not as facts but as feelings, and inevitably impart a frisson of creative tension.

Linguistic creativity allows us to fashion new and insolent meanings from the most unlikely sources, and words which seem perfectly innocuous in one setting can be cutting and cruel when on vacation in another. It is not a question of the words we use – the same words can be monochromatically dull in an everyday context, and alive with insolent meaning when taken on holiday to another. Rather, it is a question of spotting the opportunity to imbue our words with new meanings and new emotions, and of having the nerve to take these opportunities as they arise. It takes a brain and a heart, and nerve too, to bend language to our surprising new uses and meanings. Indeed, the perceived creativity of a new variation, whether to the meaning of a familiar word or to the content of a familiar expression, is often a function of its surprise value. The more familiar the expression, the more likely we are to jump to conclusions about its meaning, and so the greater its potential to really surprise us. Some variations – especially the humorous ones – are not just unexpected, but truly shocking. In the next chapter, we consider the different ways in which we might pack a surprising punch into our novel variations.

3

Shock and awe

Creating a disruption on the road more (or less) travelled

Creativity is surprising and refreshing and sometimes even shocking[1] because it is a fundamentally disruptive phenomenon. Creative thinkers achieve outcomes that often seem obvious after the act of creation, but these outcomes are far from obvious before the creative act. Producers and consumers thus play very different roles in linguistic creativity. A consumer comprehends a finished product, and works backwards from there to appreciate the creative choices that informed its production. In contrast, producers start with an empty page or blank screen, and must identify and pursue those choices for themselves. To understand the relative complexity of the tasks faced by the producer and consumer, we now consider the intricacies of the abstract search undertaken by each.

Hits and misses on the road to creativity

Our popular creativity myths have become the worst kind of clichés – the self-hating kind. Turncoat clichés like '*thinking outside the box*' urge us to disavow the clichéd and the over-familiar on our path to innovation, linguistic or otherwise. Yet thinking in clichés is not always the same thing as writing in clichés, and the creativity myth that 'originality is all' should not lead us to stifle the natural impulse to be reminded of the familiar whenever we try to imagine the novel. Rather, the most productive creators make this impulse work for them, seeing in it a steady supply of material for creative variation.

Andrew Lloyd Webber was certainly treading on very familiar ground when he decided to write a follow-on to his hugely successful musical *The Phantom of the Opera*, and must have hoped the result would be seen as a new lease of creative life for this now clichéd love story. However, the ill-fated sequel, *Love Never Dies*, was damned both by stinging reviews and by very faint praise of the 'not quite as bad as the reviews suggest' variety. We have all been bored by movies or stage plays or musicals that have failed to deliver on their promise to entertain. Besides a contemptuous yawn, we have many familiar phrases for conveying our boredom in these situations: we might say we are '*bored to tears*', '*bored to death*', '*bored out of our minds*' and '*bored beyond belief*', or claim that the experience is '*like watching paint dry*'. One influential theatre blog, *West End Whingers*, responded with a creative variation of its own, by suggesting a more apt name for Webber's new musical: *Paint Never Dries*.[2]

It's probably fair to say that more people have heard and enjoyed this creative play on Webber's title than have heard and enjoyed the musical itself. The phrase '*Paint Never Dries*' is found over 160,000 times by Google, and at least 10 per cent of these hits are about Webber's production. (The other 90 per cent are about real paint and D.I.Y. Some even allude to hangovers.) Each creative variation is a linguistic blend of sorts, a mixture of the familiar and the unfamiliar that conveys a new yet recognizable meaning, but the variation '*Paint Never Dries*' is actually a novel blend of two very familiar clichés. Webber's own title, '*Love Never Dies*' was a cliché before it ever graced the marquee of the Adelphi theatre in London's West End, and even served as the tag-line on Francis Ford Coppola's 1992 vampire remake, *Bram Stoker's Dracula*. That too was a tale of deathless love tinged with elements of gothic horror and the supernatural. As much as we might like to open their skulls and root about in their brains, there is no obvious way to retrace the mental processes that led the wags at *West End Whingers* to come up with their parody. Nonetheless, we can ask ourselves which of the following scenarios sounds most plausible. Did they start with the title, *Love Never Dies*, and from there explore the space of possible linguistic modifications until they arrived at a phrase that aptly and satirically expressed their critical viewpoint? Or did they start with the familiar phrase '*like watching paint dry*', which surely came to mind as an immediate expression of their boredom, and from this visceral but unoriginal phrasing seek to find a more creative variation that was also a variation of the musical's own title?

To a computationally-minded thinker, such as a computer scientist, a cognitive scientist or anyone with a passing interest in algorithmic complexity – let's call these people *computationalists* – these two scenarios are worlds apart. In the former, we imagine the creative producer wandering around a large conceptual space, each step yielding new avenues to explore and new choices to consider, all the while looking for the switch to that AHA! lightbulb. In the latter, we imagine the creative producer wandering around the same conceptual space, but this time the producer has a well-defined starting point (strong feelings about the play *and* the familiar phrases that these feelings evoke) and a well-defined end point (the play and its title). If it were a race, as it so often is in quick-draw wit, a producer who framed the problem in terms of the latter scenario would surely be the odds-on favourite.

We frequently think of creative behaviour using search metaphors. When seeking a creative solution, we prefer to not '*follow the herd*' but to '*explore new avenues*' and take '*the road less traveled*'. While '*looking for answers*', we frequently say that we are '*searching for a solution*' or '*exploring new options*'. When a search goes badly, we may feel that we've '*hit a dead-end*' and need to '*find a work-around*', or feel '*lost*' and '*need to backtrack*'. But if creativity involves search, metaphorical or otherwise, what exactly are we searching for, and in what terrain do we search? The most compelling answer, it turns out, is offered by computer science, where the search perspective offers a solid foundation for automated problem-solving. Indeed, the search metaphor is so conventionalized in Artificial Intelligence (AI) that it is often derisively referred to as *good old-fashioned AI*, or *GOFAI*. As conceptualized by AI pioneers such as Allen Newell, Herbert Simon and Cliff Shaw,[3] the terrain that is searched in GOFAI is not a physical terrain, naturally enough, but a *conceptual state space*. Each problem gives rise to its own state-space, where each space is an inter-connected topology of conceptual possibilities (or states) that a problem-solver can traverse from an initial problem description (called the *start* state) to an acceptable solution state (often called the *end* or *goal* state). Viewed through the prism of GOFAI, the key to intelligent behaviour in humans or in machines is an ability to quickly find a cost-effective path from the start state to a goal state. The GOFAI search paradigm, most famously associated with grandmaster-toppling advances in computer chess,[4] is thus viewed by AI researchers as the epitome of rational intelligence in humans and computers.

Though state-spaces are not conventional 3-D spaces, it helps to visualize them as such. In Figure 3.1, we see a somewhat whimsical state-space, visualized as a 3-D surface, with a signposted start state (e.g. *Love Never Dies*) and a variety of goal states, depicted as flowers. The footprints scattered hither and thither show the wanderings of a creative agent, human or otherwise, as it searches for a viable goal state (e.g. *Paint Never Dries*).

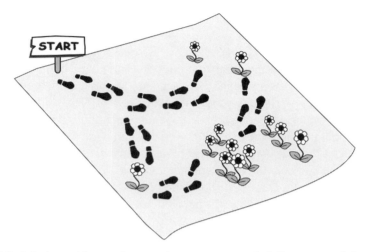

FIGURE 3.1 *A problem solver explores a space of different possibilities and solutions. The shoeprints show the path of an explorer wandering through the space. The flowers are valid end-points of acknowledged value, such as creative linguistic expressions.*

Each footstep corresponds to a different cognitive action, such as pun substitution (e.g. *Dies → Dries*), and yields a successively different partial solution. Only those sequences of actions that lead to a viable goal state are considered to be well-formed solutions. Note that the conceptual space in Figure 3.1 has a rather uneven distribution of goal states. For many problems, viable high-quality solutions tend to cluster together in conceptual space, while great swathes of the space remain barren areas for search. Elaborating the AI search metaphor into a gold prospecting metaphor, the creativity researcher David Perkins pithily refers to these fertile search areas as *Klondike spaces*.[5] As with the discovery of real gold along the Klondike river that precipitated the Yukon gold rush of the nineteenth century, the discovery of a Klondike space for a given problem can attract a great many prospectors to the same part of the search space, to discover a succession of valid but relatively homogeneous solutions to the same problem. As we'll see in Chapter 7, original thinkers often move on to new uncharted territories when a creative sweet-spot has become too crowded and too fashionable to support genuinely novel creativity.

   A flat and featureless space offers little or no scope for intelligent decision-making, creative or otherwise. Without discernible features to guide the search, our explorers are reduced to fumbling in an undifferentiated conceptual space. Fortunately, interesting problems have interesting search spaces. Though still a highly stylized depiction, Figure 3.2 presents a more structured search-space with an intriguing geometric quality: the space appears to fold

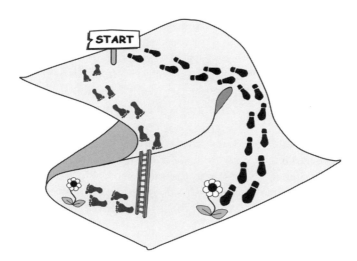

FIGURE 3.2 *Different problem solvers explore a structured space of conceptual possibilities.*

over onto itself, like a kinked sheet of paper. Such a discontinuity or kink can be viewed in two different ways by two different kinds of explorer. The first views the discontinuity as an obstacle to exploration, and effectively goes around it, charting the circuitous course represented by the shoeprints of Figure 3.2. The second considers the nature of the discontinuity, recognizes that it is not a hard obstacle but a potential *shortcut*, and formulates a means of exploiting this shorter route. The path of this more nimble thinker is depicted by the barefoot trail in Figure 3.2, while the thinker's creative approach to the discontinuity is depicted as a simple ladder. As a result of this insight, the second explorer traverses the space more quickly and efficiently, and as shown in Figure 3.2, is even capable of identifying solutions that a more conservative thinker might miss.

It's worth noting that each of the explorers depicted in Figure 3.2 acts in an entirely rational manner. Each is an intelligent explorer that reaches a viable goal using a well-informed search process. However, only one of these explorers – the nimbler, barefooted one – deserves to be considered *creative*, for only this explorer engages with the conceptual space to identify a novel or unconventional route to the goal. We whimsically represent this thinker's creative approach to the discontinuity in the space with a ladder, in part to suggest that this new route remains in place for future explorers. Those who follow in this explorer's creative footsteps will find a shorter path to the goal, but successive uses of this shortcut diminish its status as a creative insight. With continuous use, the ladder may even become an integral feature of the space, every bit a fixture as the discontinuity itself. We'll return to the mathematical qualities of this discontinuity later, when we consider its subversive role in the workings of narrative jokes.

For now, why should we care what computationalists think? The computational approach is reductive, to be sure, but it is the best approach we have for cutting through the mythology that pervades our thinking about creativity. Though readers and listeners (the *consumers*) must engage with speakers and writers (the *producers*) in the construction of creative meanings, the producer and consumer play very different roles under very different computational conditions when engaging in a creative act. Production is not simply consumption in reverse, and the processes employed to understand and appreciate linguistic creativity provide only part of the answer as to how that creativity is produced. After the fact, a creative insight can usually be explained as a collection of simple actions, knowingly performed in the right sequence to go from an intended meaning (and little more than a blank page) to a finished form, such as a pithy text. The consumer's task is to find the most sensible way of re-imagining these steps from a given text back to the producer's intended meaning ('so long a chain, and yet every link rings true', as Dr Watson might say). Though non-trivial, this task is heavily constrained by the consumer's expectations, not just of the text, but of the producer and of the world. In contrast, the producer's task is to find a sequence of steps from the intended meaning to a final linguistic form that has not yet been identified. The producer may well be guided by unstated constraints that derive from an understanding of what the consumer expects and of what the consumer can realistically comprehend, yet even when this sequence is short, the space of possibilities is still huge. In computational terms, the producer faces a vastly more complex search problem than the consumer.

While GOFAI search is inherently algorithmic, creativity theorists such as Margaret Boden and David Perkins have nonetheless embraced the notion that creative behaviour can emerge from the exploration of an abstract conceptual space. However, Boden argues that the most striking creativity arises whenever a producer transforms the space itself, to effectively change the rules of the game. For instance, Arnold Schoenberg's development of his influential twelve-tone technique challenged the convention that well-composed classical music must be played in a specific key.[6] In fact, Schoenberg created a novel system of *tone rows* to ensure that all twelve notes are given equal importance in a composition, so that none is so prominent as to be considered primary or key. Schoenberg's innovations were considered radical in their day, and were classified by the Nazis – along with jazz, of course – as *degenerate* art. In a very real sense, Schoenberg created a new conceptual space for musicians to explore, by transforming a space that had been so thoroughly explored by more traditional composers. Boden gives the name *transformational creativity* to this kind of game-changing innovation.[7]

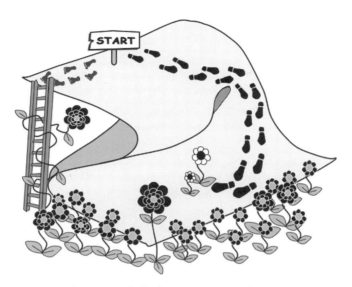

FIGURE 3.3 *A transformational thinker re-imagines the defining constraints and conventions of a genre, to create a new search space, rich in untapped possibilities.*

Figure 3.3 offers a visual metaphor for Boden's notion of transformational creativity.[8] A creative explorer, unwilling to explore the conceptual space as conventionally defined, decides to climb *outside* this space, in the hope of finding viable solutions of even greater novelty and value beyond the presumed limits of the conventional space. The solutions that one finds outside the conventional space may have markedly different qualities than the solutions explorers have traditionally found inside the space. As in Schoenberg's case, it then becomes necessary to 'sell' these new kinds of solutions to a skeptical audience. We'll consider such a *buying and selling* model of creativity in the last chapter.

Of course, non-transformational exploration, or what Boden calls *exploratory creativity*, can also yield very satisfying results. A gifted chess player, for instance, can formulate creative strategies without changing the rules of chess, and we owe the music of Mozart to his relatively narrow but wonderfully productive exploration of the space of tonal music. However, given the immensity of the search space for even simple-seeming problems, producers cannot afford to be ploddingly exhaustive in their search, and must bring as many constraints to bear on their explorations as possible. It is in the use of such constraints to cut away great swathes of the search space and to identify other areas as potential sweet-spots (or *Klondikes*) for creativity, that the computational perspective comes closest to providing a concrete basis for such metaphysical notions as insight and inspiration. For linguistic producers do have one key advantage over linguistic consumers: they know *before* the creative act the meanings they want to communicate, and also appreciate the full range of feelings and resonances that their linguistic forms are intended to evoke in the consumer. This diverse collection of conflicting constraints may well fight each other for dominance, but if properly harnessed, these constraints can collectively exert a coherent influence on the choice of conceptual and linguistic pathways that are explored by the creative producer.

The key to cooperation lies in viewing constraints as *soft* preferences rather than *hard* demands. In this way, conflicting constraints can avoid deadlock by nudging the producer's exploratory processes towards those paths of least resistance where the smallest number of constraints are violated. Such a view of creativity – which can aptly be described as the 'constraints welcome!' view – has been championed by Douglas Hofstadter, a physicist turned cognitive (and computer) scientist who argues that the interaction of competing pressures and constraints is the means by which creativity produces such diverse and unexpected results.[9] Robert Frost compared the disorientating lack of formal constraints when writing free verse to playing tennis with the net down,[10] while Orson Welles once described the absence of constraints as 'the enemy of art'.[11] Hofstadter would surely agree; he has argued, from a literary and a computational perspective, that the interlocking constraints of metre and rhyme allow both humans and computers to more effectively navigate the space of creative poetic expression.[12] Constraints are a necessary part of any satisfying challenge, and though they may often seem a nuisance, in creativity they are a blessing: not only do they help us negotiate immense search spaces, they can make the results of our explorations seem rich with secondary meanings, clever resonances and semantic tension.

When solving a problem, it is reassuring to have a time-tested plan of attack as well as an agreed definition of what constitutes a good or even optimal solution. Nonetheless, exploration of a complex search space can be a *divergent* process, much like beheading a Hydra: each head we cut off may lead the beast to grow several more in its place. Should we choose not to embrace this divergence, we can instead attempt to constrain it, by pursuing a divide-and-conquer strategy that successively narrows the search space and forces the search to converge towards a single possible solution. But if we want a diversity of solutions that exhibit a range of complementary strengths, we should use what the psychologist J. P. Guilford has called *divergent thinking*.[13] Guilford argued that this ability to generate a diverse range of different solutions, or to pursue a diversity of different search avenues at once, is a key enabler of creative behaviour. In practice, however, truly divergent thinking in a large search space is not sustainable if each of the divergent paths that we pursue branches and forks into combinatorially more avenues and laneways. Computers cannot handle the ensuing combinatorial explosion, but neither can humans, creative or otherwise. Creative people instead seem to select a manageable number of different pathways through a conceptual space. So while a chess-playing computer will crunch millions of different positions and possibilities to arrive at a move, a human grandmaster considers a much smaller basket of options. The trick is to know which avenues to pursue and which to avoid. In the end, it is not how many avenues we search, but the novelty of our trajectory that makes the difference. So to the extent that a producer can reconcile different constraints and conflate different search avenues into a path less travelled, the result can seem quick-witted, novel and insightful.

Two conflicting constraints or search avenues can often be reconciled with great concision in a single linguistic form that combines elements of two different solutions. Remember the variations *'sleight of tongue in cheek'* and *'sleight of foot in mouth'* in the last chapter? The cognitive linguists Mark Turner and Gilles Fauconnier describe this kind of combination as *blending*.[14] Blending is an integration of two or more sources of knowledge, whether linguistic or conceptual or both, to achieve a combined result that is novel yet familiar. So governor Ann Richards of Texas used blending when, in 1988, she described George H. W. Bush as a poor little rich-boy who *'was born with a silver foot in his mouth'*.[15] This much-quoted phrasing is a clever combination of two idioms that often come to mind when thinking of politicians in the Bush clan. Rather than rejecting either for its over-familiarity, Richards simply conflated both to cut short the divergent search for an equally concise replacement. In a memorable *Garfield* cartoon – how often do we get to say that? – the fat tabby passes a dog with a sign that says *'Will eat homework for food'*. Both dogs and hobos beg for food, yet we rarely view one in terms of the other. Blending not only allows us to conflate the two, it produces a hybrid result that is more than a dog and more than a hobo. Though quite a sophisticated blend, it is motivated by an overlap in two familiar phrases, *'will work for food'* and *'the dog ate my homework'*.

Most non-trivial blends, and virtually all of the clever ones, involve some degree of compromise. Fauconnier and Turner describe blends as selective projections from two or more knowledge sources: some elements get highlighted, and perhaps even exaggerated, and others get cast aside so that the grand combination can actually work. This kind of semantic compromise has been given the name *slippage* by Douglas Hofstadter and Melanie Mitchell.[16] When we, as producers, encounter something that just doesn't work, it is slippage that allows us to transform the troublesome element into something more accommodating. But once again, slippage is a divergent phenomenon, since we can often transform a blocked constraint or a violated expectation in a variety of meaningful ways. Thus, if Hillary Clinton were to become US president, we could refer to Bill Clinton as first *lady*, or first *man*, or first *husband*. If Bill were to balk at 'first lady', Hillary could still keep this title for herself.

She would, in a strong sense, truly be *first* lady, but many of our expectations of what the title means would have to slip away. Hofstadter's notion of slippage plays an important role in the production of any creative variation. When we replace 'dies' with 'dries' or 'love' with 'paint' in '*Love Never Dies*', or 'witness' with 'apostle' in '*witness protection program*', we are engaging in slippage at a phrasal level. These replacements are not arbitrary but governed by an intuitive sense of what can be substituted with what. In Hofstadter's terminology, the space of slippage possibilities can be captured by a *SlipNet*, a network of terms and ideas in which those that have the potential to slip into one another are explicitly connected by weighted links.

So a mastery of slippage allows for a mastery of creative variation. In general, one idea can slip into another to the extent that both are similar, while two words can slip into each other if both denote *SlipNet*-related ideas. Some slips have more semantic support than others, as reflected in the observation that witnesses and apostles are more similar to each other than hands are to wings or burqas are to sunglasses. But semantic similarity alone is no guarantee of slippage potential, and for slippage to work gracefully, we should intuitively feel that one word or idea can sensibly be compared and contrasted to the other. Burqas and sunglasses are both items of clothing; witnesses and apostles are different kinds of informer; hands and feet are each a kind of body part and so on. In a good pun, a rare thing indeed, the slippage of one word into another is based on phonetic *and* semantic similarity, or is motivated by strong conceptual grounds (as in *Paint Never Dries*). In the very worst *groaners*, violence is done to the structure of a larger word to shoehorn a weak phonetic substitution into place. Even creative slippage has limits that must be respected, though it takes insight to know exactly what those limits are. When we stretch the slippage potential of a word or idea too far, as in a dreadful pun or a lame substitution, that groan we hear is the sound of elastic about to snap.

Many creative linguistic blends stretch the slippage elastic half-way, to identify a noteworthy midpoint between two conceptual positions. A 2008 cover story in *Esquire* magazine[17] described the bodybuilder-turned-politician Arnold Schwarzenegger as 'the President of 12 per cent of Us'. At the time, Arnold was riding a wave of voter satisfaction as governor of California, before the state was to become bogged down by serious financial difficulties. Late-night comedians had often joked about the prospect of Arnold actually becoming president of the United States, though the Austrian-born politician would be ineligible to run without a prior change to the constitution. Nonetheless, Arnold surprised many by winning the governorship of California in a recall vote for the monochromatic incumbent, Gray Davis. His early successes as governor also surprised a great many political commentators, who found it odd to imagine this likeable but wooden star of the *Terminator* and *Conan* movies suddenly wielding so much power in America's largest state. The label 'Governator',[18] coined as a blend of *Govern*or, his new job, and Termin*ator*, his iconic role, quickly stuck. Arnold may not have become president of the United States, but he became the next best thing: leader of the US state with the largest population and the biggest economy, contributing 12 per cent of the nation's GDP. We see here two acts of creative slippage: governors are like presidents at the state level, so 'president' can slip into 'governor' and vice versa with little semantic resistance; and California is a microcosm of the United States, and can accurately be described as '12 per cent of the US' (or '12 per cent of Us' if you are American). This slippage allows us to stretch the elastic half-way, to the point at which the most optimal innovation is produced. Because Arnold is governor of California, he is also – with a generous pull on the elastic – 'President of 12 per cent of the US'.

Creativity is a restless patient that vigorously resists the straitjacket of formal definition, especially the one-size-fits-all variety. The most that any formal perspective can do for us is shed light on just one aspect of this multi-faceted phenomenon. J. P. Guilford was right to emphasize the importance of divergent production in creativity, and the need to reward both *fluency* (the ability to generate many different ideas) and *flexibility* (the ability to generate different kinds of ideas), yet Guilford's is just one valid perspective among many. The pioneers of good old-fashioned AI (GOFAI) alternately emphasized the importance of intelligently navigating a complex space of solution possibilities, while Margaret Boden has emphasized the sometimes transformative role of creativity in redrawing the boundaries of these spaces. For his part, Douglas Hofstadter has emphasized the importance of compromise and slippage when dealing with the many interacting soft constraints of a challenging problem, and even goes so far as to view constraints as welcome grist to the creative mill. John McCarthy, one of the founders of modern AI – he and Marvin Minsky first coined the term *Artificial Intelligence* back in the 1950s[19] – has argued that a solution to a problem is creative if it employs a concept that is not explicitly mentioned in the specification of the problem.[20] In other words, McCarthy emphasizes the role of *insight* in creativity and even provides a rather good working definition for this often mysticized notion. Arthur Koestler had earlier suggested that the roots of scientific, artistic and humorous insight lie in a single cognitive process called *Bisociation*.[21] His ideas, which were to be greatly elaborated and reworked by Gilles Fauconnier and Mark Turner in their model of *conceptual blending*, view creativity as emerging from the reconciliation of very different mental representations, or in Koestler's own rather quaint terminology, *matrices*.

There are also shades of Koestler in what has become the dominant theory of verbal humour, the *General Theory of Verbal Humour*, or GTVH,[22] of Salvatore Attardo and Victor Raskin, just as there are shades of the GTVH in

Fauconnier and Turner's blending theory. As we'll see next, the GTVH views the humour of jokes as arising from the bisociative friction between, and logical reconciliation of, similar but diverging scripts.

Departing from the script: Tell me a (slightly different) story

Improvisational comedy, or 'improv', bills itself as the kind of live comedy event that throws away the script. Rather than following a pre-scripted course, improv comedians ask the audience to suggest their own topics and themes for spontaneous play-acting. In fact, even though the audience appears to call the shots, improvisational comedy remains utterly dependent on scripts; not the stage scripts written by professional humorists and gag-writers, but the routine scripts that we all follow in our everyday lives. Most topics suggested by the audience, such as 'going to the dentist' or 'ordering dinner in a snooty French restaurant', are evocations of familiar scripts that the improv troupe should play out with a humorous twist. So the humour of improv is only superficially script-free. Deep down, it relies on the creative variation of scripts that are so well-known that no-one has ever bothered to write them down or give them a name.

Are these everyday routines really scripts? Most cognitive scientists think so, at least in an abstract sense. For them, a 'semantic script' is a schematic mental structure that captures our shared experience of a stereotypical routine, by binding together information about its typical setting and participants, as well as the expected sequence of actions and their effects. The term 'script' was popularized in the 1970s by Roger Schank and Robert Abelson,[23] influential AI researchers who viewed scripts as chunks of common-sense knowledge that one needs to really understand natural language. They argued that neither a computer nor a human can make sense of a story about, say, going to a restaurant, unless it knows what usually happens when a typical person goes to a typical restaurant. Without a restaurant script, an ill-informed observer could not, for instance, infer that a diner enjoys a meal from the fact that the waitress receives a large tip, or infer that a diner dislikes a meal from the refusal to leave any tip at all, or a refusal to even to pay the bill. A novel experience prompts us to either learn a new script or revise an existing one. Yet sometimes we get it wrong, and find ourselves triggering a script that merely seems appropriate, but which is actually truly and deeply inappropriate to a given setting.

This happens all the time whenever we read *whodunnit* novels with devious twists, or watch movies by artful directors who trick us into jumping to the wrong conclusions. But this tendency to apply a script before we know for sure that it apt is most often exploited by jokes, which delight in tricking us into applying the wrong script to a narrative. The moment of truth arrives with the punchline, which reveals our folly and playfully punishes us for our rush to judgement. Consider what is undoubtedly the most analysed joke in the humour literature, as brought to us by the humour theorist and computer scientist Victor Raskin. It concerns a young man who pays a visit to the doctor's office. With a low bronchial whisper, the man asks the doctor's pretty young wife 'is the doctor in?', to which the wife replies, with a smile, 'No, come on in'. So what starts out as an apparent instance of the *visit-to-the-doctor* script instead turns out to be an instance of the *affair-with-a-married-woman* script. With this realization, we reinterpret what has gone before: the young man's bronchial whisper is not a symptom that needs a doctor's attention, but a clichéd ruse to avoid the doctor's attention in the first place. The linguist and humour researcher Wallace Chafe argues that it is only the absurdity of the way the affair is conducted that gives the joke its humour,[24] yet it's hard to see much in the way of absurdity here. Recall, however, Kakuzo Okakura's claim that the most successful art engages and draws in the audience, making the viewer complicit in the resulting work. This joke is certainly no masterpiece, but the same principles of engagement and complicity apply as much to jokes as they do to paintings or poems. By hinting at the possibility of immoral behaviour, and fuelling the reader's lewd suspicions, the joke succeeds in making the reader complicit in the conduct of an illicit affair. In other words, the joke offers a knowing wink and a smile to those of us with dirty minds.

The notion of script opposition lies at the heart of an influential theory of humour first proposed by Raskin in 1985. His theory, the *Semantic Script Theory of Humour*, or SSTH,[25] builds on Schank and Abelson's view of scripts as the tectonic plates of text understanding. In this view, the most coherent interpretation of a text is given by the most appropriate script that provides the most explanatory coverage. However, as we've seen, two or more scripts can be triggered by even a short text, and humour can arise at the fault lines where two scripts compete to provide an overall interpretation of a text. This opposition typically comes to a crunch point at the end of the joke, when the punchline forces a wrenching collision. Yet script opposition is not itself a guarantee of humour,[26] and though an opposition can prompt us to ditch an inappropriate script for a more appropriate alternative, a marriage of both scripts together should still be possible at another level of interpretation. Humour theorists approach the mysterious marriage of sense and nonsense that lies at the heart of a joke in different ways, and with different terms. Neal Norrick refers to it as the 'method in the madness' of a joke[27]; Jerry Suls,[28] as well as Victor Raskin and Salvatore Attardo,[29] refer to it as the 'resolution' of the incongruity of a joke; and Elliott Oring, the cultural anthropologist and folklorist, describes it as the 'appropriate incongruity' of a joke,[30] reflecting sociologist Erving Goffman's view that 'any accurately improper move can poke through the thin sleeve of immediate reality'.[31] Yet however we define the incongruity,[32] and whatever we call the resolving operation that makes sense of it, the principle remains the same: a joke must allow us to salvage sense from nonsense to gain a useful insight into the incongruity.[33]

Figure 3.4 demonstrates how a joke narrative can be created as a blend of two very different scripts. In this case, each script establishes a tone and a theme that seems incongruous when viewed from the perspective of the other. Nonetheless, both can be woven together, with a little snip here and there, to produce a narrative that reads coherently. If the resulting script seems to veer madly from tragedy to farce, then that is precisely the point of the exercise. One script provides the tragedy, the other the farce, and the sudden transition from one to the other provides the comedy, provided of course that the transition is well-timed and the result is understandable as a coherent narrative.

Most narrative jokes employ creative variations on familiar scripts. This variation mischievously makes one script look like another, a *false friend* of sorts, causing the listener to initially trigger the wrong one.[34] When the moment of truth arrives, we are forced to see our mistake, switch scripts and perceive a

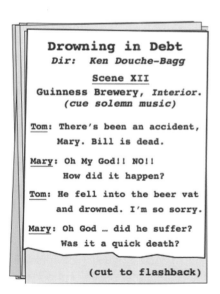 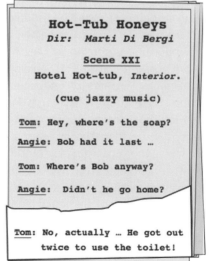

FIGURE 3.4 *Most narrative jokes employ a cross-over of different scripts. We understand the body of the joke using one script, but are finally forced to switch to another. The white fragments above (read from left to right) form an emergent narrative of their own.*

logic to the incongruity. But jokes are not just variations on scripts; they are often variations on other *jokes*. If you've heard an ethnic joke that makes fun of Irishmen, you can be confident that someone, somewhere, is using the same template to make fun of Germans, or Poles, or some other cultural target. Deep reuse occurs when two jokes put very different flesh on the same logical skeleton. Consider the following pair of jokes. Two English businessmen, with bowler hats and umbrellas, are waiting for a train. One proudly says to the other, '*My great-grandfather died at Waterloo, don't you know*'. The other replies, witheringly, '*Oh? which platform?*'. Now, compare this gag from the late great Bob Monkhouse: '*I still have sex at 75! I live at number 74, so it's no trouble at all*'. These two jokes seem very different, yet both employ the same logical device. What appears to be a temporal signifier, of an impressive age (*75*) or a historical event (*Waterloo*), is instead interpreted as a banal physical location. In the commuter joke, the shift from historical significance to mundane insignificance is used to undermine the speaker and puncture his pomposity. In the Monkhouse joke, the shift from a distinguished age to a mundane place next door undermines his boastful claim to have a vigorous sex life. If humour research was stamp-collecting, we'd have good reason to put both of these jokes in the same plastic pocket.

Douglas Hofstadter has coined the term *Ur-joke*[35] to refer to the notional first uses of a joke on which later variations are based. *Ur-joke* is a creative variation on *Ur-text*, a term used by literary scholars to describe an imaginary reconstruction of an earlier text that has since been lost to history. So *Ur-joke* nicely captures the evolutionary nature of jokes, suggesting with a wink that many contemporary jokes are variations on long-lost gags that once echoed in the ancient cities of the Old Testament. Conversely, in their *General Theory of Verbal Humour*, or GTVH, Salvatore Attardo and Victor Raskin argue that jokes exhibit deep similarities because they employ the same logical mechanisms to create humour. The GTVH is an elaborate and much-used theoretical framework[36] built on the script-based foundations of Raskin's earlier SSTH. Attardo, Raskin and others have since identified tens of unique logical mechanisms that generalize over thousands of superficially different jokes.[37] You may remember the joke about a mad scientist from (insert country of choice) who builds a rocket to fly to the sun, but launches at night to avoid being burnt to a crisp. We see here the logical mechanism of *false analogy*: the sun isn't a lightbulb that is hot only when it's bright and turned on in the daytime, and cold when it's seemingly dark and turned off at night. How about that old Russian chestnut in which a factory worker steals a different wheelbarrow every night, from right under the noses of the factory guards? This one derives its humorous logic from the mechanism of *figure-ground reversal*: the guards are so fixated on what the worker might be hiding in his wheelbarrow that they fail to see the wheelbarrow as an object worth stealing in itself.

We can think of Hofstadter's *Ur-jokes* as the notional roots of a large and tangled family tree of jokes, while the logical mechanisms identified by the GTVH are a key part of the genetic information inherited by variations from their forebears. Undoubtedly, some jokes are lineal descendants of others, and this would be represented in our family tree as a parent/child relationship. When Winston Churchill said '*I am easily satisfied by the very best*' he was clearly channelling Oscar Wilde, who had earlier said '*I have the simplest tastes. I am always satisfied with the best*'. However, some creative variations are more easily recognized as logical borrowings than others, and many jokes that share a deep similarity have a less obvious kinship. Another aphorism commonly attributed to Churchill is used to explain the left-to-right trajectory of his political career: '*If you're not a liberal at twenty you have no heart, if you're not a conservative at forty you have no brain*'. No one is entirely sure whether Churchill actually said this, or even words to the same effect, but earlier variants of this phrase have also been attributed to Georges Clemenceau and Otto von Bismarck. The variant that commonly attaches to Clemenceau is '*Any man who is not a socialist at the age of 20 has no heart. Any man who is still a socialist at the age of 40 has no head*'. One might also recognize in these aphorisms a certain similarity in structure and sentiment, if not in political inclination, to a witticism coined by the British politician and writer Horace Walpole over a century earlier: '*Life is a tragedy for those who feel, but a comedy for those who think*'.

In other words, sensitive liberals lack a rational brain, while rational conservatives lack a sensitive heart. Both Walpole and Churchill (or Clemenceau or Bismarck) seem to agree that the latter is the preferable state of affairs. What these two witticisms have in common goes far beyond a shared logical mechanism, for each offers a different creative expression for precisely the same political world-view. Yet both are different, and both are original, even if the sentiment itself is old. In contrast, Vladimir Putin was clearly trying to sound Churchillian when he quipped that '*Whoever does not miss the Soviet Union has no heart. Whoever wants it back has no brain*'. Nonetheless, for all that it presumably owes Churchill, Putin's remark is still funny, and still creative, if not entirely original. In the words of Giora and Hanks, Putin has given us an optimal innovation, a novel exploitation on a familiar quotation that packages its own unique meaning into a form that has already proven its comedic value.

Creating a fuss on the road more travelled

When given very few lines to speak, it can be hard for an actor to make a memorable impression on an audience. Bit players are rarely given the most important lines, yet what they have to say can be just as vital in maintaining the flow of a narrative. In *Macbeth,* Shakespeare provides just five lines to a character called *Seyton*, Macbeth's lieutenant, but one of these lines is absolutely pivotal to the play. When a conscience-stricken Lady Macbeth dramatically kills herself, and her death scream prompts Macbeth to ask '*Wherefore was that cry?*', it is Seyton who delivers the grim news with the line '*The Queen, my lord, is dead*'. Though lacking a certain poetry, the play would simply stop in its tracks were this line to be omitted. Yet, as theatrical legend has it, this is precisely what happened when Donald Wolfit, a Shakespearean actor famed as much for his ego as his acting, took *Macbeth* on the road over half a century ago. Wolfit had given the part of Seyton to an ambitious young actor, who, when his ambitions were thwarted, found a most ingenious way to extract his revenge. When Wolfit next played Macbeth, Seyton did not give Shakespeare's familiar reply to the question '*Wherefore was that cry?*', but a show-stopping variation, '*The Queen, my Lord, is very much better*'.[38] Like a tiny but well-placed explosive, this creative variation would have had a hugely disruptive effect on the flow of the play, leaving other actors in a state of confusion and stunned silence.

Though verging on the tasteless, the concept of an improvised explosive device, or IED, offers a useful metaphor for the workings of the most surprising variations. In a 2010 letter to *The Economist*, a former US army combat engineer named Charles Rei lamented the military's over-reliance on 'gee-whiz gadgets' for neutralizing the threat of roadside IEDs in Iraq, adding that the military had 'continually underestimated the intelligence and creativity of the soldiers and insurgents'.[39] Rei offers his own view on what form this creativity should take: 'The easiest way to predict the location of an IED is to look at a map and think, where would I put one? Choke points, avenues of approach, intersections, areas of routine use; these are the places where IEDs are found'. He further notes that 'an insurgent wouldn't waste resources building, placing and watching over an IED that had little chance of success'. Insurgents target choke points because they are highly vulnerable to the application of a small but unexpected force. Indeed, the tighter the choke point, the less force that is needed to achieve a devastating effect. So, though Shakespeare offers Seyton a most meagre role, his fifth and final line is a significant choke point in the narrative of *Macbeth*, and it is in this line that the disgruntled actor can lay his trap. With the unstoppable dramatic force of the play barrelling through this point of the narrative, it only takes a little well-timed pressure to derail the whole show.

Most well-crafted jokes in the script-switching tradition are deliberately constructed around a similar choke point in the narrative, a point where maximum surprise can be achieved with a minimum of effort. For once a listener triggers the wrong script and becomes fully committed to a certain avenue of interpretation, it takes just a little force from an 'appropriate incongruity' or

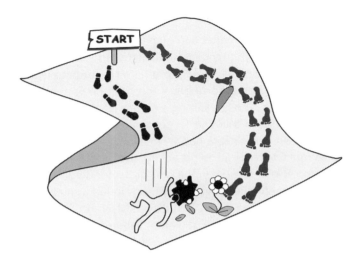

FIGURE 3.5 *A joke-teller and joke-listener navigate the search space of possibilities very differently. In a reversal on Figure 3.3, the joke-teller takes the longer 'safe' way through the space, while the joke-listener takes the more obvious but ultimately 'fatal' route.*[40]

an 'accurately improper move' to stop the listener's advance with a sucker-punch of a punchline. So while joke tellers and joke listeners navigate the same conceptual space, only one has a map. The teller, who already knows the ending to the joke, understands the space intimately, while the listener, who may have no specific knowledge of the terrain, must use more general common-sense knowledge of the world as a guide. This, of course, turns out to be a mistake, for the most obvious route to the goal is not a viable route at all. As shown in Figure 3.5, and in a subversive switch to the roles depicted in Figure 3.3, it is the knowledgeable joke-teller (depicted as the more nimble, barefoot explorer) who takes the circuitous route through the conceptual space. The discontinuity is not a short-cut, but a logical trap, into which an unsuspecting listener (the plodding, heavy-shoed explorer of Figure 3.5) awkwardly falls.

You could say that the discontinuity at the heart of a joke proves to be a *catastrophe* for a naïve explorer, in logical terms at least, while the joke-teller glides smoothly around this pitfall. And in mathematical terms you would be right. The kinked surface depicted in Figures 3.2, 3.3 and 3.5 is widely used in a branch of mathematics called *Catastrophe Theory*. Invented by French mathematician René Thom in the 1960s, catastrophe theory[41] allows us to study the geometry of discontinuous forms, where a small change in an input variable can cause an abrupt and extreme change in output value. Catastrophe theory has been used to model everything from stock market crashes to the moods of bipolar artists to the sudden collapse of empires and civilizations. The mathematician John Allen Paulos has used catastrophe theory to sketch a theory of humour along the lines discussed here.[42] Though schematic in outline, the account offered by Paulos is nicely consonant with the view of creativity as intelligent search in a space of many different conceptual possibilities. In each case, what makes *creative* behaviour different from regular *intelligent* behaviour is the way the explorer exploits the discontinuous contours of the conceptual space, either as logical shortcuts in the race to find novel solutions quickly and efficiently, or as logical deathtraps in the humorous misdirection of a good joke.

In mathematical terms, the perceived incongruity of a joke corresponds to a sudden discontinuity in conceptual space. An unthinking listener who plows through the space on the basis of conventions, expectations and habitual readings will need very little pressure to be tipped over into the chasm of the discontinuity. Just as the tightest choke points need the least force to achieve a dramatic effect, the merest incongruity in a punchline can be enough to force the listener into a radically different interpretation of a text. So to be creative with language, it helps to think like an insurgent, and ask: where are the choke points in this phrasing? What discontinuities between words or phrases and their habitual meanings can I exploit? The most vulnerable points are those that the permit the greatest leverage, so that the most subtle variation can turn its meaning upside down. Often, we need only to vary a single word in a familiar form to turn a glowing tribute into a wounding insult, as when talk-show host Clive Anderson asked author Jeffrey Archer *'Is there no beginning to your talent?'*. Even the subtlest logical nuance can carry a humorous wallop if it is couched in a familiar but misleading form, as in this gag from the British sketch-writer Barry Cryer: *'Four Jewish ladies of a certain age are having lunch in a restaurant. The waiter comes over and asks "Is any*thing *all right?"'*.[43]

Déjà vu all over again

Of course, there is a much simpler and altogether more obvious way of up-ending the meaning of a text. It's called negation – we simply add 'not' to any phrase whose meaning we want to invert. Negation may be the most obvious way to achieve this effect, but it is hardly the most creative, even if teenagers still think it is clever to place negation markers at the very end of a statement as a sarcastic signal of displeasure. In language, teenagers may be the ultimate insurgents, but the sentence-trailing 'Not!' is a crude IED that is lacking in surprise and is easily neutralized. Nonetheless, teenagers do plant their little sarcasm bombs in the right place. An unexpected variation at the end of an utterance has maximal surprise value, leading an audience down the garden path towards an interpretation that is never realized. Likewise, an unexpected deviation from a familiar script can be just as shocking when it arrives at the end of a joke. Some jokes even go as far as to employ repetition in the body of the text to reinforce an expectation that is finally dashed in the punchline. As in the story of the boy who cried 'wolf!', the final variation is all the more surprising for diverging from a pattern that has been established within the narrative itself. In abstract terms, these jokes employ what is called an AAB[44] pattern structure, in which two or more examples of an event-type A are followed by an incongruous event B. For instance, the following witticism employs an AAB structure: *George Washington couldn't tell a lie; Richard Nixon couldn't tell the truth; and Bill Clinton couldn't tell the difference*. Here, an A-type event is the use of the word 'tell' to denote an act of verbal communication, while the final B-type event is the use of the same word to denote an act of mental differentiation. The joke suggests that Clinton is less truthful than Washington, more truthful than Nixon, but less discerning than either.

The AAB pattern is a structural feature of many songs in the Blues tradition. A typical Blues verse comprises a line (A) which is sung twice in succession, followed by a different line (B) which ends the verse. As in jokes, the final (B) can be a playful departure from the content of (A), as in this verse from Tab Benoit's 'Garbage Man'[45]:

> *My Baby, she run away with the garbage man,*
> *Yeah, My Baby, she run away with the garbage man,*
> *Well I need you so bad, so you can empty my garbage can.*

But this music is called *The Blues* for a reason, and most AAB verses are not humorous and joke-like. It takes more than a surprising divergence from A to B to make AAB funny. Humour theorists insist that B must seem incongruous when following A, yet be resolvable as meaningful and appropriate in its relation to A. The above AAB verse can thus be understood as a humorous script variation in the mould of the GTVH. Though we trigger the familiar script of failed romance, we later realize that the singer does not pine for his lover, but for the lover's new partner, not because he misses the comforts of a steady romance, but because he misses the convenience of regular garbage collection.

When used as a rhetorical strategy, the AAB pattern allows a speaker to gain some positive momentum in the run up to a negative put-down, at which point a killer B punch is delivered. Perhaps the most memorable use of the AAB pattern in this vein occurred during the 1988 US presidential elections,[46] when the following exchange took place in the vice-presidential debate:

> Senator Dan Quayle: I have as much experience in the Congress as Jack Kennedy did when he sought the presidency . . .

> Senator Lloyd Bentsen: Senator, I served with Jack Kennedy, I knew Jack Kennedy, Jack Kennedy was a friend of mine. Senator, you are no Jack Kennedy.

You almost have to feel sorry for Dan Quayle here, as Bentsen counters Quayle's altogether reasonable claim to have amassed sufficient experience for the presidency with an unstoppable roundhouse punch. Bentsen squeezes in an additional A element to lengthen the buildup to his put-down, reducing both the social distance and the conceptual distance between himself and Kennedy with each step, so that each successive affirmation just adds increased force to the negation when it finally comes. Quayle can only respond by noting, weakly, 'that was really uncalled for, Senator'. To appreciate the contribution of the AAB pattern here, just consider if Bentsen would have landed such a resounding blow with the simple response 'but you're not Jack Kennedy'.

Recent work by cognitive scientists Jeffrey Loewenstein and Chip Heath shows that the AAB pattern in stories – which they call the *repetition-break plot structure*[47] – is considered more enjoyable by readers than the equivalent AAA (unbroken repetition) or ABC (no repetition) patterns. Many narrative jokes use explicit repetition to enforce an AAA pattern in the minds of an audience, so that AAB repetition-break comes as an incongruous and potentially humorous surprise. There are whole genres of jokes involving a priest, a rabbi and an imam; or an Irishman, and Englishman and a Scotsman; or a trio of nuns, hookers, husbands or some other stock characters, in which two of the three act somewhat predictably while the zany actions of the third provide the humorous departure. But there are many more jokes that do not rely on explicit repetition. Yet these jokes might still be said to obey an (AA)B pattern if prior familiarity with A and a superficial similarity between A and B causes the AA lead-in to be tacitly assumed. This implicitness is also a factor in the creative variation of familiar phrases, but even this kind of variation can benefit from the use of explicit AAB repetition. The AAB pattern gives an audience the opportunity to compare and contrast a novel variation to its more familiar norm, so that the meaning of any substitutions can be fully appreciated.

Moreover, the explicit use of repetition in an AB or AAB pattern can make the relationship between variation and norm all the more apparent, as in the following triad:

> *When in Rome, do as the Romans do.*
> *When in Athens, do as the Greeks do.*
> *When in Paris, do as the Germans do.*

The A-script here is the standard 'when in a city, do as the locals do'. The B-script is altogether more subversive, 'when in a conquered city, do as its military occupiers do'. The explicit AA repetition and B divergence is not strictly needed here, since the first A is a cliché through and through. Nonetheless, the repetition does remind the audience of some received wisdom in need of a cheeky make-over. It may be appropriate to act like a true local, but who wouldn't prefer the freedom to act like a debauched invader instead?

The final B line of the above triad subverts the A cliché that spawned it, but many variations simply *clone* a convenient norm to lend it a modicum of freshness and contextual fit. For instance, the 'When in Athens' variation in the second line is more an attempt to localize the familiar 'Roman' norm than to wring any humour from it, since it adds little but contextual detail to the original, and fails to generate any kind of non-obvious incongruity, semantic tension, or surprise. We'll return to the topic of lazy variation in Chapter 7, where we'll discover why linguists use the intriguing label 'snowclones' for these rather obvious forms.

Appropriately improper

The sociologist Erving Goffman coined the phrase 'accurately improper move' to describe how the charades that shape our day-to-day social interactions – what Goffman called 'expression games' – can be deliberately undermined with a creative action that is, at once, improper *inside* the charade, but sensible and proper when viewed from *outside*. In this light, Lloyd Bentsen's memorable put-down of Dan Quayle can be seen as an accurately improper move: Quayle had, after all, merely hinted that JFK might be an apt vehicle of comparison for himself and did not go so far as to make his comparison explicit. In this sense, Bentsen's response is improper, or as Quayle described it, 'really uncalled for'. Nonetheless, Bentsen needed to neutralize even the hint of a comparison to JFK, justifying his rhetorically accurate if socially improper retort with the defence 'You are the one that was making the comparison'.

In other words, Bentsen accurately saw Quayle's expression game for what it was and improperly ended the charade.

If our aim is to show the unreasonableness of unearned praise, half-baked opinion or habitual expectation, then like Bentsen, our most creative move is also an 'accurately improper' one. Such a response achieves what Elliott Oring calls an 'appropriate incongruity', a B where an A is expected to show these expectations to be nothing more than the rules of a game we can choose not to play. However, the sociologist Thomas Scheff suggests that Goffman's simple prescription may be hard to fill[48]:

> Devising a phrase or sentence that is 'accurately improper' in this sense would seem to be a formidable task. One must first hit upon an important commonly held assumption, then exactly counter it with an equally plausible assumption.

Ironically, if Scheff is right, the key to devising a creative and 'accurately improper' insight is an ability to recognize, and duly hit upon, 'an important commonly-held assumption'. In language, the names we give to these widely-accepted truisms are also commonly perceived as antonyms for creativity itself: the *cliché* and the *stereotype*.

In our received wisdom, clichés are never bubbling or energetic, fresh-faced or innovative, surprising or clever; rather, the poor devils are inevitably flyblown, dust-covered, tired, jaded, stale, lifeless, pale or limp. Nonetheless, just as we can't have surprise birthday parties without birthdays, excitement without boredom, pleasure without pain or relief without anxiety, we can't properly conceive of a creative departure from the norm without a well-developed conception of what is conventional and normative and, well, *boring* in language. If anything, stereotypes get an even worse press than clichés, perhaps because we are prone to stereotype our stereotypes as prejudicial and small-minded, just as we are wont to condemn clichés with more clichés (or, in the words of critic Christopher Ricks,[49] with cliché-clichés such as 'flyblown', 'stale' and 'limp'). The A of the AAB pattern is every bit as important as the B, but is condemned to play a largely unsung or misunderstood role in the workings of creative variation. Nonetheless, clichés and stereotypes have a fundamental role to play in linguistic creativity, and so we shall do our best to redress the imbalance in the next chapter.

4

Round up the usual suspects

Stereotypes as the building blocks of creative language

Mary Poppins sang that 'a spoonful of sugar makes the medicine go down', and when it comes to creativity, a liberal coating of the familiar can certainly make the strange and the unfamiliar all the more palatable to an audience. We take comfort from the familiar, and so use clichés and stereotypes as a touchstone for inference in hectic, distracting or uncertain situations. But if we wish to master language, rather than be mastered by it, we must exploit our familiar stereotypes thoughtfully and creatively. In short, we must learn to separate the familiar from the obvious, so we can exploit the immediacy and the evocativeness of the former without falling into the trap of the latter. If used thoughtfully, we'll see that our stock of cultural stereotypes allows us to create combinations that can be both familiar and surprising.

Poster boys and *Bêtes Noires*

Words that evoke strong emotions or deeply-held beliefs can easily slip from the moorings of their literal meanings. Because the link between these words and the feelings they evoke is so strong, the feelings persist even when the words are used with newly minted figurative senses. Thus, while it may seem trite to call someone 'Judas!' for betraying a shared belief system – as Bob Dylan was memorably called in a 1965 concert in Manchester shortly after he went 'electric'[1] – the resulting metaphor is both unambiguous and visceral. Name-calling doesn't have to be witty or creative to be emotionally effective, and a language like English provides a range of stock names and phrases for conveying a recognizable feeling with a powerful, if rather obvious, punch.

Yet creativity is sometimes a necessity, especially when the feeling that we want to convey is neither simple nor commonplace – 'Judas!' ticks both of these boxes – but complex and nuanced, and lacking an obvious signifier in language. For instance, consider this playful description of a wine from a guide for beginners:

> Riesling is the Kenny G of the wine world: technically brilliant, but oh-so-lacking in credibility.[2]

Judas and *Kenny G* are familiar figures in pop-culture, though it is a rare event to see them both mentioned in the same breadth. To appreciate the creativity of the wine comparison, and the total lack of creativity in the Dylan incident, it is important that we distinguish between familiarity and obviousness. The use of *Judas* in a description of Bob Dylan was both familiar and obvious, since nothing draws to mind the concept of betrayal more effectively than *Judas Iscariot* (even *Benedict Arnold* and *Vidkun Quisling* are also-rans in this race). In contrast, the use of the saxophonist Kenny G to describe Riesling is familiar but *non*-obvious. A hallmark of creativity is the way it makes the non-obvious seem so obvious *after* the fact, and at first blush the comparison does indeed seem non-obvious: a wine described in terms of a popular musician? But on closer inspection, Kenny G – a technically-gifted musician whose music has become a near-constant accompaniment to elevator rides the world over – proves to be an ideal poster-boy for the realization that credibility and virtuosity do not always go hand in hand. This realization, the comparison assures us, is as relevant to our appreciation of wines as it is to our appreciation of musicians. And if Kenny G suffers unnecessarily in the expansion of someone else's wine vocabulary, then the gratuitous sideswipe only adds to the humorous creativity of the comparison. Take that, Kenny G!

Whenever a simile or metaphor describes an X as a Y, we say that Y acts as a *vehicle* for carrying certain qualities of Y over to X.[3] Though it hardly seems fair, Kenny G is an established stereotype for virtuosity without credibility, and has thus become a popular vehicle for ascribing those qualities to another person or idea. Search the web with the Google query '* *is the Kenny G of* *' and one can find over a 1,000 variations on this double-edged compliment. Most use the stereotype to damn another musician with faint praise; thus,

Yanni is the Kenny G of keyboards, while *Eric Clapton is the Kenny G of the blues*. Of course, it could be worse: *Ringo Starr* is a stereotype for the weakest and least talented member of a group, as evidenced in the large number of web-comparisons that use him as a vehicle. Linguists refer to descriptions like this, with the form '*X is the Y of Z*', as XYZ constructions,[4] for obvious reasons. Many XYZs are neither figurative nor creative, as in '*Barack Obama is the president of the United States*', but those that use a proper-named individual as a vehicle in the Y position are usually figurative and – depending on the balance of obviousness to familiarity – creative.

Every domain of experience has its own familiar stereotypes which can be leveraged into an XYZ construction to denote a whole category of similar people or things. The use of individuals to denote categories is not really that unusual, in creative language at least: recall Lloyd Bentsen's use of the put-down 'you're no Jack Kennedy' in the last chapter. Indeed, Sam Glucksberg[5] and his collaborators[6] argue that this is how all metaphor works, after a fashion. For example, the 'jail' in the metaphor 'my job is a jail' doesn't denote a penal institution but a broader category of environments that are unpleasantly restrictive; *jail* is used here as a stereotypical vehicle for any kind of confining situation.

When we come to study stereotypes in metaphor, the capitalized Ys in proper-name XYZs make these vehicles easy to harvest from the web. Here's a taste of what we find:

Paris Hilton is the Zsa Zsa Gabor of the 21st Century

Victoria Williams is the Yoko Ono of the folk scene

Chris Manion is the Woody Guthrie of the right

Qifa Nabki is the Winston Churchill of the Islamic Resistance

Nick Denton is the William Randolph Hearst of the blog world

P. D. Q Bach is the Weird Al Yankovich of the classical music world

David Wetherell is the Warren Buffet of the internet

Steve Jobs is the Walt Disney of the tech world

Ben Bernanke is the Tony Robbins of the financial world

Newt Gingrich is the Trotsky of the Hard Right

David Cameron is the Tony Blair of the conservative party

Michael Jordan is the Tony Hawk of the basketball world

Milton Caniff is the Rembrandt of the comics

Scipio Africanus is the Tommy Franks of the Roman legions

Peter Brett is the Tolstoy of the F train

Daniel Melingo is the Tom Waits of the contemporary tango
Shahruhk Khan is the Tom Cruise of the Bollywood Industry
Edward Abbey is the Thoreau of the desert
June Wanniski is the Thomas Paine of the Reagan revolution
Bill Gates is the Thomas Edison of the tech industry
Nicholas Sparks is the Stephen King of the mush-brained romantic novel

It goes without saying that such comparisons work best when the Y cuts a more familiar figure than the X it is used to describe. This familiarity need not mean that such comparisons are always obvious, though most uses of the figurative XYZ construction on the web do exhibit a certain inevitability. For instance, most draw their Xs and Ys from the same domain, and so, in the sample above, we see musicians compared to musicians, writers to writers, artists to artists, athletes to athletes and businessmen to businessmen. In a web sample of 500 XYZs, with a political figure (like *Tony Blair* above) in the Y position, we find that almost two-thirds of the examples also contain a political figure in the X position. The sample is worryingly conservative in other ways too: four-fifths of the examples compare a male X to a male Y, about a tenth compare a female X to a female Y and a tenth are cross-gendered. Moreover, an XYZ in our web sample is twice as likely to be backward-looking (where the X is more contemporary than the Y) as to be forward-looking, while the Y component is four times more likely to be a fictional character than the X component (nine out of ten examples draw both their Xs and Ys from the real-world). A similarly conservative parade of obvious uses for familiar figures is observed when we sample XYZs from the sports domain and from the music/ art domain.

Yet it need not be like this, and some XYZs put familiar figures to creative, non-obvious uses. Let's focus on a particular figure, the basketball player *Michael Jordan*. Our sports sample contains 21 web XYZs with *Jordan* in the Y position. The corresponding Xs are listed below, with the corresponding Zs in parentheses:

Manny Pacquiao (Philippines), *Andrew Gaze* (NBL), *Chet Snouffer* (boomerang), *Garry Kasparov* (chess), *Mwadi Mabika* (WNBA), *Vince Young* (NFL), *Pádraig Harrington* (golf), *Tiger Woods* (golf), *Randy Couture* (martial arts), *Daryll Pomey* (Philippines), *Tony Hawk* (skateboarding), *Champ Hallett* (wheelchair basketball), *David Berg* (courtroom), *Bronwyn Weber* (cakes), *Michael Chabon* (literary), *the tuna sandwich* (mid-day meal), *Billy Bob Thornton* (movies), *Ralph Appelbaum* (museums), *Allan Bloom* (seminars), *Britney Spears* (pop), *Randall Ross* (rare books)

Some comparisons are more obvious than others, and most of these Xs are sportsmen; yet three Xs are female, and nine are from non-sports domains. The description of *Britney Spears as the Michael Jordan of pop* is a double-whammy, bucking the trend to conserve both gender and domain in a figurative XYZ comparison. Of course, the least obvious uses of a stereotypical person are those in which the stereotype is used as a vehicle to describe a non-person, such as when X is a product, an animal or a plant. The sample above shows that even the humble tuna sandwich is thought to possess *Jordanesque* qualities on the web, and the list below provides further evidence that web XYZs sometimes use familiar stereotypes in non-obvious comparisons:

Der Sturmer is the Rush Limbaugh of the Third Reich

DSL is the Rocky Balboa of the fast-access future

Alfa Romeo is the Quentin Tarantino of the automotive world

Facebook is the Patrick Henry of the 21st Century

Apple's iThingy is the Paris Hilton of mobile phones

Chicken Inasal is the Oprah Winfrey of the menu

Nintendo is the Ned Flanders of the console world

Samsung DLPs are the Lindsay Lohan of the television market

Pac Man is the King Lear of the 1980's 8-bit videogame revolution

The Razr is the Kate Moss of phones

The Borgata is the Julia Roberts of casinos

Bradley's Battleship is the John Travolta of board games

Piper Cub is the Henry Ford of the aviation world

Krug is the Dorian Gray of the wine world

Red meat is the Donald Trump of cancer

Copy-protected CDs are the Dick Cheney of the music industry

Tungsten is the Cleopatra of the elements

The K750i is the Chuck Norris of the photography world

Toyota Prius is the Che Guevara of the [eco-friendly car] movement

The Manhattan is the Cary Grant of cocktails

Mac Mini is the Bruce Lee of the computing world

Big Bordeaux is the Barry Bonds of the wine world

The Montrachet is the Angelina Jolie of the pack [wines]

Jimmy the Parrot is the Robert De Niro of the bird world

Moby Dick is the Samson of the ocean

The Blue Marlin is the Muhammad Ali of the fish world

Pit Bulls are the Mike Tyson of the K9 world

The Boxer is the George Clooney of the dog world

The Northern Pintail is the Audrey Hepburn of the duck world

The potato is the Tom Hanks of the vegetable world

The most creative examples appear to have the least obvious interpretations, and resemble riddles in the way they refuse to serve up their meanings on a plate. To understand '*The Razr is the Kate Moss of phones*' it suffices to know that Moss is a stereotypically skinny supermodel, while '*Jimmy the Parrot is the Robert De Niro of the bird world*' might be understood as a reference to De Niro's oft-parodied habit of aggressively repeating his lines. But '*Red meat is the Donald Trump of cancer*' is a puzzle that does not yield its meaning so readily. While we know, for instance, that Trump is a famously aggressive property tycoon, that cancer is scariest when it spreads aggressively, and that aggressive predators tend to be voracious consumers of red meat, this puzzle is still missing a piece. Its meaning only becomes clear when we look to the original web-text (a Vegan website[7]) in which this XYZ was originally coined. Here the author notes that since red meat has been implicated in the development of many different kinds of cancer, it can thus be categorized, metaphorically, as an aggressive and opportunistic *builder* of cancers. It makes sense then that 'the Donald', who is the very model of an aggressive and opportunistic property developer, should fill the Y role in this wonderful comparison.

No real people were harmed in the making of these comparisons. The *Robert De Niro* that is employed here is merely our stereotype of the intense method actor, gleaned not from first-hand experience but from his many repetitive film roles. These are simplified conceptual models, mental doppelgangers in which a useful stereotypical property is recognizably grounded[8]: thus, Tom Hanks is *versatile*, Rocky Balboa is *resilient*, Chuck Norris is *implacable*, Muhammad Ali is *graceful*, Kate Moss is *super-slim*, Donald Trump is *aggressive*, Audrey Hepburn is *elegant*, Cary Grant is *sophisticated* and Angelina Jolie is both *voluptuous* and *full-bodied*. These stereotypes are simplistic, of course, but only present a problem when they are used lazily, to '*enjoy the comfort of opinion without the discomfort of thought*' as John F. Kennedy memorably put it.[9] Creative speakers do not abhor the use of stereotypes, but exploit the familiarity and immediacy that stereotypes offer in non-obvious ways.

Our goal in this chapter is to explore the world of stereotypes more generally, to look beyond stereotypical individuals to consider the wide variety of mundane (and often prejudicial) stereotypes that pervade our everyday language. Behind every creative riff on a familiar form lies an equally familiar idea or stock mental image, and we'll explore how stereotypes are used to anchor our most common similes, to see how similes are used to perpetuate the shared knowledge of a culture. We'll also see how we can use similes to harvest a cast of thousands of common stereotypes from the web, using a search engine like Google. As counter-intuitive as it may seem, stereotypes are the building blocks of creative language, so the more we (or our computers) can acquire, then the more varied the descriptive toolbox we have at our command. Finally, we'll show how we can use stereotypes to build a simple but effective metaphor generation system, called *Aristotle*.

The proverbial stereotype

The term 'stereotype' does not usually receive a good press, for generally good reasons. We tend to use the term as a short-hand for unjustifiable preju-dices and biases that are in turn rooted in irrational social anxieties. Though social stereotypes can sometimes flatter a particular category of person, albeit in a way that is often double-edged and self-serving, most social stereotypes are negative. Consider the stereotypes that inform our opinion about different nationalities. The European Union, for instance, is not just a common market for goods and services; it supports a brisk trade in stereotypes too, though most of these long pre-date the foundation of the E.U. Even in 1772, the '*Encyclopédie, ou dictionnaire raisonné des sciences, des arts et des metiers*' of Diderot and d'Alembert[10] noted that '*it's a kind of proverb to say: as frivo-lous as a Frenchman, as jealous as an Italian, as serious as a Spaniard, as malicious as an Englishman, as drunk as a German, as lazy as an Irishman, as deceitful as a Greek*'. These associations are stereotypes not because they are necessarily wrong, but because they lazily assume that nations correspond to classes, and that the distinctive characteristics of any class can be safely attributed to all of its individual members. Stereotypes based on geography, race and nationality are easily fostered, and though prone to subtle changes over time, they do not retire gracefully. In 1919, the writer Hereward T. Price claimed that:

> [t]he Russians are as muddle-headed and stupid as the Englishman of a *Daily Mail* nightmare, and as quick in perception and polished as a Frenchman, as fond of tea and talk as an Oriental, as open-minded, acute, and subtle as an Athenian, as lazy as a Spaniard, as passionate as an Italian, as cold at heart and calculating as an Irishman, honest, simple, and kindly as the German of the good old fairy tales, yet, in their wrath, as brutal as the Tartars from whom they spring, and, in revenge, as cunning and implacable as a Jew.[11]

As stereotypes are echoed and reinforced by the language we use, they inevitably become entwined with the fabric of the language itself, in the guise of proverbs and clichés like Price's *as-as* similes above. As a result, linguistic devices like simile provide a convenient means of packaging a stereotypical belief into a concise, reusable form, and also provide a powerful lens for detecting and analysing the stereotypes that become woven into these familiar forms. Generally speaking, the more commonplace a simile, the more entrenched the stereotypical world view that it communicates. For instance, the simile '*as drunk as a German*' from Diderot and d'Alembert's *Encyclopédie* can be found just five times on the web if we search for this phrase using Google.

Looking at these solitary hits in the screen-shot of Figure 4.1, we can see that one of these is a reference to the *Encyclopédie* itself, another is a like-minded quote from the Enlightenment philosopher Montesquieu (who, incidentally, considered climate to be a contributing factor in the development of national character[12]), and two are not to German *people* at all, but to German *huskies*. Despite the enduring popularity of Oktoberfest, the idea of Germans as drunkards simply refuses to crystallize in the language of the web.

FIGURE 4.1 *Screen-shot of Google results for the query* 'as drunk as a German'.

Likewise, Diderot and d'Alembert's stereotype of the '*lazy Irishman*' finds just three hits on Google, of which two are again from the *Encyclopédie* and Montesquieu. In dramatic contrast, however, is the stereotypical notion of the drunken Irishman, conveyed by the simile '*as drunk as an Irishman*'. As shown in Figure 4.2, this phrase finds over 1,300 hits on Google. This extraordinary number attests to the popularity of a stereotype that has become entrenched in a range of habitual language patterns. To this day, police vans used for the transport of prisoners are known by the slang term *Paddywagon*, arising from their once frequent use in the transport of boisterous Irishmen (or 'Paddies', after the diminutive 'Paddy' for 'Patrick', a common Irish name), usually from the scene of a violent disturbance in a public house. In a similar vein, the use of the word 'hooligan' to mean a violent and unruly person derives from the surname of a fictional Irish family whose rowdy exploits were celebrated in a music hall song of the late nineteenth century.[13] Social stereotypes plainly lag behind the world they are intended to capture. While this is an unfortunate fact for groups that are ill-served by a mean-spirited caricature, it is a generally positive fact for language as a whole, since uncreative language benefits

FIGURE 4.2 *Google results for the scurrilous query,* 'as drunk as an Irishman'.

from the appearance of solidity that these anchor concepts can provide, and creative language benefits from having an uncreative but familiar foundation it can exploit and subvert.

Wherever we find rules and conventions, linguistic or otherwise, we are sure to find exceptions, and sure enough, we find that the ironic phrase '*as sober as an Irishman*' is also a habitual form in the texts of the World Wide Web. Figure 4.3 below shows that this phrasing finds over 500 hits via Google, less than half that of the phrase '*as drunk as an Irishman*', but more than enough to suggest a firm presence in the popular imagination. Looking to the first snippet in Figure 4.3, we see that the author takes the 'sober' variation as an indicator that the surrounding text is merely an ironic parody of what it pretends to be. Other snippets show even more elaborate variations of the same simile; the fourth uses '*an Irishman on Paddy's Day*' to evoke a state of extreme intoxication, while the fifth evokes the image of '*an Irishman in a brewery*'. In each case, the ironic variation succeeds only because the norm is already so entrenched in the public imagination, via the widely-shared stereotype of the drunken Irishman.

Most stereotypes are founded on a dash of empirical observation mixed with a giant helping of convenient fiction. Nonetheless, social stereotypes

FIGURE 4.3 *Google results for the unthinkable query,* 'as sober as an Irishman'.

persist because they lend a comforting sense of solidity to our vague and often uninformed impressions of others. Indeed, the term 'stereotype' can be taken to literally mean a 'solid impression', since 'stereo' is derived from the Greek for 'solid' or 'firm', and 'type' is derived from the Greek for an engraved 'mark' or 'impression'. Surprisingly, however, the cognitive and social sense of the term comes to us by way of the world of printing, in which a 'stereotype' is an engraved metal plate for firmly imparting a printed impression onto the page. By happy *un*coincidence, the word 'cliché' also originates in the world of printing, where it once denoted a block of movable type corresponding to a frequently used phrase; the availability of a metal cliché (the word derives from the sound made by the metal type) meant that individual letter blocks did not need to be re-composed each time the phrase was reused. So, a stock printing block for a stock phrase then. Printing provides an apt metaphor for how mental stereotypes are used to guide our social reasoning. Just as a printer's plate stamps the same text onto every page, we use stereotypes to make inferences about others as if they too were empty pages, blanks lacking any idiosyncratic detail that might transcend the general template to which we have assigned them.

We owe this social-psychology notion of a 'stereotype' to the journalist Walter Lippmann, whose 1922 book *Public Opinion*[14] introduced the idea of a stereotype as a partial model of the truth of a complex situation. As Lippmann notes, 'Our stereotyped world is not necessarily the world we should like it to be. It is simply the kind of world we expect it to be.' Lippmann's terminology captured a powerful insight into the mind's use of schematic structures, or categories, in dealing with the minutiae of everyday life. Rather than construct a detailed and unique representation for everything and everybody that we encounter, we instead assign them to stereotypes that allow the same details to be shared by many different entities. When an entity exhibits some key features of a stereotype, we naturally assume that it possesses *all* of the features of the stereotype. As Lippmann rather sadly puts it in *Public Opinion*,[15] 'There is neither time nor opportunity for intimate acquaintance. Instead we notice a trait which marks a well known type and fill in the rest of the picture by means of the stereotypes we carry about in our heads'.

From cliché to stereotype, and beyond

The power of a stereotype lies in its ability to simplify the world, allowing us to focus on the salient features of an entity that have already proven their inferential worth many times over. As such, stereotypes suffer from the same bad press as do verbal clichés: both capture knowledge that, on deeper reflection, can appear simplistic, exaggerated or just plain wrong.[16] Nonetheless, this knowledge is an essential part of good communication. The philosopher Hilary Putnam notes mischievously that 'Communication [about tigers] presupposes that I have a stereotype about tigers which includes stripes, and that you have a stereotype about tigers which includes stripes, and that I know that your stereotype includes stripes, and that you know that my stereotype includes stripes, and that you know that I know . . .'.[17] In other words, stereotypes are inference-rich categories[18] that collectively provide a repository of *mutual knowledge*,[19] one that speakers tacitly use to establish a common ground when interacting with one another.[20]

Stereotypes and clichés provide complementary perspectives on our psychological tendencies toward simplification and idealization, but they are not the only perspectives. Other useful type structures include the 'prototypes' of cognitive psychology and the 'archetypes' of Jungian psychology,[21] both of which have their own unique connotations. Archetypes have gained an almost metaphysical connotation from their use in the work of psychologist Carl Jung, who viewed them as psychological distillations of humankind's collective experiences. In particular, Jung used the notion of an archetype to identify key personality types that represent different expressions and needs of the human psyche, from the archetype of the *child* to the *hero* to the *mother* to the *trickster*. These are resonant ideas that influence our understanding of human behaviour at a mythic level, from the symbols we use to the rituals we perform.

Prototypes similarly stick in the mind as resonant ideas, not as metaphysical tools to interpret the world and our actions within it, but as empirical observations about how humans cognitively divide the world into categories with more or less typical members.[22] Cognitive psychologists see prototypes as the most familiar and representative members of a category, making them the ideal yardsticks for performing typicality judgements. So when Mr Blond in *Reservoir Dogs* talks about his need to 'get a regular job job-type job'[23] to appease his parole officer, his laboured phrasing makes it clear he is referring to the prototypical view of a job and not to the kind of criminal job he would much prefer to have. It is meaningful to talk not just of prototypical jobs but of prototypical birds, prototypical trees, prototypical weapons, prototypical games or of the prototype of any category at all. As shown in Figure 4.4, robins, crows, eagles, penguins, ostriches and chickens are all members of the category *Bird*, but they are not all equally typical or representative. Cognitive psychologists like George Lakoff view *Bird* as a *radial* category,[24] with the most typical members residing at or near the centre, and progressively less representative members residing further out, towards the periphery.

Members of other categories that share some of the most salient properties of *Bird* can be imagined to lie outside the boundaries of the category, but

FIGURE 4.4 *The usual suspects: More or less typical 'birds', and some non-birds that lie outside the category while still sharing salient properties with the prototypical bird.*

at a distance reflective of their inherent similarity to the prototype. Thus, as shown in Figure 4.4, we might imagine bats, airplanes and mosquitoes and other winged entities as lying outside the boundaries of *Bird*, yet not so far away that a creative speaker couldn't playfully sneak them inside. The stretchiness of radial categories means we can sometimes view – with a little creative licence – obvious non-members as though they were members, as in the quip '*the state bird of Minnesota is the mosquito*'. We might even suggest that '*the official bird of Washington state is the 747*', since Boeing has its headquarters in Seattle.

Prototypes, archetypes, stereotypes and clichés all denote similar ideas from different perspectives about what is normal and unexceptional in the world. Yet no perspective is entirely reducible to any another, and none properly subsumes all the others. In his essay *From Cliché to Archetype*, Marshall McLuhan finds an awkward middle ground with his term 'cliché-archetype'.[25] Noting that the term 'archetype' implies a somewhat high-brow sensibility, McLuhan adopts a less metaphysical approach than Jung, and views an archetype as a highly conventionalized association that finds its verbal equivalent in the cliché. For McLuhan, the facts that flags typically hang on flag-poles and oil typically flows through pipelines are archetypes that form 'complex retrieval systems',[26] conceptual networks in which the retrieval of one archetypal idea inevitably leads to the retrieval of others. Archetypes are thus aspects of a conventional world view; these aspects hang together to form complex 'cross-quoting' structures via overlapping clichés and other *non*-linguistic norms. As such, a flagpole with a flag is more representative than a flagpole without a flag, while a pipeline carrying oil is more representative than one that is empty. In this way, McLuhan's notion of an cliché-archetype also seems to reconcile itself, to a degree at least, with the cognitive-psychology notion of a prototype.

Like 'cliché-archetype', the term 'stereotype' is just as applicable to cars, books, animals and other objects in the real world as it is to people, countries and social groups. Consider the traits that are most salient in our stereotypical conception of a good cup of espresso. While espresso can vary from one café to another, there is an idealized conception of the perfect serving (nicknamed *'the god shot'* by aficionados) that is widely shared. Whenever we order an espresso, it is this stereotype that guides our expectations of what it will look like, feel like and taste like. These expectations are echoed in language in a variety of clichéd evocations of the qualities of espresso. Figure 4.5 presents a *word cloud* of those qualities that are stereotypically associated with espresso in everyday language. A word cloud is a simple visual device that is commonly used on the web to reduce a large document or set of words to its most frequent elements, which are displayed with a proportionately larger font size. In Figure 4.5 the most salient properties of Espresso – which we take here to be the properties most frequently ascribed to Espresso in similes – are foregrounded in a larger, bolder type.

Of course, the precise salience of each property in Figure 4.5 – from *intense* to *Italian* – will vary from drinker to drinker, but the general landscape should be similar for all. These properties are not usually articulated (e.g. you don't, as a rule, ask for an 'Italian espresso' or a 'strong espresso'), but are assumed whenever one orders an espresso, and generally only made explicit

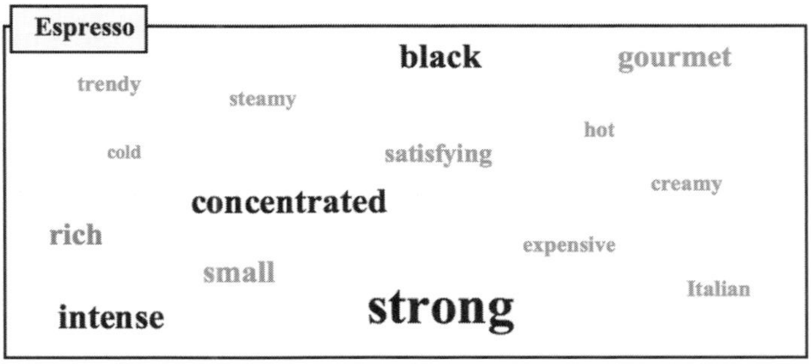

FIGURE 4.5 *Word cloud for the concept Espresso, in which salient traits are foregrounded.*

when a particular cup is either very good or very bad. Stereotypes condense a great deal of related information into a single mental structure, to form inference-rich categories that, in Lippmann's words, allow us to quickly 'fill in the rest of the picture' whenever we are presented with an incomplete view of a situation.

Once again, language serves as a lens through which we can see the stereotypes that exist in a linguistic community. Figure 4.6 shows the results of using Google to determine the prevalence of '*as strong as an espresso*' on the web. Over 500 documents attest to the fact that espresso is stereotypically strong, while unsurprisingly, no documents at all are found for the contrary position '*as weak as an espresso*'. A speculative search for other properties on Google finds 787 hits for 'as *intense* as an espresso', 699 hits for 'as *dark* as espresso' and 65 hits for 'as *rich* as espresso'. If we use Google's * wildcard to broaden our search via the generalized simile '*as * as espresso*', we net an even bigger catch that also includes 'as *bitter* as espresso' and 'as *aromatic* as espresso'. Similes and stereotypes enjoy a productively symbiotic relationship: while similes leverage the descriptive power of stereotypes to paint evocative but concise word-pictures of a topic, they also prove to be the perfect packaging for the wider dissemination and cultural reinforcement of the stereotypes they exploit.

FIGURE 4.6 *A Google-search shows the prevalence of the expectation* 'espresso is strong'.

The simple art of simile

There is something undeniably democratic and unpretentious about similes. Not only are they pervasive in language, they are at home in any register of speech and in any genre of text, from tabloid newspapers to scientific texts to hardboiled detective fiction to romantic poetry. We can easily mint our own, and very often do, but most languages and cultures also conveniently provide a wealth of pre-fabricated similes to choose from. Speakers do not need to invent their own creative descriptions, but can draw on a large back catalogue of cultural tropes to clearly convey their impressions of a topic, as in *'as strong as an ox'*, *'as sober as a judge'*, *'as pale as a corpse'* and *'as white as a sheet'*. But these formulaic similes are more than a linguistic shorthand; they also open a window onto society that allows us to identify the key stereotypes in a language and a culture. One of the finest expressions of this viewpoint comes to us by way of Charles Dickens, who opens *A Christmas Carol* by describing stock similes as an inherited source of cultural wisdom, one that is not always fully appreciated by speakers of a language:

> Old Marley was as dead as a door-nail. Mind! I don't mean to say that I know, of my own knowledge, what there is particularly dead about a door-nail. I might have been inclined, myself, to regard a coffin-nail as the deadest piece of ironmongery in the trade. But the wisdom of our ancestors is in the simile, and my unhallowed hands shall not disturb it, or the country's done for.[27]

Towards the end of the book, when Scrooge awakes on Christmas morning to the happy realization that he is still very much alive, Dickens uses a stream of formulaic similes to lend Scrooge's euphoric outburst an immediate and unmeasured tone:

> I am as light as a feather, I am as happy as an angel, I am as merry as a schoolboy. I am as giddy as a drunken man. A merry Christmas to everybody![28]

Orwell might disagree, but it would seem utterly contrived for Scrooge to utter a stream of elaborately creative similes in a situation like this. In language, using the right tool for the job means that the tired and familiar will occasionally trump the new and creative.

How big is the inventory of stock similes that members of a given culture can draw upon? Naturally, it depends on how you define a stock simile. If by 'stock' we mean phrases that are so commonplace that they earn a place in print dictionaries or in specialist books of proverbs and other cultural sayings, then English has an inventory of about 400 stock similes. For instance, Neal Norrick[29] based his influential 1986 analysis of stock similes on a set of 366 similes found in the 1970 edition of *The Oxford Dictionary of Proverbs*. The linguist Rosamund Moon, who based her 2008 study of similes on common phrases mined from a variety of text corpora such as the *Bank of English* corpus, found a comparable collection of 377 stock similes.[30] In contrast, the folklorist Archer Taylor used neither a corpus nor a dictionary, and collected thousands of proverbial similes from American speakers for his classic 1954 study, *Proverbial Comparisons and Similes from California*.[31] If a system as pervasive and extensive as the World Wide Web had existed in Taylor's day, he would doubtless have found a great many more, covering every point of the spectrum from the formulaic to the truly creative.

Come all ye similes (and bring your stereotypes with you)

While metaphors are masters of disguise, similes are fundamentally unsuited to undercover work of any kind. Similes inevitably stand out by virtue of their 'as' or 'like' markers, and while aging metaphors eventually become part of the literal establishment in language, even the oldest and most hackneyed simile remains, defiantly, a simile. Whereas Taylor's painstaking collection took years to compile, it is entirely feasible for a computer to harvest tens of thousands of similes from the web in a matter of hours.

Google provides a special interface for just this kind of automated harvesting (and other search engines, like Yahoo, are just as helpful). We use an automated process to send successive waves of related queries to Google, such as *'as * as a tiger'* and *'as tough as a *'*, and sift through the snippets that are returned to find genuine similes, as opposed to simple comparisons.[32] A surprising number of these web-similes are ironic, like 'as tanned as an Irishman' and 'as sober as a Kennedy', but let's put the topic of irony aside until Chapter 6. For now, we remove these mischievous comparisons by hand, to produce the ultimate database of web-similes: over 12,000 in all, ascribing over 2,000 properties to over 4,000 common objects, or stereotypes. Figure 4.7 presents a word cloud of the most oft-used stereotypes in our database of similes.

In turn, Figure 4.8 shows a word cloud of the properties that are most frequently ascribed to the descriptive nouns in these web-similes.

Two striking realizations arise from this analysis of common web-similes. The first concerns the unusually high frequency of ironic comparisons, a

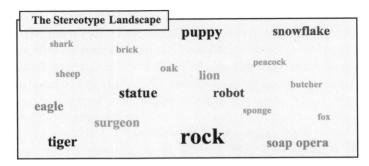

FIGURE 4.7 *Word cloud of the most common simile vehicles found on the web with Google.*

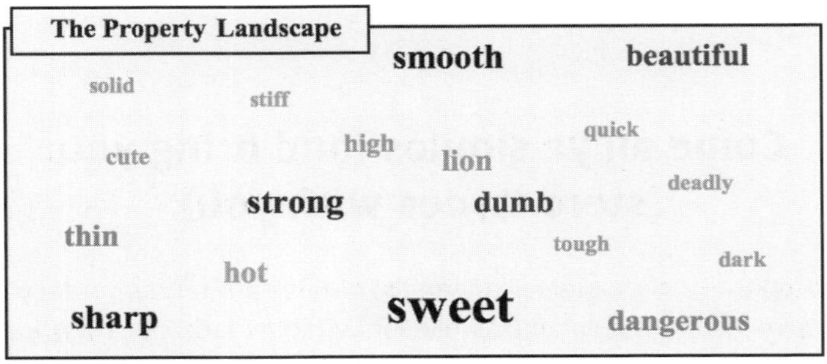

FIGURE 4.8 *A word cloud of the properties most commonly highlighted in web-similes.*

consideration of which we defer until later. The second realization is less immediate, but just as remarkable: even in the twenty-first century, our comparisons involve many of the same stereotypes that would have been used in Dickens' time. This observation is a testament to the cultural nature of stereotypes, which are meant to be shared and inherited by the speakers of a language. They constitute a key part of what Dickens calls 'the wisdom of our ancestors', which may go some way toward explaining why, in the twenty-first century, we still find it useful to compare people to peacocks, wolves, lions and eagles. Figure 4.9 presents a breakdown of the stereotypical vehicles we find in our database of similes from the web.

Notice that animals account for the largest share (indeed, the *lion*'s share) of vehicle categories in Figure 4.9, followed closely by people (22 per cent) and tools (15 per cent). The web, it seems, it is awash with figurative animals. When we look more closely at the similes found on the web (and retrieved in the snippets that are returned by the Google API), we are led to a remarkable conclusion: as descriptive vehicles, animals are more often used to

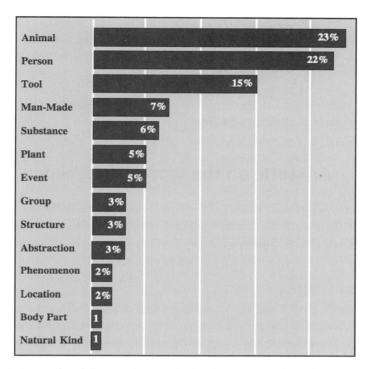

FIGURE 4.9 *A breakdown of the vehicles found in web-similes, by semantic category.*

describe people than they are to describe other animals. We use animals for a wide-range of uses in real life, as food, clothing, vehicles, farm implements and pets, so perhaps it should not be so surprising that we extend this catalogue of uses into the world of linguistic description. Nonetheless, even in this capacity animals show more usefulness in describing the traits of people than in describing the traits of other animals. The writer Thomas Love Peacock nicely captures the descriptive need of man for animals in this extract from his 1816 novel *Headlong Hall*:

It appears to me that man may be correctly defined an animal, which, without any peculiar or distinguishing faculty of its own, is, as it were, a bundle or compound of faculties of other animals, by a distinct enumeration of which any individual of the species may be satisfactorily described. This is manifest, even in the ordinary language of conversation, when, in summing up, for example, the qualities of an accomplished courtier, we say he has the vanity of a peacock, the cunning of a fox, the treachery of an hyaena, the cold-heartedness of a cat, and the servility of a jackal.[33]

Curiously, everyday language engenders a sense of familiarity with animals that most of us will only ever see in zoos, in movies or in documentaries on the Discovery Channel. As our nearest counterparts in nature, animals continue to exert a poetic force on our collective imagination, allowing us to view ourselves stripped of the artificial trappings of the civilized world. Despite the march of technological progress, this force plainly continues to make itself felt in the similes of the World Wide Web.

Aristotle on the World Wide Web

The reason we generally believe lions to be brave, fierce and noble is that language tells us they are so, via conventionalized similes like '*as brave as a lion*'. Children grow up in a language environment where such stock phrases are the common coin, and so believe the truth of these linguistic chestnuts long before they ever have a chance to observe it first-hand. By harvesting large quantities of similes from the web, a computer can go a long way toward learning this knowledge for itself. This turbo-charged process allows a computer to acquire, in one fell swoop, Dickens' 'wisdom of our ancestors' that humans take years to acquire. For instance, the similes acquired for the vehicle 'funeral' allow a computer to identify the following properties as most salient:

  {sad, orderly, unfortunate, dignified, solemn, serious}

Naturally, these properties will be shared by other vehicles as well. For example, similes on the web also provide us with the following stereotypes for the property 'solemn':

  {monument, owl, judge, funeral, temple, dowager, lighthouse, gravestone, pathologist, crow, funeral_march, oracle, prayer, wake}

Now consider the simile '*his wedding was like a funeral*', which asks us to adapt our knowledge of funerals to our understanding of weddings. In other words, the simile directs us to look for salient properties of 'funeral' that can be transposed onto 'wedding'.[34] Our knowledge of funerals is given by the property set above, but there is nothing in the lexical semantics of 'wedding' (as found in a dictionary, say) that tells us that weddings can be solemn, unfortunate or sad. Rather, the simile requires us to exploit our tacit, experiential understanding of these events, such as the fact that weddings occur in a (solemn) church, and are sometimes forced (unfortunately) for non-romantic (sad) reasons. A computer system does not have an experiential grasp of events like weddings, but fortunately, it can tap into the written reflections of those that do, by using the web as a corpus that can be queried on demand. A curious computer can thus generate six queries, one for each hypothesis – 'sad wedding', 'orderly wedding', 'solemn wedding', 'unfortunate wedding', 'dignified wedding' and 'serious wedding' – and use a search-engine like Google to determine the relative web-frequency of each hypothesis. Given in order of decreasing frequency, they are:

sad	wedding	11,700 hits
serious	wedding	5,020 hits
solemn	wedding	2,750 hits
unfortunate	wedding	1,450 hits
dignified	wedding	736 hits
orderly	wedding	207 hits

If we take frequency to be a rough correlate of likelihood, then the most frequent phrases will describe the most likely hypotheses. We can thus conclude that a *funereal wedding* is a sad and serious affair, conducted in a solemn manner for some unfortunate reason, yet in a way that is dignified and orderly. Of course, the speaker may have an entirely different and context-dependent meaning for the simile – the happiest weddings often resemble an Irish wake – but all we can expect of a computer (or an otherwise uninformed human) is an interpretation that respects common-sense. By combining the salient features provided by other web-similes for 'funeral', and web-frequencies that suggest whether (and how much) these features make sense for a 'wedding', a computer can make an educated guess at this common-sense interpretation.

Now consider the reverse simile, '*her funeral was like a wedding*'. The web-similes our computer acquires for the vehicle 'wedding' identify the following salient properties:

{joyous, joyful, decisive, glorious, expensive, emotional}

A computer can adapt this knowledge of weddings to the topic 'funeral' by generating the following hypotheses/queries: 'joyous funeral', 'joyful funeral', 'decisive funeral', 'glorious funeral', 'expensive funeral' and 'emotional funeral'. In order of decreasing frequency, these hypotheses as found on the web as follows:

emotional	funeral	20,900 hits
expensive	funeral	5,760 hits
glorious	funeral	1,010 hits

joyous	funeral	456 hits
joyful	funeral	310 hits
decisive	funeral	35 hits

The observation that funerals and weddings are typically expensive events is not a fact that one expects to find in a typical knowledge representation, or even in a typical dictionary. However, a computer system that acquires its understanding of figurative categories from web-similes, and again verifies the possible implications of a figurative interpretation via queries to the web, can acquire and use this kind of encyclopaedic knowledge with ease.

Search engines like Google make it easy – and a little too tempting – to view the web as a vast, unstructured encyclopaedia for just about any topic. The lexicographer Adam Kilgarriff has dismissively referred to the use of the web in this way as *Googleology*, and goes as far as to say that 'Googleology is bad science'.[35] Certainly he is right to suggest that the web-counts reported by commercial search engines should be taken with a generous measure of salt,[36] and for fine-grained analysis the unfiltered web lacks the quality of curated resources such as dictionaries, almanacs and encyclopaedias. Yet the web excels at providing large quantities of dynamic material, on diverse topics, that can be statistically used to give a broad sense of a topic. These collected materials can be used to estimate whether a given proposition (expressed as a query) has widespread acceptance on the web, or to determine whether one proposition has more widespread support than another. Suppose we want our computer to generate metaphors on a topic of popular interest, such as the famous-for-being-famous Paris Hilton. We might ask this system to focus on metaphors that highlight the fact that our topic is unnervingly skinny. Turning to its database of over 12,000 stereotypical associations, our system will note that skinny is a salient property of 35 different stereotypes and simile vehicles, namely:

> {twig, rail, rake, toothpick, broomstick, flagpole, pole, needle, pencil, snake, noodle, rake handle, lamppost, broom, chopstick, scarecrow, supermodel, mosquito, whippet, marathon runner, tadpole, cadaver, rope, pool cue, flamingo, beanstalk, string bean, sapling, stick, pin, post, stick insect, thread, miser, matchstick}

Any of these vehicles can be used to generate an explicit simile for the desired property, such as '*Paris Hilton is as skinny as a flagpole*', or an implicit open simile such as '*Paris Hilton is like a cadaver*', or a metaphor such as '*Paris Hilton is a mosquito*'. In each case, however – even in the case of an explicit simile with a stated property – the combination will insinuate that the topic also possesses other salient properties of the vehicle as well, to the degree that these properties are semantically transferable to the topic. To evaluate the potential of each vehicle to figuratively describe a topic, a system will need to determine the aptness of each of these other properties. Once again, the web can be viewed as a mass of reverberating opinions in which the frequency of a certain proposition can be used as a rough indicator of its general acceptance or aptness.

If one were to choose the charming metaphor 'Paris Hilton is a mosquito', our system would find the following salient properties of mosquito in its stereotype database:

{annoying, weak, tiny, insignificant, miniscule, skinny, worthless, nasty, irritating, insistent, bothersome}

Mosquitoes are clearly viewed with a dim eye in the 'wisdom of our ancestors'. But does the web have an equally dim view of Paris Hilton? To find out, the system simply generates a hypothesis-query for each of the above 11 salient features of 'mosquito', yielding the following document counts on the web in support of each:

weak	Paris Hilton	2,950 hits
nasty	Paris Hilton	1,570 hits
skinny	Paris Hilton	1,100 hits
worthless	Paris Hilton	578 hits
irritating	Paris Hilton	456 hits
annoying	Paris Hilton	435 hits
tiny	Paris Hilton	303 hits
miniscule	Paris Hilton	310 hits
insignificant	Paris Hilton	5 hits
bothersome	Paris Hilton	5 hits
insistent	Paris Hilton	2 hits

It follows that describing Ms Hilton as a 'mosquito' will not only imply that she is skinny, but that she has a host of other undesirable qualities as well. In contrast, 'matchstick' has just three salient properties in our simile database – thin, skinny and spindly – so a comparison with 'matchstick' yields a more focussed effect, supported by:

skinny	Paris Hilton	1,100 hits
thin	Paris Hilton	307 hits
spindly	Paris Hilton	1 hit

However, since *skinny* is the property of 'matchstick' that is found most often as a descriptor of Paris Hilton on the web, it does seem that the metaphor *'Paris Hilton is a matchstick'* is a excellent candidate for conveying this very property. Not very original, perhaps, but a good foundation on which to base further creative word-play.

A version of this approach can be accessed online, at *www.educatedinsolence.com*, in the simplified guise of the *Aristotle* system[37] shown in Figure 4.10. *Aristotle* invites users to enter a topic and a property of this topic to highlight, whereupon the system presents a list of the stereotypical vehicles that possess this feature. In addition to displaying detailed aspects of these vehicles (e.g. that wolves exhibit *rapacious decisiveness*), *Aristotle* also reveals how the highlighted property might be interpreted in the specific context of the chosen topic.

Having no knowledge of the mean things writers say about stereotypes and clichés, *Aristotle* exploits them freely, as though they are something to be proud of. And why not? As a software system, it simply has no sense of the disdain in which clichés and stereotypes are generally held, and the special scorn reserved for them by polemicists like George Orwell. But this focus on stereotypes makes *Aristotle* a starting-point rather than a dead-end.

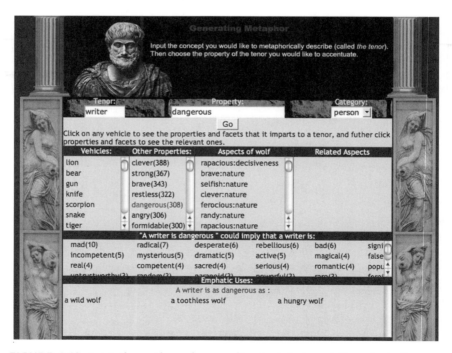

FIGURE 4.10 *Aristotle on the web, an online tool that exploits web-similes as a source of knowledge for generating and understanding metaphors.*

When harnessed properly, in well-crafted combinations, stereotypes can also be the stuff of truly creative language. *Aristotle* has yet to learn how to formulate more interesting combinations for itself, but we hope – and expect – that it will, in time. As we shall see in Chapter 6, there are so many easily harvested examples of the creative manipulation of stereotypes on the web that *Aristotle* will not lack for the guidance it needs to generalize and learn.

Conclusions: Metaphor cleansing versus metaphor renewal

It's easy to be snooty about clichés and stereotypes. Proscriptive writers regularly use them for target practice, as when George Orwell claimed *'there is a long-list of fly-blown metaphors which could similarly be got rid of if enough people would interest themselves in the job'*. This awful job sounds suspiciously like the sinecure that Winston Smith held in the *Ministry of Truth*.[38] The problem, of course, is that these writers all too easily succumb to cliché themselves when writing of the very dangers of cliché. This complex attitude to cliché, characterized by sharp insight in recognizing cliché but a plodding banality in describing what to do about it, lead the critic William Empson to memorably describe Orwell as *'the eagle eye with the flat feet'*.[39] Empson's put-down offers a marvellous repudiation of the whole anti-cliché movement, since it is itself a creative turn of phrase built from a blend of two rather hackneyed, even flyblown, clichés: the cliché that an observant person has 'the eyes of an eagle', and the cliché that a plodding thinker is 'flat-footed'. Likewise, Christopher Ricks, in *The Force of Poetry*, notes with some humour that Orwell's listing of his least favourite clichés – *'jackboot, Achilles' heel, hotbed, melting pot, acid test, veritable inferno'* – has an accidental but vital poetry about it, as if clichés long to be grouped into creative combinations.[40] Did Orwell succumb to a subconscious desire to use cliché creatively, Ricks wonders, since he so evocatively followed *jackboot* with *Achilles' heel* (what better way to protect an exposed heel?), *hotbed* by *melting pot* (as if the same heat is used to warm both), and *melting pot* by *acid test* and *veritable inferno* (as if this metaphorical heat offers a searing test of truth)?

As demonstrated by Empson and Ricks, clichés and stereotypes are worthy of scorn only when they are used lazily, as a substitute for careful thought and well-crafted composition. When used with care, clichés and stereotypes are no more or no less scorn-worthy than words themselves, and no less limited in how they can be combined. In the end, whether they are used for banal or creative purposes depends on how they are varied and combined,[41] and how well they are integrated into what it is we want to say. What is true for clichés is equally as true of Jung's archetypes, McLuhan's cliché-archetypes, and Lippmann's stereotypes. All are familiar, but all can be used in surprising new ways.

This chapter has examined the strong link between conventional patterns of thought and conventional patterns of language. These conventional patterns are so pervasive in the language of the web that this link can be exploited to automatically acquire a large body of stereotypical associations. Computers may lack the real world experience to form biases and impressions and stereotypes of their own, but they can certainly acquire these indirectly, from the web, in a simplified and turbo-charged version of how humans learn from the language of others. Though the source of many a hackneyed thought and phrase, this body of mutual knowledge also provides the normative foundations on which linguistic creativity must ultimately be grounded. The *Aristotle* system, though just a start, shows how this knowledge can be parlayed into a computational model for generating and understanding simple but useful metaphors.

In the next chapter, we drill deeper into metaphor, and investigate its close ties to two other heavy-hitters in creative language – analogy and conceptual blending.

5

Pimp my ride

Customizing language with metaphor, analogy and blending

Much of what we know and feel about the world is shaped not by direct experience, but by words. Language is at its most persuasive when it creates new pathways for information to flow between ideas, so that strong feelings for one topic can become equally strong and vivid feelings for another. In effect, creative language is a form of conceptual rewiring that allows us to influence, with words alone, how ideas are connected and emotions are channelled in the heads of an audience. Having already looked at simile, we now look at how metaphor, analogy and blending enable us to customize language to our own ends.

Vehicles of creativity

Henry Ford famously joked that customers could buy his new model-T in any colour they liked, so long as it was black.[1] Ford could afford to be dismissive of a customer's desire for personalization; when his assembly-line first started to crank out the model-T, car ownership was thousands of times less common than it is today, and the act of owning a car – *any* car at all – was itself a supreme act of social differentiation. Yet, as ownership grew and cars became more commonplace, automakers like General Motors capitalized on the new demand for variety, offering cars in a wide range of colours, sizes and styles.

Variety is not just the spice of life, but of language too. Plain folks may prefer plain language, but even the plainest of us occasionally feel the need to trick out our ride, linguistically speaking, and inject a little individuality and flair into how we communicate. Plain language is, in many ways, the model-T of communication: sturdy and affordable, a normally reliable vehicle for our meanings, but a vehicle that often appears dull and unsophisticated. Mono-chromatic prose is fine as far as it goes, and as George Orwell argued (in Chapter 1), plain speaking is often the best way to get our meanings across, yet speakers strive to customize their use of language in many different ways. Henry Ford may have been dismissive of the bells and whistles that consum-ers would later come to demand, but buying a new car is now as option-ridden as buying a coffee in Starbucks (or should that be the other way round?). Our shared facility for linguistic creativity makes home mechanics of us all, allow-ing us to invent our own add-ons or just copy and perhaps even improve upon the road-tested 'mods' of others.

No modern writer better represents the model-T school of monochromatic prose than Dan Brown, author of 'The da Vinci Code'[2] and its various prequels and sequels. Though critically reviled, Brown has enjoyed immense commer-cial success; readers love his fast-paced plots larded with historical details that are presented in the most unchallenging airport-friendly prose. The British stand-up comedian Stewart Lee has memorably lampooned Brown as the kind of author who writes sentences like 'The famous man looked at the red cup'.[3] It's a curiosity of language that we can mock a writer like Brown for being capable of this level of blandness, yet consider a comedian like Lee to be creative for attributing this blandness to Brown. The difference is one of context and purpose: as a writer, we expect a higher level of linguistic innova-tion from Brown; but as a comedian, Lee seems to have perfectly distilled this purest drop of eau de Brown. In truth, Brown is not a bad writer, no more than the model-T was a bad car. But the creativity of the model-T lay in its method of mass production, which made it the world's first affordable car. In contrast, critics are sceptical of any art that smacks of the production line, and expect instead to find the creativity on the canvas, screen or page.

Of course, we expect critics and sharp-tongued comedians to be mean, but other writers are just as eager to get into the Brown-bashing business too. When speaking at the University of Maine in 2005, Stephen King unchari-tably described Brown as 'the intellectual equivalent of Kraft Macaroni and Cheese',[4] conveniently forgetting that he himself has not always been appre-ciated by the critics for his shelf-crowding best-sellers. Two decades earlier,

King had described his own work as *'the literary equivalent of a Big Mac and large fries'*,[5] which shows what a difference 20 years can make to one's self-image. Popular writing shares many qualities with popular food: both are convenient to buy and quick to consume, and both can be satisfying in an unhealthy but lip-smacking fashion. Naturally, by comparing popular art to fast food, the implication is that both are junk, and that each is the lowest common denominator of its respective domain. Brown and King are household brands, and so are naturally compared to other high-profile marques. Here is critic Peter Conrad reviewing Brown's sequel to *The da Vinci Code* (named *The Lost Symbol* in true Brown fashion) in 2009:

> Brown, like Coke, is a global brand. . . . The writing is as bad as Brown's admirers have come to expect: imagine Coke gone flat.[6]

The Coke metaphor works well for Conrad, and he goes on to elaborate it as follows:

> Brown relies on italics to carbonate his limp language.

Yet, Brown must not use enough italics for Conrad's liking if the result resembles 'Coke gone flat'. The capper, however, is Conrad's conclusion:

> Dan Brown's latest blockbuster is the literary equivalent of Coca Cola and will no doubt sell as well.

How is it that Brown can be ridiculed for his clunky prose, but the critics themselves can get so much creative mileage out of well-worn tropes like these junk-food[7] metaphors? Indeed, if these metaphors all have the same conceptual foundation, which views an easy read as junk food, how can these metaphors ever escape their own critical judgement?

As these examples show, we can analyse metaphors at different levels of form and content. At one level, a metaphor can be viewed as a playful combination of words that allows us to describe one idea or domain of experience with the words we normally reserve for another. At a deeper level, we might view metaphor as the use of one conceptual structure to organize our understanding of an entirely different concept or domain. Adopting this conceptual perspective, we might even conclude that metaphor is much more than a linguistic phenomenon, and that language is just one possible medium for the expression of metaphorical thinking. In recent decades, influential scholars like George Lakoff,[8] Mark Johnson[9] and Ray Gibbs[10] have been at the vanguard of this shift from the linguistic to the conceptual understanding of metaphor. This shift has posited a new and more profound role for metaphor in thought.

No longer just a tool of effective communication, the *conceptual* metaphor is now widely seen as a fundamental part of our cognitive apparatus. Because each conceptual metaphor is a productive schematic mapping between the mental representations of two different domains, a single conceptual schema can give rise to a thriving family of related linguistic metaphors.

Thus, a schematic mapping like Low-Brow Fiction is an Unhealthy Foodstuff can be superficially realized in many different ways at the linguistic level. For instance, we've seen that this conceptual metaphor can be rendered in words so that popular fiction is described in terms of a calorie-rich Big Mac and fries, perhaps to emphasize how this fiction can be big (like most of Mr. King's offerings) and filling, yet frowned upon by serious nutritionists (read: critics), or in terms of macaroni and cheese, whose homely convenience bears as much relation to real Italian food as Mr. Brown's writing bears to serious literature. Each linguistic realization elaborates the underlying conceptual metaphor in different ways, allowing us to visualize the rather generic notion of an Unhealthy Foodstuff in a way that appeals more directly to our senses and to our specific experience of the world. Like Ford's model-T, or the 'prefabricated henhouses' that Orwell worried about, Big Macs are produced on an industrial scale, with millions pouring off the McDonald's assembly line every year. Likewise, we know that Kraft's Mac & Cheese is loved by generations of kids whose appetites have yet to develop more sophisticated tastes, while Coca Cola dominates the market for sugary drinks that can widen the waist and rot the teeth. All are comfort foods with their own unique properties that can easily be transferred to the domain of popular fiction. Different critics can use the same conceptual metaphor of Low-Brow Fiction is an Unhealthy Foodstuff, yet each may bring something fresh to the way it is rendered anew each time.

In fact, this conceptual metaphor is itself an elaboration of an even more generic metaphor that views Ideas as Foods, commonly rendered in stock phrases such as '*food for thought*', '*the meat of an argument*', '*chew over the issues*' and '*digest the news*'. Drilling deeper, we see evidence in our everyday use of language that an even more generic metaphor is at work here, one that views Mental Content as a Physical Substance, as when we talk about the '*substance of a message*', '*the density of information*' or '*an insubstantial argument*'. Indeed, we find it hard to talk about ideas at all without invoking some kind of conceptual metaphor to view the products of cognition as the physical contents (or 'content') of the mind. As noted by John Barnden,[11] a computer scientist who has extensively studied everyday metaphors of mind, we '*grasp*' ideas, '*bounce*' ideas off one another and '*push doubts to the back of our minds*'.

At the conceptual level then, the metaphors from King and Conrad above employ the same underlying conceptual structure and convey broadly the same meaning. In fact, Mr. King employs the same conceptual schema twice, once to modestly describe his own work and again to attack the work of Dan Brown. Yet, to focus entirely on the conceptual level is to miss the linguistic nuances that make these snarky remarks so much fun; each barb may instantiate the very same schema, but their creativity lies in how this schema is elaborated at the level of words. For it is at this level that considerations of style and technique take centre stage. A fixation with schematic conceptual content would force us to conclude that two pictures of the same scene or topic have the same artistic merit when clearly they would not. If we give marks for effort, then Conrad's use of the schema beats both of King's, since Conrad at least attempts to use the schema in a systematic manner. He begins by noting that the status of the Brown brand is as globally entrenched as that of Coke, by some measures the most valuable commercial brand in the world. He then quickly builds on this to compare the products themselves, likening Brown's writing to the taste of a *flat* Coke. The use of 'flat' is key here, since a great many of Conrad's readers may actually like the taste of Coke. Conrad is forced to qualify his comparison so that it yields the negative inferences he wants (and needs) to yield. He goes on to describe Brown's irritating use of italics as an attempt to add fizz to his writing, perhaps implying that overuse in either case is liable to leave the reader with a bad case of gas.

Though the conceit here is somewhat counterproductive at a schematic level – Conrad has already described Brown's writing as 'flat' in the non-effervescent sense of a stale beverage – it does allow him to use that wonderful (if metaphorically mixed) combination of words '*carbonate his limp language*'. In fact, it is Conrad's use of the BROWN IS COKE metaphor, a simple elaboration of the schema LOW-BROW FICTION IS AN UNHEALTHY FOODSTUFF (or, more charitably, POPULAR FICTION IS A POPULAR FOODSTUFF) which in turn elaborates the IDEAS ARE FOODS schema, that allows Conrad to carbonate his own review of Brown's writing. In other words, the conceptual schema is just a starting point, and a rather commonplace one at that; the creativity of Conrad's review derives from how he uses the schema at the linguistic level, as a structure from which he can hang a whole series of related similes, metaphors and analogies.

Scheming with schemas

Good metaphors deliver a concentrated burst of information and feeling, in such quantity that, like jokes, they are poorly served by rational explanations of what they mean. The lazy use of conceptual schemas can make our metaphors seem mechanical, gimmicky and insincere, while creative one-offs can seem striking and immediate because they make us feel first and analyse second, if we consciously analyse them at all. Suppose a new colleague you know little about is described by the office gossip as a *'busted flush'*. Even if you have no idea of the rules of poker, you'll still get the gist of this put-down straight away, since it's a tough sell to compliment anyone with the label 'busted'. But if you *are* familiar with the rules of poker, this metaphor can convey so much more, by tapping into your experiences of poker and of the highs and lows that a good game of chance can produce. The label *'busted flush'* nicely compresses the compelling drama of a good poker game into a simple two-word phrase, communicating a sudden shift from high to low, from hope to failure and from prospective winner to certain loser. This shift is disappointing enough in a game context, but when applied to another person, the phrase evokes a near-tragic sense of loss and squandered promise.

Look beneath the minimalism of *'busted flush'* and you'll find a whole world of meaning, as deep and as resonant as you care to imagine. Though the gist is simple, almost every scrap of poker knowledge that is brought to bear on its elaboration can yield additional insights. For instance, poker players know that a flush – five cards of the same suit – is a risky all-or-nothing strategy to pursue. When aiming to turn three-of-a-kind into four-of-a-kind, or two-pairs into a full house, players know that failure to improve their hands will still leave them in a pretty good position. In contrast, a partial flush is worthless; all the pieces must come together for it to work, and either one has a complete flush or nothing at all. The card that finally busts a flush is the poker equivalent of a tragic character flaw, as when someone who seems to promise so much is shown to be lacking some vital quality.

Though our appreciation of this metaphor can certainly be enhanced by a recognition of the conceptual schema LIFE IS A GAME, the most important part of the metaphor obeys no such schema. We often view different kinds of life situations through the lens of game play – as when we describe ourselves as *'being in a stalemate'*, or *'stuck behind the eight-ball'*, or *'backing a loser'* – but there is no general metaphoric tendency to view different kinds of people as different configurations of playing cards. What makes poker such a good metaphor for life in general is the array of feelings that the game can evoke, strong feelings such as anxiety, joy, hope and disappointment that are common to many different situations in everyday life. The sudden rush of disappointment that follows a misplaced investment in a busted flush mirrors that which follows a misplaced investment in another human being: both promise a great deal but finally deliver nothing at all. It is these shared feelings, rather than an overarching conceptual schema, that make poker (and other high-tension games) such a powerful vehicle for metaphor.

Structure matters

Strictly speaking, is this use of poker to re-frame our conception of language a kind of simile, a metaphor or an analogy? As it happens, it is a mix – or a hodgepodge, if you are feeling uncharitable – of all three together. Generally speaking, the more elaborate the conceit, the less likely it is to fit neatly into a single category of creative language. Rather, as a conceit is developed through the course of a text, it can meander from one category of expression to another, manifesting as a simile here and a metaphor there, whichever is most conducive to the author's current purpose and temperament. Remember, the conceit is the insight *behind* the creative expressions, which suggests that one domain of experience can be re-framed in terms of another, while the linguistic metaphors and similes are often just a means to an end, to convey that conceptual insight in the most resonant form that the author can muster. But if we can veer from one expressive form to another when communicating a single underlying idea, what keeps all the pieces in place and ensures the overall coherence of the resulting text?

The answer to this question comes in two forms. If the conceit is an elaboration of a well-understood conceptual schema – such as POLITICS IS SPORT OR THEORIES ARE BUILDINGS – then that schema will impose its own consistent stamp on all of the individual expressions that successively develop the conceit. When talking about romantic relationships, for instance, we might hop between different but related aspects of the LIFE IS A JOURNEY[12] schema, such as the road the lovers are travelling along (bumpy roads are a sure sign of a troubled romance), the lovers' vehicle (perhaps a bicycle made for two, as in HAL 9000's favourite song 'Daisy, Daisy'[13]) or the ultimate destination (marriage, parenthood or the divorce courts?). Though we might use different similes and metaphors along the way to develop these aspects, these expressions will all tend to be mutually coherent because they are all rooted in the same underlying schema. Alternately, if the conceit is an original one, like the offbeat notion that we can look at people through the prism of a poker hand, then our stock of conceptual schemas like LIFE IS A GAME will be of little help, offering just modest opportunities for elaboration around the edges of an otherwise novel arrangement of ideas. In this case, we have to rely on a structural analogy to keep all the pieces neatly in place.

Many of our most elaborate similes and metaphors are also analogies, insofar as they establish a coherent mapping of elements from one domain of experience onto another. Students familiar with the SAT college-entrance examinations[14] will likely have a hate-hate relationship with the *A:B::C:D* format for analogies,[15] as in *dog:bark::cat:meow* or *computer:processor::car:engine*. While similes are grammatically noteworthy for their use of 'like' or 'as', and metaphors are just as noteworthy for their lack of an explicit comparison tag, high-school students learn to verbalize an analogical relationship with expressions of the form 'A *is to* B *as* C *is to* D'. Aristotle, in his *Poetics*, considered this kind of proportional analogy to be a sub-category of metaphor, since the proportion *A:B::C:D* implicitly underpins metaphors of the form *A's* B or *C's* D, as when we talk of a computer's engine, or more fancifully, of a dog's meow. The same kind of implicit proportional analogies underpin the *kenning* riddles of old English.[16] In Beowulf,[17] for instance, the sun is described as the '*world candle*', exploiting the analogy *room:candle::world:sun*, while the sea is described as a '*whale road*' or '*whale path*' via the implicit analogy *person:road::whale:sea*.

SAT-like tests do not use proportional analogies to enlighten but to challenge and evaluate. To ensure an objective marking scheme, each analogy is posed as a multiple-choice riddle for which there is a single correct answer. So, given a source-domain pairing *A:B*, a student must identify the correct mapping *C:D* from a given set of candidates. All but one of these are distracters, sirens designed to lure unwary students onto the rocks. The following example is more prosaic than those of Beowulf but is typical of the SAT:

BIRD :   NEST ::

(a) squirrel :   *tree*

(b) horse :   *horsebox*

(c) dog :   *kennel*

(d) beaver :   *dam*

(e) baby :   *nursery*

A hapless student might be tempted by a number of false harbours in this example: just as birds live in nests, squirrels live in trees, dogs live in kennels and beavers live in dams; likewise, while young birds are reared in nests, human babies are reared in nurseries. Option (b) is quickly discarded, since horses occupy horseboxes just for the purposes of transportation, but option (d) is worthy of further consideration, since birds both construct their own nests and dwell in them, just as beavers construct and dwell in their own dams. Squirrels do not build their own trees, nor dogs their own kennels, nor babies their own nurseries. So, the best answer is the most systematic answer, that is, the answer that represents the most coherent and extensive mapping between domains: (d).

The simple form of a proportional analogy can be deceptive, as these analogies often draw on obscure aspects of our knowledge of the world. As noted by Aristotle, analogy and metaphor often work hand in hand, as in this rather enigmatic witticism from Sigmund Freud in his treatise on jokes and the unconscious: '*A wife is like an umbrella. Sooner or later one takes a cab*'.[18] Freud offers a curiously Victorian interpretation of his joke, in which he claims that 'One marries in order to protect oneself against the temptations of sensuality', but the joke can better be explained if we summarize it as a proportional analogy in the Aristotelian fashion, as follows:

Wife : Prostitute :: Umbrella : Taxicab

The analogy can only be properly understood if we view it as an instance of creative categorization. Freud asks us to see the parallels between a wife and an umbrella in the context of a contrast between umbrellas and taxicabs. The resolution arrives when we categorize wives and umbrellas as the private facilities of individuals, in contrast to taxicabs, which can be categorized as a public facility, hired and shared by the masses. The missing piece of the puzzle is the concept *Prostitute*, which like a wife is both a woman and a lover, and which like a taxicab is 'accessible in return for money'. So, to understand Freud's riddle, we must see it as a problem of analogy (viz. what corresponds to what?) and of categorization (viz. what do corresponding elements have in common?).

Thankfully, students undergoing modern SAT-like tests are unlikely to encounter analogical riddles of the psychosexual variety beloved of Freud, but the analogies they do encounter may nonetheless require a nuanced understanding of both words and the world. For instance, the proportion *hack:writer::mercenary:soldier* hinges upon our sense that there is something equally disreputable about hacks as writers-for-hire and mercenaries as soldiers-for-hire, and so this proportion is, in its way, a more contemporary (and less sexual) counterpart to Freud's object-for-hire analogy. While even scholars may scratch their heads at that museum piece of cryptic Victoriana, it is worth noting that computers can do rather well on modern SAT-style analogy tests. Using a semantically organized computer-readable dictionary-cum-thesaurus like WordNet,[19] a computer can just about scrape a passing grade on a test with real SAT analogies.[20] In fact, computers can approach human levels of performance on the SAT if they look beyond the confines of the dictionary and tap into broader intuitions about the world. While these intuitions are not given an explicit form in a conventional dictionary, they do have a linguistic form, implicitly at least, on the World Wide Web.

Consider how a human student might solve the earlier *bird:nest* analogy. Our student might characterize the relationship between *bird* and *nest* via the set of possible linking phrases that can meaningfully be squeezed between them, such as 'in their', 'builds', 'lives in' and 'returns to', and then find another word pair with a similar range of linking phrases. Computers have no linguistic experience of the world to draw upon, yet they can still scan the Web to find the most popular linking phrases across a wide variety of texts. By also noting the frequency of each linking phrase, a computer can build a vector representation for each word pair (such as *dog:kennel* or *beaver:dam*) in a high-dimension space. A comparison of the vectors for any two word-pairs yields a numeric measure of how similar they are in terms of the relational phrases that can link them, which turns out to be a very good proxy for the relational similarity of the two word-pairs. Since proportional analogies hinge on relational similarity, a computer using only the text of the Web (harvested via a search engine like Google) can do surprisingly well. Using these techniques, in a model he calls *Latent Relational Analysis* (LRA),[21] the Canadian computer scientist Peter Turney has developed systems that can score above 55 per cent on tests with real SAT analogies, whereas random selection in a five-way choice will yield just 20 per cent on average. Above 55 per cent is a pass rate for humans, and pretty close to the average score obtained by human test-takers on SAT analogies. Not enough for admission to the Ivy league, to be sure, but a remarkably promising start for computers as they tackle a vexing human problem.

Outside the artificial context of a test paper, most analogies are not distinctively marked as such in a text, but come wrapped in the guise of a simile or metaphor, or a combination of both. Here, we see the satirical writer P. J. O'Rourke describing the appearance of the Oriental Pearl Tower in Shanghai. He tells us that the tower looks like

> a Russian Orthodox church of the twenty-eighth century, or a launch vehicle for a pair of Houston Astrodomes, or a humongous shish kebab that lost everything but two onions in a barbeque fire.[22]

The tower is such a visual novelty that it almost defies literal description. The key elements are a series of pink tessellated globes – two large and one small – mounted along the vertical length of a needle-like structure that it rooted to the ground via a tripod of legs. But such a description hardly does it justice, and the *London Independent* newspaper has memorably described the tower as looking like '*a syringe that's swallowed a pink neon disco ball*'.[23] Though fantastical, these similes do a good job of capturing the sheer implausibility of the structure; if you've seen the tower up close, and you should, there is a clear analogical mapping between the structural parts of these descriptions and the structural parts of the tower. The globes do look like disco balls, or giant onions, or the Houston Astrodome or the domes of a Russian orthodox church, while the backbone of the structure does look like a giant syringe, or a rocket, or a giant skewer or a church spire. What's more, the relationship between the parts of the description align nicely with the relationship between the parts of the tower. The giant globes do look like they've been skewered onto the tower and are about to be launched into the heavens.

Creative linguistic analogies thus fall into two broad categories: those that describe a pre-existing target domain in terms of another and those that describe a pre-existing target in terms of a specially constructed patchwork fantasy. The perceived creativity of this second kind of analogy depends not only on the pragmatic and semantic distance between the domains themselves (e.g. a tower vs a syringe) and their connotations (e.g. between reaching for the skies and searching for a vein), but also on the implausible arrangement of the elements within the vehicle domain (e.g. a disco ball *in* a syringe, or the Houston Astrodome *on* a rocket). We should be careful to note that this category of analogy is not funnier by definition, for it is a pudding that is very easily over-egged. However, because these analogies allow for intra-domain disparity (syringes and disco balls) as well as inter-domain disparity (towers and syringes), then by definition they *do* offer more opportunities for the kinds of creative tension that can result in humour.

Analogies of the form *A:B::C:D* are called proportional analogies because the pairing C and D preserves the proportion that is observed between A and B. The term 'proportion' is literally apt in arithmetic analogies such as *2:4::3:6* but applies to all analogies in a broader relational sense. There is a good reason why *The Independent* contrived to have the syringe swallow the disco ball, or why O'Rourke needed to have everything but the onions fall off his giant kebab. In each case, the author needs to establish the right spatial relationships between the parts of the description, so that these relationships will be proportional to the spatial relationships in the target domain. But the proportions in an analogy are not always visual or spatial; in many conceptual analogies, the proportions relate to the use of the same organizing relationships in the source and target domains. A is proportional to C because it shares the same conceptual relationship with B as C does with D. The abstract proportions between the elements of the source and target domains allow us to map the conceptual structure of one onto the other.

A powerful contemporary account of analogy is offered by Dedre Gentner's Structure Mapping Theory (or SMT).[24] Gentner observes that good analogies exploit a source domain with a rich relational structure to describe a target domain whose core relations (e.g. those to do with cause and effect) are organized in isomorphic ways. A classic example, and one that has inspired generations of scientists and hippies alike, is the Niels Bohr/Ernest Rutherford analogy shown in Figure 5.1. The analogy compares the structure of the atom (with its nucleus of protons and neutrons orbited by layers of spinning electrons) to the structure of the solar system (with its core, the sun, orbited by planets at varying distances). A coherent analogy thus identifies aspects of the target domain that structurally mirror key aspects of the source domain. Insightful analogies also exhibit *systematicity* by focussing on those parts of the source and target domains that are well connected in, and central to, the

FIGURE 5.1 *The Rutherford Atom and the Solar System: The classic analogy is founded on structural similarities between two very different physical scales.*

workings of those domains. Compared to Bohr's *atom as solar-system* mapping, the incendiary analogy for which Turkish politician Recep Tayyip Erdogan was jailed in 1994 seems to lack both systematicity and coherence: 'The mosques are our barracks, the domes our helmets, the minarets our bayonets and the faithful our soldiers'.[25] Erdogan's analogy, from an Islamic poem, more closely resembles a cubist painting – with its thought-provoking mishmash of conflicting perspectives and scales – than a coherent, systematic mapping with explanatory power.

Gentner and her colleagues have shown in repeated experiments that people tend to prefer analogies in which an important causal structure is shared across both domains.[26] The Bohr/Rutherford analogy is so compelling precisely because the shared structure supports causal explanation as well as mental visualization: the planets orbit the sun and do not fly off into space because the sun is so much bigger than they are and so exerts an attractive force that keeps them in orbit; the analogy suggests that a comparable force must be keeping the electrons spinning in place around the nucleus. To have real explanatory power, the analogy must be coherent: if two elements are related in the source, and both elements are mapped onto the target, then these elements must have a comparable relationship in the target. Gentner suggests that the core relationships in the source domain – which together offer the most systematic explanation for the workings of the source – are mapped identically, or with minimal transformation, onto the target. Thus, planets *revolve around* the sun and electrons *revolve around* the nucleus, planets *are attracted to* the sun and electrons *are attracted to* the nucleus, and planets *are much smaller than* the sun while electrons *are much smaller than* the nucleus.

Gentner, like Aristotle, has argued that analogy plays a central role in the workings of the metaphor. In contrast, Sam Glucksberg and his collaborators argue that metaphors are more accurately understood as categorization statements.[27] In the metaphor 'my job is a jail', Glucksberg argues that jails are not compared to jobs, rather the word 'jail' denotes a category – such as *confining and oppressive situations* – in which *jail* is a very prominent member. Thus, the metaphor tells us that the idea of a job (and 'my job' in particular) might also be included in this category. As we saw in the last chapter, prominent exemplars are often used in language as proxies for the unnamed categories they exemplify (thus, *Kenny G* has become an exemplar for people or things that are technically brilliant but which lack credibility). How else are we to understand claims like the following, made by the former Afghan minister of the interior Ali A. Jalali: '*Afghanistan is not Iraq. It is the theme park of problems*'. The word 'Iraq' has a dual reference[28] in this comparison; while it normally denotes a specific country, it refers here to a whole category of countries with Iraq-like problems that are amenable to the kinds of solutions that worked in Iraq (such as the controversial 'surge'). Likewise, 'theme-park' refers here to the category of places whose diverse challenges are as likely to inspire terror and fear as they are excitement and adventure.

Of course, we can also put on our *analogist* hats and argue that the metaphor '*my job is a jail*' establishes a systematic structural analogy between jobs and jails, in which workers are prisoners, managers are guards, cubicles are cells, the boss is the warden and the water cooler is the exercise yard. The office bully might even be the hulking white-supremacist in the bottom bunk, the one with a taste for fresh meat and a bowel-chilling romantic gleam in his eye. All of these are analogically possible and certainly add colour and humour to the interpretation, yet such an analogy might just be an interesting sideshow to a more central act of category inclusion. So, which view is correct? Earlier, when analysing Freud's metaphorical joke about wives, umbrellas and taxicabs, we saw how analogy can work hand in hand with categorization to communicate a complex figurative meaning. So, perhaps one need not choose one over the other after all?

An intriguing compromise, with the equally intriguing name *The Career of Metaphor*, has been proposed by Brian Bowdle and Dedre Gentner.[29] In this integrative perspective, a metaphor is both appreciated differently and processed differently as it ages. Bowdle and Gentner argue that novel metaphors (like '*Afghanistan is . . . the theme park of problems*') are initially understood as comparisons, so that structure mapping may be used to identify analogical similarities between the relational structure of both domains. As our familiarity with these metaphors grows, and they no longer seem quite so novel or challenging, we come instead to understand them as categorization statements. As Bowdle and Gentner put it, there is an '*evolutionary path . . . from*

comparison to categorization'. In this clever reconciliation of analogy and category inclusion, challenging new metaphors are best understood by using
the structural insights offered by analogy. But as such metaphors lose their
new car smell and become more familiar with age, it often becomes more
effective to treat them instead as inclusive categories that readily accept new
members.

Frankenstein comparisons and badass blends

In the movie *Sunset Boulevard*, the aging Norma Desmond remains convinced of her star power: 'I am big! It's the pictures that got small' she
cries.[30] The actor Ethan Hawke might well agree. When asked to write a profile of Kris Kristofferson for *Rolling Stone* magazine, Hawke had to create an
imaginary star of his own to serve as an apt contemporary comparison. For
Hawke, Brad Pitt is as meaningful a comparison as one can make, but even
Pitt's star power is but a dim bulb to that of Kristofferson when he shone
most brightly in the 1970s. To communicate just how impressive the singer/
actor/activist would have seemed to an audience in 1979, Hawke assembles
the following Frankenstein-monster from the body of Pitt and other assorted
star parts:

> Imagine if Brad Pitt had written a No. 1 single for Amy Winehouse, was
> considered among the finest songwriters of his generation, had been
> a Rhodes scholar, a U.S. Army Airborne Ranger, a boxer, a professional
> helicopter pilot – and was as politically outspoken as Sean Penn. That's
> what a motherfuckin' badass Kris Kristofferson was in 1979.[31]

Pitt comes off poorly in the comparison, but this is precisely the point: no contemporary star comes off well, because in Hawke's view, none has the wattage
or the all-round appeal that Kristofferson had in 1979. The awkwardness of the
comparison, and the fancifulness of the composite image, actually serves as
a creative meta-description of Kristofferson's achievements. In effect, Hawke
is saying 'look to what lengths I must go to find a fair comparison for this man
without peer'. Note how information actually flows in both directions in this
comparison. To create a more rounded comparison, Hawke finds it necessary
to not only mix in a few elements from other stars (such as Sean Penn), but
also to burnish Pitt's résumé with elements borrowed from Kristofferson himself. Most of this additional structure is imported directly from the target into
the source, such as when we are asked to imagine Pitt as a professional heli-
copter pilot. The other structure is imported in the form of an analogy: while

Kristofferson wrote songs for the likes of Janis Joplin, Pitt is imagined here as a songwriter for her modern counterpart, Amy Winehouse.[32]

This *Pitt 2.0* doesn't actually exist of course. Hawke's description is a *conceptual blend* that constructs a whole new source concept in its own counterfactual space. Blending is pervasive in modern culture and can be seen in everything, from cartoons[33] to movies[34] to popular fiction,[35] while the elements of a blend can come from any domain of experience, from classic novels to 140-character tweets[36] to individual words. As defined by the cognitive linguists Gilles Fauconnier and Mark Turner,[37] conceptual blending combines the smoothness of metaphor with the structural complexity and organizing power of analogy. We can think of blending as a cognitive operation in which conceptual ingredients do not flow in a single direction, but are thoroughly stirred together, as in a chef's bowl, to create a new structure with its own emergent meanings.

Fauconnier and Turner's theoretical framework gives us the formal tools to characterize the middle ground that is formed from the selective projection and integration of elements from two or more bundles of conceptual concept, called *mental spaces*.[38] For instance, we might give the name 'Astrotourist' (itself a word-level blend) to the middle-ground between an adventurous space-farer (an '*astro*naut') and a curious tourist. This blended word form[39] is more than a metaphor (an astronaut viewed as a tourist) and more than an analogy (a structural comparison of space travel for science and terrestrial travel for fun), but a true lexical and conceptual blend of both. That is, an *astrotourist* is a non-professional astronaut who travels for fun and not for science. Astrotourists also have an emergent property that comes from neither input space, since commonsense dictates that astrotourists must be very rich indeed if they are to buy their way into space (yet another blended neologism for space tourists nicely highlights this requirement: *aristonauts*). So, as championed by Fauconnier and Turner, blends are more than merely descriptive: a blend is a conceptual product in its own right, a cross-quoting and newly 'chunked' idea that can itself be cross-quoted as part of even larger conceits in the future.

In linguistic creativity, less is almost always more. The more concise and allusive a creative expression, the more buy-in it requires from an audience to flesh it out, thus allowing an audience to share just a little of the paternity of the creative act. The active participation of an audience in elaborating a highly compressed meaning can turn a listener from a passive recipient into an active constructor of meaning, more a midwife than an anxious onlooker. Whenever we say that a particular barb is dripping with satire or drenched in malice, we pay tribute to the ability of a concise phrase to serve as a sponge for our meaning, one capable of absorbing much more content that its compact form would outwardly suggest. Consider the following, said of director

Sam Mendes in the Guardian newspaper after studio bosses had chosen him to direct the 23rd film in the *James Bond* franchise: *'Appearance: Like the painting in George Clooney's attic'*.[40]

This is not a simple comparison, but a complex blend that is loaded with figurative meaning, and we require neither a prior mental image of Sam Mendes nor a knowledge of the paintings in Clooney's attic to understand its real meaning. We can be quite certain that the picture in question is not a real picture that Clooney might actually own, whether *A Rake's Progress* or *Dogs Playing Poker*, but an entirely fictional painting that we create on the fly, via Fauconnier and Turner's process of conceptual blending (see Figure 5.2). As Fauconnier and Turner might say, this is a multi-layered blend that must be unpacked[41] in several stages, and Figure 5.2 represents just the first stage of unpacking. The blend exploits our familiarity with Oscar Wilde's *The Picture of Dorian Gray*,[42] a morality tale concerning the fate of a handsome but narcissistic young man who pledges his soul so that his painted self might suffer the ravages of time in his stead. Dorian soon discovers that his portrait – the infamous painting in the attic – not only changes to reflect his true age, but also

Topical input   Cliché-archetype

Cross-quoting 'blend'

FIGURE 5.2 *Not-so-gorgeous George – The blend of George Clooney and Dorian Gray that is cross-quoted in 'the picture in George Clooney's attic'. Mapping within the blend is logical and systematic, so once we accept the analogy Clooney=Gray, the picture in Clooney's attic is not just a picture of Dorian Gray but a picture of an aging Clooney.*

holds a mirror to his inner being. As Dorian descends into moral degeneracy, his painted counterpart suffers a more physical degeneration. Dorian's portrait becomes increasingly ugly to behold as he himself remains unnaturally youthful. Wilde's story comes wrapped in a memorable and highly quotable text, and has become as potent a cliché-archetype as any that Carl Jung or Marshall McLuhan can offer.

In everyday communication, however, the cliché-archetype has collapsed into pure cliché: if an acquaintance retains a youthful vigour into late middle-age, people are just as likely to trot out the '*picture in the attic*' conceit as they are to reach for that other chestnut, '*Peter Pan*'. These uses are so formulaic that we can easily forget the full import of the Dorian Gray cliché-archetype. To suggest that a youthful oldie has a Dorian-like portrait in the attic is to imply that this person has not only withstood the physical effects of aging, but has also withstood the physical effects of *sinning*, while nonetheless becoming rotten to the metaphysical core. This often overlooked allusion to sin and degeneracy, if brought again to the fore, can lend renewed pungency to the cliché.

In the right hands, any cliché can be revitalized in a well-turned phrase, and *The Guardian* breathes humorous new life into the *Dorian Gray* cliché-archetype by embedding it within two more topical nested blends. A visual representation of the workings of this figure-within-a-figure is provided in Figure 5.3. The innermost blend re-imagines Wilde's story with a new leading man, George Clooney, whose matinée-idol good looks make him an apt substitute for the handsome youth of the original tale. Clooney has maintained his status as a Hollywood sex symbol for almost two decades, and he remains a regular fixture in the pages of celebrity gossip sheets. We find it easy to imagine a slowly decaying portrait in a dark corner of Clooney's attic, and even if the conceit has the tang of sour grapes, this just adds to its snarkily humorous effect. Note that this inner blend is more than a simile, a metaphor or an analogy, and it does more than compare George Clooney to Dorian Gray. Rather, it creates a new version of the morality tale with its very own star. In the world of the blend, Clooney really does have a portrait of his aging, sin-wracked face in the attic. This inner blend puts a new face on Wilde's tale, to create a new chunk from familiar elements that can then be recruited by other blends and other conceits, as though it had always existed in our cultural lexicon.

This outer blend works largely as a simile, mapping the appearance of the director Sam Mendes to the appearance of the fictitious portrait in Clooney's attic. It is still a blend, however, because it imagines a counterfactual world in which Clooney has made a Faustian bargain to preserve his leading-man looks. In this world of the larger blend, we have to imagine the ways in which a lesser-mortal like Mendes might resemble a physically decaying matinée idol. We infer, for instance, that Mendes might once have been quite handsome,

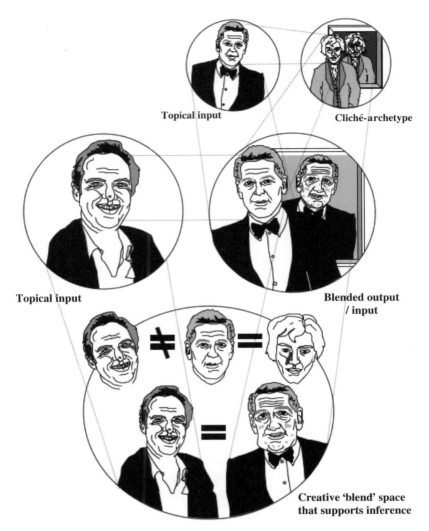

Topical input

Cliché-archetype

Topical input

Blended output / input

Creative 'blend' space that supports inference

FIGURE 5.3 *The figure-within-a-figure in* The Guardian's *comparison of director Sam Mendes to* 'the picture in George Clooney's attic'.

but now retains just a guilty hint of his youthful splendour. In short, we assume that Mendes looks like a ruined version of George Clooney, and, one supposes, like someone who has destroyed their own good looks through rakish excess. The humour of the conceit derives in part from this obvious hyperbole and in part from the gratuitous sideswipe at George Clooney. But it also derives in large part from a more subtle inference: Mendes merely *looks* dissolute and merely *looks* like one who has squandered his looks and his morals in the pursuit of corporeal pleasures; in fact, he may well have enjoyed very few (or none at all) of these pleasures, and so in a way, the poor fellow merely looks like one who is paying the physical price for someone else's dissolute behaviour.[43]

In the end, the reason *The Guardian* uses George Clooney is quite simple: Mendes has a passing resemblance to Clooney, more so than to the other Hollywood stars (such as Johnny Depp, say) on whom the mantle of Dorian Gray may sit more comfortably. The Wildean/Faustian version of George Clooney is a classic example of what Gilles Fauconnier and Mark Turner call a *middle-space*,[44] a manufactured middle ground that facilitates a larger mental leap between two more distant frames of reference.

But do readers really go to such lengths to analyse a passing remark in a snarky newspaper column of no great import? Perhaps many do not, but the potential for deep analysis, and thus for deeper enjoyment, is certainly present, even if everyone does not always avail of it. Moreover, even a cursory analysis will suggest to the reader that there is more meaning and resonance to be had if one cares to look, and this perception – even if it doesn't always spur deep analysis – can still add to our sense of enjoyment. Most readers will be aware of the remark's broad allusions (such as to Dorian Gray, Faustian bargains, Hollywood excesses and so on) even if no conscious attempt is made to completely connect the dots. Conversely, we might also ask whether the author of the throwaway remark deliberately imbued it with the complex meanings that our analysis has credited to it, or whether have we simply *over*-interpreted it for our own purposes. However, in the final analysis, does it really matter if a witticism turns out to be more funny and more resonant than its author had first intended? Creative expression is a process of discovery for both writer and reader alike, even when this expression is a throwaway quip in the gossip section of a daily newspaper.

Seeing the world through *metaphor eyes*

Researchers in *Psychology*, *Linguistics* and *Cognitive Science* (and the blend of all three, *Cognitive Linguistics*[45]) have collectively pieced together a compelling story about the workings of metaphor, analogy, simile and blending. This story goes some way toward demystifying the mechanisms of creative language production and consumption, by committing to specific mental processes and conceptual representations. But the real test of this story is not how convincing it seems or how well the scholars agree but the practicality of computational implementation.[46] Ultimately, it comes down to this: does our story have enough detail to allow us to build a realistic computer model?

Computer scientists have been working on the problem of creative language for decades, to produce working (if limited) models of metaphor,[47] analogy,[48] simile[49] and even blending.[50] The recurring bottleneck in all of these efforts is, inevitably, knowledge: algorithmic processes are all well and good, but where does a computer acquire the common-sense knowledge that these processes are supposed to operate upon? There is a flip side to this dilemma, however, for if a computational model is good enough, it can make a little knowledge go a very long way. We have developed one such model in the guise of the *Metaphorize* system, which is robust enough and just about knowledgeable enough to run on the Web (at www.educatedinsolence. com). *Metaphorize*[51] acquires its stereotyped knowledge of the world from three different sources: the abundance of similes on the Web (as described in Chapter 4); the abundance of questions, rich in presuppositions, that are commonly posed to Web search engines (e.g. 'why do pirates wear eye-patches?' and 'why do dogs bury bones?'); and manual knowledge-engineering, in the GOFAI tradition of the *Cyc*[52] project, in which engineers enrich the system with the most useful cliché-archetypes[53] (e.g. that soldiers carry guns or that guns fire bullets). At present, *Metaphorize* contains over 100,000 simple stereotypical beliefs about the world. Figure 5.4 shows a snapshot of the application as it appears online, showing its analysis of the tongue-in-cheek assertion 'Google is a cult'.

Metaphorize is a brainstorming tool that allows users to pose figurative *what-if* questions such as '*hackers are terrorists*' or '*scientists are artists*'. For each what-if, *Metaphorize* introspects about the further questions that are entailed by this perspective – this is relatively easy for the system, since much of its knowledge comes from questions in the first place – and then uses linguistic knowledge to identify those avenues that are most likely to bear creative fruit for the user. For instance, when asked to consider 'hackers as artists', *Metaphorize* ponders the meaningfulness of 'hacker art', 'hacker techniques' and 'hacker studios'. Likewise, if asked to imagine 'hackers as hobbyists', the system ponders the plausibility of 'hacker clubs'. The presence of established uses of these phrases on the Web lends credence to the corresponding hypotheses, so *Metaphorize* gives the highest ranking to the hypotheses with the most linguistic support.

Metaphorize also supports blending, and to a degree it even supports blends within blends, but it is not yet capable of anything close to the sophistication and effortless virtuosity of the *Dorian* blend in Figure 5.3. Nor will it be, realistically speaking, for some time to come. Right now, the system can handle simple blends like 'media empire' or 'space tourist', by using Web evidence to determine, for example, which aspects of an 'empire' are most salient in the world of media, or which aspects of science transfer most readily to the space domain. So, the acceptability of ready-made phrases like 'media dynasty' and

FIGURE 5.4 *Brainstorm for one, please: we can use computer models of creative language processing as tools for exploring conceptual what-ifs and stimulating human creativity.*

'media fortune', or 'space laboratory' and 'space experiment', dictates which aspects of empires and scientists are highlighted in their respective blends. The combination of these functionalities allows *Metaphorize* to handle more complex blends like 'astronauts are space scientists' or 'matadors are Flamenco dancers', though at present the human user is still very much in the driver's seat as to which blends are actually interpreted by the system. Clearly, we have a long way to go before tools like *Metaphorize* can manipulate words and ideas with anything like the creative fluency of humans. In the interim, however, our computer models can still serve two very important goals. First, they can show us whether our cognitive theories are on the right track and humble us by highlighting the practical limitations of those theories. Second, and most rewardingly, robust computer models can enable new software applications to provoke, stimulate and perhaps even to enhance creativity in humans.

Conclusions: New model, original parts

True motor-heads worship classic cars, yet are not afraid to tinker with a classic. In fact, to car aficionados, no vehicle is beyond custom modification. Custom paint-jobs, rear spoilers, alloy rims, turbochargers, superchargers, performance camshafts and other modifications can all improve the look, the feel and the power of a vehicle. Who cares what the manufacturer's specifications say? These specifications are designed for conventional owners and serve only as a starting point for those who really want to explore what their vehicles can achieve. In this chapter, we've argued that creative language has much the same relation to conventional language as custom cars do to the mass-produced vehicles that roll off a factory's assembly lines. A creative speaker does not totally reject or seek to obliterate the conventional but augments convention with powerful 'mods' like metaphor, analogy and blending to build something better and more individualistic.

Whenever we are tempted to think of creative language as merely the eye-catching packaging that we put on our thoughts, we do well to remember Goethe's maxim that words are often most useful precisely when ideas fail us.[54] For, we express ourselves creatively not just for the benefit of an audience, but for our own benefit also. Words are our handles on ideas, and our complex ideas need expressive but uncomplicated handles; in fact, the simpler the better. Anyone can articulate a complicated idea in a complicated way, but it takes genuine insight to reduce it to its simplest form without loss of meaning or the potential for subsequent elaboration. Our struggle to find this most convenient handle is our struggle to identify the real essence of an idea, and creative expressions can provide concise handles for ideas that are still taking shape. The more creative the handle, the more room a new idea has to breathe, to develop into something more, something that may further surprise and delight us. If we were forced to articulate new ideas in wholly literal terms, our most promising darlings would almost certainly be strangled at birth.

6

Six ridiculous things before breakfast

Finding method in madness and sense in nonsense

All creativity is surprising at some level, since it challenges our habitual assumptions about how things can and should be. Humorous creativity goes further still, and seemingly revels in the nonsensical and the absurd. Yet, even the most outrageous humour merely flirts with the ridiculous, for to be genuinely creative, humour must show us that there is folly in conventional wisdom and wisdom in unconventional foolishness. In this chapter, we consider how apparently illogical actions – such as saying the opposite of what we really mean or using deliberate ambiguity and outlandish imagery to communicate deeply felt sentiments – can be sensible and efficient strategies for achieving our communicative goals.

Hatter and anti-Hatter

The White Queen boasted to Alice that she could sometimes believe as many as six impossible things before breakfast.[1] This is quite a claim, even in Wonderland, yet the morning news that promises to 'tell it like it is' is liberally peppered with enough metaphoric descriptions and literal impossibilities to put even the Mad Hatter off his breakfast. Most of the metaphors we encounter everyday employ the language of literal impossibility to say something meaningful, *and* possible, on a non-literal level. For, even the most conventional metaphors flit along the boundaries of sense and nonsense: we cannot literally '*catch* a cold' or '*empty* our minds', no more than we can '*beef up* an idea' or '*kill* a proposal'.[2] Like the incongruity of jokes, it often seems that non-literal meanings come wrapped in forms that are, superficially at least, absurd. Yet, it is the appearance of nonsense that challenges us to seek out a deeper figurative meaning beneath the surface. The Hatter may have been mad, but even he would not bet his breakfast on the claim that there is never any logic to illogicality nor sense in nonsense.

Indeed, there is scarcely a logical fallacy that logicians think fatal to sound argumentation that comedians do not routinely exploit for humorous ends. Logicians tell us to avoid the *fallacy of equivocation*[3] – using the same word in different senses in the same argument – but language would be robbed of a remarkably productive strategy of humour if we could not exploit ambiguity in this way. Logicians also caution us to stay clear of the *fallacy of accent*[4] – placing a misleading emphasis on one part of an argument over others – but much of the deliberate misdirection in jokes relies on viewing this emphasis not as a fallacy but as a narrative strategy. Moreover, humour exploits a whole range of what logicians call *fallacies of presumption*,[5] from the fallacies of *sweeping generalization*[6] and *hasty generalization*[7] to the fallacies of *false analogy*,[8] *false cause*[9] and *irrelevant thesis*.[10] That's a lot of fallacies, which leads us to conclude (if not too hastily) that logic plays a pivotal role in humour, not as a guardian of meaning but as a reverse barometer of meaningful absurdity. The most successful comedy duos – from Hope and Crosby to Lewis and Martin to the magicians Penn and Teller – divide the comedic responsibilities in two, with the *straight man* acting as the logical foil for the often illogical antics of the *funny guy*. Needless to say, the logical straight man must also serve as the fall guy, yet it is the two together, the mix of logic and anti-logic, that yields the humorous creativity. Even without a straight man on stage, there is always one in the audience, for we bring our own expectations to bear every time we understand a joke.

Logicians pay great heed to fallacies because logic is annihilated by the anti-logic of fallacy just as surely as matter is annihilated by anti-matter. In language and argumentation, the anti-logic of absurdity must, therefore, be handled with great care. While we want to use absurdity – or the threat of absurdity – to destroy the arguments of others, we must be extremely careful that it does not annihilate the substance of our own arguments too. Conventional language gives us special 'containment chambers' to contain the effects of absurdity, to make it a viable threat to others without destroying our own arguments as well. The comedian George Carlin harnessed illogicality in this way when he argued that *'A smoking section in a restaurant makes as much sense as a peeing section in a pool'*.[11] His argument is striking and humorous because of the ruthless way in which it wields the anti-logic of stupidity. Using 'as' to keep the absurdity at arm's length, Carlin evokes the ridiculous idea that a swimming pool might actually allow us to urinate into its waters, provided we do so in a specially designated area of the pool. The image is disgusting (perhaps we imagine the discoloration of the water or people complaining of the odd taste) and defies commonsense: urine would spread throughout a pool just as surely as smoke throughout a restaurant. This is precisely Carlin's point, of course: if the idea makes no sense in a swimming pool, it surely makes no sense in a restaurant or on an airplane. By herding absurdity into specially constructed linguistic devices and using it to eat into the arguments of others, comedians like Carlin show that good arguments can be effective *and* silly; one need not preclude the other. We'll return shortly to this intriguing use of 'as' to compartmentalize and channel absurdity for creative ends.

Another safe (albeit less subtle) container for absurdity is negation. If the proposition *X* is silly or absurd, then wrapping it in the container (*not X*) safeguards us from this silliness. You may question the benefit of stating the obvious in this way, but the specific interaction of negation and absurdity can yield unexpected insights. When John Donne asserts that *'no man is an island'*,[12] his negation does more than turn the absurd into the obvious, but asks us ponder how close a man might come to being an island, if only figuratively. In a more modern context, the lyric *'I'm no Superman'*[13] from the TV series *Scrubs* uses negation to turn a fanciful claim into a meaningful articulation of human limitations, and in particular the practical limitations faced by doctors in their practice of modern medicine. As Michael Reddy pointed out in his critique of the conduit metaphor of language,[14] meaning does not reside in an utterance like the contents of a box. Rather, listeners collaborate with speakers to construct meaning among themselves.[15] When a speaker negates the absurd or the ridiculous to create the obvious, listeners collude with the speaker to find a meaningful and insightful middle ground between both extremes.[16]

Indeed, we often derive meaning from the negation of propositions that no sane person would ever assert or believe. Imagine a well-to-do wife, in an opulent house in the suburbs, shouting at her husband: *'I'm not your maid!'*. Since this wife is nobody's maid, her assertion is perfectly truthful, but is, on the face of it, no more sensible than the equally true assertion *'I am not Mike Tyson!'*. However, if this wife is weary of her husband's indifference to her housekeeping efforts, it can be meaningful to assert that his indifference resembles that of a lord of the manor to a lowly scullery maid. Though patently obvious, this kind of negation amounts to what Erving Goffman describes as an 'accurately improper move [that] can poke through the thin sleeve of immediate reality'.[17] The wife effectively punctures the shared pretence of her subservience, to say something like: '*Stop treating me like a maid, expecting me to pick up your clothes, serve your meals and wash your dishes, without any show of gratitude. You may not think of me as a maid, but that is how you act'*. The husband may reply with the equally accurate '*I never said you were my maid*', but this merely addresses the superficial charge, and fails to deflect the argumentative force of the wife's improper but accurate assertion.

Rachel Giora and her colleagues have conducted a range of comprehension experiments on how people understand negated assertions like these.[18] Their results suggest that negation can be used to induce a metaphoric interpretation; so when membership in a familiar category like *maid* is negated, listeners bring the figurative aspects of the category to the fore in their interpretation. Recall that Sam Glucksberg[19] views such situations as examples of dual reference: the word 'maid' typically denotes the class of domestic servants, but it can also refer to the figurative category of people who are treated like servants and who are expected to perform menial household tasks. Giora has shown that when we negate the blatantly false or the literally absurd, speakers quickly move to a metaphoric understanding that is not so silly. So, parents aren't just stating the obvious when they tell their kids that life *is not a popularity contest*. For the same reason, it is still meaningful to remind politicians of what is so obvious to everyone else: fund-raising over the Web may now be the norm, but the internet *is not an ATM*.

Explicit negations that seem uninformative from an objective viewpoint may nonetheless establish a playful pretence that carries a good deal of subjective information. When American tennis pro Vitas Gerulaitis finally beat Jimmy Connors in 1979, his win ended a losing streak of 16 straight losses against Connors. Exultant, he joked '*And let that be a lesson to you all. Nobody beats Vitas Gerulaitis 17 times in a row!*'[20] If the strident tone of the negation strikes us as delusional, then this is precisely the point of the witticism, which tries – and fails, with humorous modesty – to salvage some dignity from such a poor run of form. And if one had expected Gerulaitis to feel vindicated by his ultimate victory over Connors, Gerulaitis uses his ridiculous warning to remind us that he is only too aware of the score sheet and that to harbour any sense of vindication would be equally ridiculous. What emerges from this simple negation is a witty blend of two extremes: the arrogance of the victor, tempered by the modesty of a perennial loser.

Both negation and nonsense mark out extreme positions from which a listener can infer a creative speaker's true intent. Thus, what seems like a pointlessly explicit negation can allude to a more figurative meaning that is left unspoken. Implicit negation yoked to apparent nonsense can achieve the same effect. Consider the following examples from the Web, in which an absurd situation is couched within an absurd-seeming conditional:

> If he was any more Christmassy, he'd be a mince pie
>
> If Tweety was any more latent, he'd be a set of fingerprints on CSI: Miami
>
> If he were any more laid back, he'd be a snooker table
>
> If Bill Clinton was any more 'low rent', he'd be a Spring break destination
>
> If the guy's suit was any more empty, he'd be a freaking coat hanger
>
> If he was any more stupid, he'd have be watered twice a week
>
> If he was any more flaming, he'd be a Tiki Torch
>
> If he was any more composed, he'd be a Beethoven symphony
>
> If he was any more shallow, he'd be a mud puddle
>
> If he was carrying any more water, he'd be a camel
>
> If he was any more relaxed, he'd be in a coma
>
> If he was any more chilled out, he'd be a polar bear
>
> If he was any more cold and stiff, he'd be a corpse
>
> If he was any more wooden, he'd be a pine post

Since the consequent in each case is clearly ridiculous, the antecedent must also be false to prevent the assertion of this silly (if not impossible) state of affairs. Thus, since a human being cannot possibly be a mud puddle, or a snooker table, the referent of 'he' cannot also be any more shallow or any more laid back, in a metaphorical sense at least. Notice also how the *fallacy of equivocation* is frequently exploited in these examples through the use of ambiguous properties that can be used in two different senses at once: one sense applies to the target (e.g. 'shallow' as in 'superficial') while another applies to the vehicle (e.g. 'shallow' as in 'not physically deep'). The logician's handbook of fallacies is, after all, copied from the comedian's handbook of joke strategies, and the use of obvious equivocation is just another signal of the speaker's playful lack of sincerity.

Implicit negation is also signalled by a speaker when an implausible claim is labelled as the product of mere perception. If X merely *looks* like Y, then X is *not* Y. In fact, if it seems ridiculous to assume that X can even look like Y, then we must question our perceptions and recalibrate accordingly. So, when Niccolo Machiavelli – the author of *The Prince* and a writer who is held up as the model of cynical self-interest – is perceived as naïve in the following examples from the Web, we do well to doubt our senses:

> He makes Machiavelli look like a kindergarten teacher.
>
> Karl Rove makes Machiavelli look charmingly naïve.
>
> A schemer who makes Machiavelli look like Mother Teresa.
>
> Peter Mandelson – he makes Machiavelli look like Mary Poppins.
>
> Locke makes Machiavelli look touchy-feely.
>
> This guy makes Machiavelli look like a social worker
>
> A man who makes Machiavelli look like an amateur.
>
> Lorne Michaels makes Machiavelli look like Ronald McDonald.
>
> This man makes Machiavelli look like the hero of a Frank Capra movie.
>
> Cheney makes Machiavelli look like Mickey Mouse.
>
> LBJ . . . makes Machiavelli look like Santa Claus.
>
> Hillary Clinton makes Machiavelli look like a second-grader.
>
> [He] makes Machiavelli look like a saint and Torquemada look like a philanthropist.
>
> A true Washington insider makes Machiavelli look like a real prince.

One can use the altogether lazier phrasing 'Machiavelli on steroids' to communicate the idea that a particular person or group possesses Machiavellian qualities in abundance. But the fun of these examples is that they ask us to suspend disbelief for a moment, to imagine the master manipulator being placed into new categories and contexts where he clearly does not belong. We might imagine how It's A Wonderful Life would turn out if the main character was Niccolo Machiavelli instead of George Bailey, and wonder how the now miscast Jimmy Stewart would handle his new role. Alternately, we might briefly imagine Machiavelli in Disneyland, humiliated in a mouse-ears cap, or what Machiavelli in a Santa suit would do to a child's faith in the Christmas spirit. These look like blends, but the pretence required by each is so ridiculous that the blended elements do not mix, and quickly separate again. This is the point, of course: the instability of each blend only highlights the extreme nature of the comparison, prompting us to infer that what is highlighted is not a warm and fuzzy anti-Machiavellian quality, but a cold and grasping ultra-Machiavellian trait. The 'look' in each of these examples is a reminder that we are dealing with appearances and that things may not be as they seem. As such, our sense of the ridiculous is an excellent guide to the use of creative pretence in language. However, as we'll see next, ironic pretence is often a good deal more subtle, and the use of implicit negation is not always so clearly sign-posted.

Double-edged words

Scholars have articulated a variety of nuanced views on irony, but most agree that irony is a calculated exploitation of the *cooperative principle*, the assumption – most famously articulated by the philosopher of language H. P. Grice[21] – that speakers choose their words so as to effectively communicate their intentions to an audience. So, while irony is often challenging and sometimes devious, it is a manner of speaking that is designed to be understood and appreciated by an audience. Irony may involve pretence,[22] but it's a superficial pretence, not a deep deception. Irony may involve inappropriate language, but it is a *relevant inappropriateness*[23] whose relevance is discernible to an audience. Likewise, though irony demands a degree of insincerity from a speaker, it is a *pragmatic insincerity*[24] that does not rise to the level of mendacity. It's one thing to utter a misleading statement if one's goal really is to mislead, and another entirely to utter an apparently misleading statement when one's goal is for an audience to see through the pretence and pierce 'the thin sleeve of immediate reality'. But if irony constructs a flimsy facade that is designed to be pierced, why bother with pretence in the first place? We bother, of course, because irony is much more than simple pretence for its own sake.

To be ironic, one does not have to say the opposite of what one means, though it can often seem this way. Indeed, as argued by Rachel Giora, even simple negation is not so black and white but is often far more nuanced than classically minded logicians would like to think. Thus, the implicit negation of irony does not crudely invert our apparent meaning, rather it mitigates[25] this superficial meaning so that the speaker's intention is recognized as a selective, contextually understood blend of what is said and its negative inversion. Certainly, when we say '*Thank you!*' to someone who has been rude and who does not deserve to be thanked,[26] an ironic tone can give our remark the same meaning as '*Screw you!*'. But we also say '*Thank you!*' to remind the violator that we, at least, know how to preserve the unspoken social contract of good manners, even if they do not. In these exchanges, we see the pragmatic insincerity identified by Sam Glucksberg and his colleagues: our ironic utterances may actually be true at some level, yet we do not mean our words in the way that they would normally be interpreted. Thus, there is a pragmatic insincerity in the apparent hubris of Vitas Gerulaitis at a 1–16 score line, much as when we say '*oh, you're too helpful*' to a friend whose eagerness to help is actually detrimental to our efforts. Irony often uses pragmatic insincerity to couch a rebuke in a form that is conventionally, and sometimes conveniently, taken as a compliment.

So, there are eminently logical ends to the apparent illogicality of irony after all. Though it seems roundabout and wastefully indirect at first glance, irony actually allows us to achieve remarkable concision and cutting power with words. For, we squeeze two levels of meaning into an ironic utterance: an allusion to an expectation that has been violated, by pretending it has not been violated at all, and a reminder that we have noticed this violation, which often acts as a rebuke to the offending party. In most uses of verbal irony, the pragmatic insincerity is detected by noting the inappropriateness of the utterance to the context. There is no reason to say *'Thank You!'* when someone rudely ignores you, and no cause for triumphalism in a 1–16 score line. Some utterances, however, make use of a fully self-contained form of verbal irony, in which the utterance establishes and dashes its own expectations. That is, the ironic part of a description is semantically or pragmatically incongruous with the rest. Some utterances of this kind have earned the status of proverbial similes in the English language. For instance, we might say that a dense lecture on Hegelian philosophy is *'as clear as mud'*, or that a supposedly straight road is *'as straight as a rainbow'* or that an apparently crazed individual is actually *'crazy like a fox'*. These formulations are so commonplace and clichéd that we tend not to think of them as instances of irony, but ironic they are.

One can argue that the description *'clear as mud'* lacks irony because it seems to mean more or less what it says. On a scale of clearness, mud will occupy some extreme point far removed from clarity, and it is this degree of clearness that is communicated by *'clear as mud'*. There are two problems with this get-out-of-jail card. First, when used as an answer to the question *'Is that clear?'*, the phrase relies on equivocation to make its point, for the questioner's sense of 'clear' (the specific achievement of clarity) is not the same as the respondent's sense of 'clear' (the scale of clearness more generally). This equivocation is deliberate and rises to the level of pragmatic insincerity on the part of the respondent. Second, there seems little doubt that the phrase is structured so as to humorously create an expectation (*'yes it is clear . . .'*) before then dashing this expectation (*'. . . clear as mud, you fusty old fool!'*). The insincerity is fleeting and the phrase rights itself in the end, so that it seems to make its true meaning explicit. Yet, this eventual explicitness does not make the phrase any less ironic: its time frame may be compressed, and its insincerity may not extend beyond the boundaries of the utterance, but its allusion to an expectation (e.g. that a good lecture *should* be 'clear') and its subsequent dashing of this expectation marks it out as irony. Because these phrases offer a self-contained form of irony that encapsulates expectation and response in a single phrase, they can serve as the perfect laboratory guinea-pig for experimenting with irony.

Whereas negation can be explicitly conveyed with semantic markers like 'not', 'never' and 'nobody', irony typically uses a more subtle intimation of the ridiculous to achieve the same ends. Our experience of the world furnishes us with much of the knowledge that is needed to identify whether a particular assertion is sensible or ridiculous, as in the false politeness of a disgruntled customer or the false hubris of a perennial loser, but sometimes we need a little extra help from a speaker, especially when this flirtation with the ridiculous assumes a more subtle guise. This help can come in many forms, such as the curl of a lip, the wink of an eye, the raising of an eyebrow or the tone of the voice. However it is done, speakers who engage in creative pretence often signal their status as unreliable narrators. By hinting that their perceptions may lack precision, they give the stronger hint that the conventional mapping of words to meanings is not to be trusted. Lexical markers of imprecision like 'about', 'almost' and 'nearly' and verbs of mere appearance like 'look' and 'seem' can thus mark a speaker's desire to be accurately improper. As we'll see, listeners ignore these markers at their peril.

The ironic Web

Ironic similes like '*as crazy as a fox*' and '*as clear as mud*' are unlikely to light up any conversation. Yet, writers like Raymond Chandler have used the form of the ironic simile to craft some wonderfully imaginative lines.[27] Classic Chandlerisms include '*He looked about as inconspicuous as a tarantula on a slice of angel food*'[28] (to describe a hulking white man stomping about a black neighbourhood) and '*The people who run that place are about as sympathetic as Georgia chain-gang guards*'.[29] Notice Chandler's use of the word 'about' in these similes. The lexicographer Rosamund Moon has suggested – based on a corpus analysis of frequent similes and a small set of ironic similes – that 'about' always prefigures the use of irony in a simile.[30] Analysis of the long tail of less frequent 'about' similes on the Web will allow us to see whether this is indeed so or whether 'about' is a signal of creative pretence more generally.

Instances of the 'about as X as Y' pattern are widespread in the texts of the Web, and so the pattern points us to a rich if impure vein of creative comparisons that can easily be harvested using a search engine like Google. Our goal, as before, is to see how stereotypes are used in figurative comparisons, both for and against type. As in our previous Web-mining efforts in Chapter 4, the resulting matches are sometimes banal and difficult to understand outside their specific contexts of use; so we filter any comparisons in which reference is made to properties established outside the simile, or to the broader context of the utterance, and we keep those whose properties derive from the use or abuse of obvious stereotypes. We build on the results of the earlier search for simple 'as'-similes by using queries with the form '*about* as * as *', and once again we conduct a widespread if non-exhaustive search of the Web by asking Google for 200 hits for each query. Since we are especially interested in finding similes that use elaborate and sometimes ridiculous combinations, we accept all similes whose vehicle is a well-formed noun phrase, no matter how many words it contains or how complex is its syntactic form. We also accept those that use familiar personages with obvious stereotypical associations, such as *Stephen Hawking*, *Albert Einstein* and the much-maligned *Kenny G*.

In all, Google gives us just over 45,000 matches for our 'about' patterns. Just 1 in 8 of these matches is found more than once in our 200-hit horizon, suggesting that most 'about' similes are disposable one-offs crafted for just a single use. Others are well-established proverbial similes in the Archer Taylor[31] sense (such as the clichéd '*about as useless as tits on a boar*'), though 'about' does seem to mark a speaker's desire to invent a simile on the hoof, even if one does ultimately lapse into cliché by the time the second 'as' arrives. Many of the retrieved matches cannot be understood without specific contextual knowledge of the topic that is being described. Nonetheless, we find that the broad intent of over half of the matches (53 per cent) can be understood from the simile alone, because they use vehicles with obvious qualities that are widely accepted as cultural 'facts', such as the widespread belief that Machiavelli was cynical, Buddha was fat and Adolf Hitler was evil. This presents us with approximately 20,000 similes whose meaning pivots around a broadly understood stereotype or a combination of stereotypes. It's worth noting that just 1 in 7 of these 'about' similes uses a vehicle with a single content-word (as in '*about as smart as a rock*'), and overall, 'about' similes use an average of three content words per vehicle. Moreover, the overlap between the 'about as' similes harvested here and the simple 'as' similes harvested in Chapter 4 is negligible: chop off the 'about' marker and just 3 per cent of these new similes are also found in the earlier corpus of simple similes. The presence of the 'about' marker thus leads us to harvest an almost completely different set of similes.

Recall that Dickens referred to conventional similes as a relatively stable form of cultural wisdom that is inherited from 'our ancestors'. In contrast, creative one-offs are typically coined without a concern for their place in history, and we find that 12 per cent of 'about' similes on the Web make use of well-known names from the current pop-cultural and political climate. Only 1 in 7 or so (14 per cent) highlights a positive aspect of a famous personage, and most view prominent figures as reliable targets of humour and ridicule. Indeed, a list of the most commonly dropped names offers a roll-call of topical hate figures such as ex-president George W. Bush, his political advisor Karl Rove, the socialite Paris Hilton and the filmmaker Michael Moore. These figures are evocative enough to serve as complete vehicles in their own right, yet occur just as frequently in combination with other scene-setting concepts, as in these two examples from the Web: '*about as lost as Paris Hilton in a library*' and '*about as frustrated as Stevie Wonder in an Easter egg hunt*'. It is hard to imagine either of these having any linguistic currency in a 100 years from now or to imagine a future Dickens puzzling over their origins.

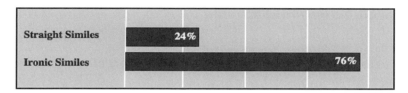

FIGURE 6.1 *Breakdown of ironic and straight (non-ironic) instances of 'about' similes.*

We hand-annotate all 20,000 'about' similes as either straight or ironic by determining whether the highlighted property is stereotypically associated with the vehicle (hence the simile is *straight*), or whether the vehicle describes an idea that, stereotypically at least, we would strongly expect *not* to exhibit that property (hence the simile is *ironic*). In other words, we use implicit negation as a criterion for deeming a simile to be ironic. As shown in Figure 6.1, we find that just a quarter of 'about' similes (24 per cent) are straight, insofar as they use a vehicle for which the highlighted property is salient and apt, and three quarters (76 per cent) are ironic, since they use a vehicle that subverts rather than reinforces this property. The 'about' marker, it seems, is a magnet for irony.

The strong propensity for irony with the 'about' form suggests that the double-hedging of 'about' and 'as' together is intended to prepare an audience for a description that is not just imprecise, but which may also involve implicit negation. This mitigates the risk that the author's true intent is misunderstood. But the 'about' marker does not always signal irony, as evidenced by the 24 per cent of 'about' similes that are not deemed ironic. By looking at the wide range of creative similes on the Web, we can refine Rosamund Moon's hypothesis about the role of 'about' in signalling irony, and more accurately claim that 'about' prepares the listener for a challenging comparison that may demand deeper figurative analysis. The frequency with which 'about' is used in ironic similes means that when there is doubt as to the aptness of a vehicle for a given property, the presence of 'about' will likely sway the listener towards an ironic interpretation. Indeed, the 'about' marker is informative even for similes that do not explicitly use it. If an 'about' variant of a simile can be found on the Web, this is a strong indicator that the unmarked variant has an ironic intent also. This criterion, among others, now allows computers to achieve a modest competence at detecting irony in similes.[32]

An ironic fist in a velvet glove

Regardless of your politics, you are likely to understand the simile *'about as insightful as George W. Bush'* as ironic. You may well believe the ex-president to be capable of genuine insight, as many commentators on the Right do

believe, but will likely know that many others consider him incapable of profound thought. In this either-or situation, you will probably come down on the
side of irony, while perhaps disagreeing with the sentiments expressed by this
interpretation (you do not have to agree with an ironic statement to recognize it
as irony in the first place, though it must be said that people with the most fixed
beliefs also seem to be the most impervious to the charms of irony). Or consider these non-political examples from our Web-corpus, which each suggest
similarly imaginative dilemmas both for their protagonists and their audience:

> *about as decisive as a horny bulldog in a pound with no cages*
>
> *about as decisive as a kitty in a room full of catnip*

Without a specific context, it really is a judgement call as to whether these
descriptions are intended ironically or not. On one hand, conventional wisdom tells us that cats are drawn to catnip almost as much as male dogs are
drawn to potential mates. With no obstacles to bar their way, we easily imagine each making an unhesitant beeline for their objects of desire. On the other
hand, these animals do seem rather spoiled for choice, so it only takes a little
anthropomorphism to imagine each paralysed by indecision and torn between
the many choices on offer. Looking to the specific Web-documents that use
these examples, we see that the word *decisive* is actually used in a somewhat
anthropomorphised sense in each case, to mean 'the ability to make a single
choice, and stick to that choice'. The irony of the second example becomes
clearer when we see the larger context in which it is couched: '*Rather than
stick with that bad decision, they backtrack, looking about as decisive as a
kitty in a room full of catnip. And for what?*'.[33] While context is always helpful, the point of the 'about' marker is that context is not always completely
determinative. As we'll see, 'about as' has a generally souring effect on any
adjective that it precedes: if the adjective has a negative sentiment, 'about
as' intensifies its unflattering effect; if the adjective has a positive sentiment,
then 'about as' encourages us to take this sentiment as an ironic criticism.
Thus, we can non-ironically rephrase the above descriptions without any loss
of meaning as follows:

> *about as indecisive as a horny bulldog in a pound with no cages*
>
> *about as indecisive as a kitty in a room full of catnip*

Just as water prefers to flow down an incline, not up, irony generally prefers
to downshift the sentiment of a description, so the 'about' marker seems
idempotent in the context of a clearly unflattering description. This becomes
clearer when we look in our Web-corpus for 'about' similes with an obviously

positive property like *useful*. In the list of vehicles below, any that is used ironically is marked with an asterisk:

about as useful *as . . .*

*a chocolate teapot   *a one-legged man at an arse kicking contest

*tits on a bull   *a chocolate tea kettle

*a chocolate fireguard   *a screen door on a submarine

*a cow's fifth teat   *a steam engine in getting to the moon

*buying one shoe   *a coalman on a maglev monorail

*a fish on a bicycle   *looking at tea leaves

*a football bat   *an appendix

 a clock   a microscope

*tits on burnt bacon   *a third nipple

*crystal balls   *an infected scrotum

*knickers on a kipper   *teats on a bull

*biodegradable house paint   *an ashtray in a motorcycle

*a 10-ton rock in a canoe   *a useless thing

*teats on a boar   *side pockets on a cow

*polka dots to a polar bear   *a one-armed man on a building site

*a chocolate fireplace   *a dog chasing a parked car

*a dead house plant   *an old vacuum tube

*a raincoat in the desert   *teaching aerobics to the homeless

*a fridge at the North Pole   *scuba diving with an umbrella

*tapeworms   Google Scholar

*a hat full of busted assholes   *a blunt pocket knife

*a case of jock itch   *a penis on a priest

*watching paint dry   *an asshole hole on my elbow

*a solar telescope   *a fart in a spacecraft

*Ouija boards   *truth at a political convention

*handles on a banana   *an old pair of underwear

*tits on a nun   *a wet cowpie in the summer sun

*bloodletting   *a van full of 8 track cartridges

*a tinfoil hat   *mammary glands on a chicken

*toilet paper for a fish   *a knock on the head

*square wheels   *training wheels for tricycles

*a bag full of farts   *a knife in a gun fight

*a hole in the head   *a chocolate saucepan

*an inflatable dart board   *a condom machine in the Vatican

*a snow cone in Siberia   *a broken pencil

*a clutch on a walrus   *air conditioning on a motorbike

*a pork chop in a synagogue   *a cautery on a wooden leg

*a foam hammer   *bucket brigades in fighting fires in skyscrapers

*a warm bucket of spit   *a pocketknife in a laser tag arena

*an umbrella in a volcano   *a windshield wiper on a goat's ass

Asterisks abound! But now consider the remarkable lack of asterisks when we look at the most frequent vehicles for the contrary property, *useless*, in our web-corpus of 'about' similes. The vehicles that are used with both *useful* and *useless* are highlighted in bold:

about as useless *as* . . .

a screen door on a submarine   **tits on a bull**

JPEGs to Helen Keller   the Windows firewall

tits on a boar hog   a sore thumb

teats on a boar hog   **udders on a bull**

a football bat   **a one-legged man in an ass-kicking contest**

a hat full of busted assholes   a cat flap in an elephant house

a chocolate teapot   inviting triangles to a circle convention

a hole in the head   a marzipan dildo

an appendix   the underside of a desk in a nuclear explosion

a milk bucket under a bull   a cocktail umbrella in a thunderstorm

a solar-powered lightbulb   a three-legged cat

a flat tire   an inverted penis

a pair of tits on a boar   knees on a fish

a gun with no bullets   an old shoe

an ashtray on a motorcycle   a toothpick in a canoe

a damp squid   a pinky toe

an umbrella in the desert	a fart in a spacesuit
tits on a male dog	soggy toilet paper
mammary glands on a boar	a three-legged dog
a male nipple	riding cross country on a midget unicycle
an asshole on my elbow	a condom in a convent
the prick on the pope	a cell phone tied to a wall
the proverbial chocolate fireguard	a liberal in a gunfight
an old wart	a canoe in the middle of the desert
a 3-dollar bill	a fish out of water
an inflamed appendix	a brick
tits on a nun	a toenail in a donkey factory
a bra on a horse	a pool of runny turd at a pottery contest
a bag of condoms at a monastery	an extra navel
tits on a frog	**a fish with a bicycle**
a bikini store in Antarctica	glass hammers
a chocolate spacesuit	a broken chair
wheels on a fish	a sneaker full of shit

While both sets of vehicles are equally humorous in a sardonic vein, note the prevalence of irony in the *useful* similes and the utter lack of irony in the *useless* similes. Many of the same vehicles crop up in each set; so it is not the inherent silliness of the vehicles that makes the similes ironic, but the sentiment of the property they are used to convey. The property *useless* does not need irony to yield humour, since images of extreme dysfunction will tend to be humorous in their own right. In contrast, it is much harder to think of something genuinely *useful* that is also genuinely funny, though of course it can be done. More generally, complimentary properties like *insightful*, *decisive* and *useful* have a positive sentiment, and so are more amenable to the souring effect of ironic subversion than unflattering properties with a negative sentiment like *dumb*, *indecisive* and *useless*. The 'about' marker just makes this curdling effect more pronounced, asking us to try and find something negative and critical in what follows, and to give more credence to an ironic interpretation if a description initially seems more positive than negative. Sharp tongues, like sharp knives, are more often used to cut than to butter-up.

Nonetheless, the question of whether a property is complimentary or insulting is not always straightforward. While properties like *useful* and *useless* are mostly stable in terms of their sentiment, so that *useful* is almost always a good quality and *useless* is almost always a bad quality, others are more fickle, and can vary from one context to the next. Consider the quality *menacing*, which has a mostly negative sentiment, unless of course it is a deliberately cultivated aspect of one's personality, in which case it can be positive. For instance, boxers, wrestlers, warriors, rappers, bodyguards, guard-dogs, criminals and actors playing the roles of villainous characters all strive to create an air of menace for which the literal description 'menacing' is a positive sign of uncritical approval, and for which the ironic description 'about as *menacing* as' is a negative sign of criticism and failure. If the sentiment of a linguistic sign is contextually unstable and cannot simply be learned as if it were hard wired into the language, then we must place even greater reliance on cues like 'about' to tell us what to make of it when it is used in an unfamiliar and creative description. Let's look at all the '*about as menacing*' similes we can find in our Web-corpus (* again marks those similes with ironic intent):

about as menacing *as. . .*

*a boozy college cheerleader	*a petting zoo
*the Care Bears	*Daffy Duck
*a smile	*a college professor
*a wet kitten	*a suburban shopping mall
*the Vegas Strip	*Meg Ryan
*the Famous Five	*a gumdrop
*Iowa	*a bunion
*Uncle Fester	*a wet firecracker
*a stuffed bear	*a teddy bear
*the local under 14 netball girls	*a magnet school chess club
*my kid's rubber ducky	*a sedated goldfish
*a granola bar	*an old lady holding a nail file
*a group of weekend ramblers	*a rubber duck
*a rabid gerbil	*a toothless family dog
*the Cookie Monster	*a marshmallow
*a newborn puppy	*the corner grocer
*Count Chocula	*the Seven Dwarfs
*Vanilla Ice	*my 2nd grade teacher
*my cat	*a bit of soggy tissue
*Keystone Cops	*a herd of wet bath towels

*piss ants on a chocolate bar   *a marshmallow in bubble wrap

*a fluffy kitten   *banana pudding

*an outbreak of sunspot activity   *being mauled by a sheep

*goldfish   *Garfield

*a pregnant woman   *a canary

*a fluffy little squirrel   *sliced squid

*a toddler   *an eggplant

*an extra on Green Acres   *an ice cream cone

*Fred Rogers   *a kitten preying on a vicious ball of yarn

*a newborn mouse   *pigeons

*a handicapped chipmunk   *Big Bird

*a sock puppet   *vegetables

*a Boy Scout   *a lamp post

Few people would want to be seen as *menacing*, least of all by an interview panel, a jury or a prospective parent-in-law. Yet, to use a music analogy, words like 'menacing' are not simple notes, but complex chords that cause a range of properties, some positive and some negative, to resonate at once. The negative notes of *menacing* are most prominent when it is used to suggest creepiness, wrongdoing and a potential for physical violence, but the more complimentary notes can be heard when it is used to suggest toughness, firmness and a potential for effective physical action. All of the examples above are ironic, and none of them appear complimentary, which suggests that the irony is targeting the positive notes of the chord while de-emphasizing the negative ones.

Shotgun weddings

We owe our modern stereotype image of the chimneysweep – top hat, tails and cockney accent – to Dick Van Dyke's role as *Bert* in the 1964 Disney musical *Mary Poppins*. The top-hatted chimneysweep may never have been a historical reality, but it has, in its way, become a peculiarly modern stereotype. The Web lists over a thousand chimneysweep companies that are named after some variation on 'Top Hat', and so a computer that used the Web as a knowledge-base might be forgiven for thinking that *'about as modern as a top-hatted chimneysweep'* is not in the least bit ironic. Except that, when in doubt, the use of 'about' with a complimentary property seems to predispose us to an ironic interpretation. This is why the 'about' form (and various other constructions for corralling absurdity discussed earlier) is such a convenient support structure for linguistic creativity on the hoof. Our examples do not have to be clear-cut, and our logic does not have to be perfect, for the construction itself will do much of the work in communicating our intentions.

We observed that there is a negligible overlap (just 3 per cent) between similes harvested with the 'about' marker and those harvested with 'as' alone, but this underestimates the role of stereotypical imagery in 'about' similes. On closer inspection, we find that almost two-thirds (60 per cent) of our 'about as' similes use at least one stereotypical image that is also used in the 'as'-only similes from our earlier analysis. These longer 'about' similes do not always use stereotypes in isolation, or even to exemplify the same properties as their shorter and simpler counterparts, but they do tend to combine stereotypes in novel ways to create visceral images. For instance, the similes 'as quiet as a cat' and 'as noisy as a blender' are harvested in our 'as' sweep, while the more outrageous combination 'about as soothing as a cat in a blender' is harvested during our 'about' sweep. If this simile prompts you to imagine a screaming cat being mulched to a bloody pulp in a kitchen appliance, then feel free to partake in a villainous *Mwa-ha-ha-ha* of your own, for no one asked you to imagine that the blender was turned on! As much as we may dismiss such comparisons as tasteless, one of the joys of creative language is that it asks us to fill in the logical gaps for ourselves, making us complicit in the construction of the author's playfully subversive and sometimes cruel imaginings.

In almost one-third (30 per cent) of our 'about' similes from the Web, the vehicle is a marriage of two different stereotypes linked with a preposition, as in 'a cat in a blender'. These combinations typically employ two stock images with contrary properties, in which the negative usually trumps the positive. As David Fishelov[34] has noted, the most striking vehicles are not built from the most exotic images but from familiar stereotypes that are combined in interesting and unexpected ways. For instance, consider the lyrics of the Leonard Cohen song *Bird on a wire*[35] (the reader is invited to browse Cohen's lyrics here: leonardcohenfiles.com/album2.html#10).

In the course of this song about Cohen's search for personal freedom, the singer compares himself to two kinds of animal, a 'bird on a wire' and a 'worm on a hook', and to two kinds of person, a 'knight from some old-fashioned book' and a 'drunk in a midnight choir'. Though it is the comparison of the singer to a 'worm' that appears to be the most incongruous and disrespectful, it is the comparison of the singer to a 'drunk' that generates the most humour. The reasons for this are three-fold. First, the image of a drunk in a choir is both striking and humorously chaotic, since we expect choralists to be committed volunteers and harmonists; the image of a worm on a hook is neither. Second, though it is easy to imagine a worm on a hook, it is not quite so easy to mentally visualize the singer as a worm; in contrast, it is very easy to imagine the singer as a drunk, and especially a drunk *singing* in a choir. Third, and perhaps most importantly, the image is not just striking but ridiculous: we imagine the drunk singing with gusto while earning the enmity of the choir, and just as we would be entertained by the foolishness of a singing drunk in real life, we find the image constructed here foolish and entertaining.

A visualization of Cohen's simile from the perspective of Fauconnier and Turner's blending theory is provided by Figure 6.2. In the terminology of blending theory, *running the blend* allows us to imagine the consequences of the combination: the drunk, uninhibited and profane, exercises his freedom of expression at the expense of the choir, much like Cohen wants 'to be free' from the expectations of those around him. All the choir (and society) can do is look on and frown. So, as depicted here, Cohen's comparison is not so

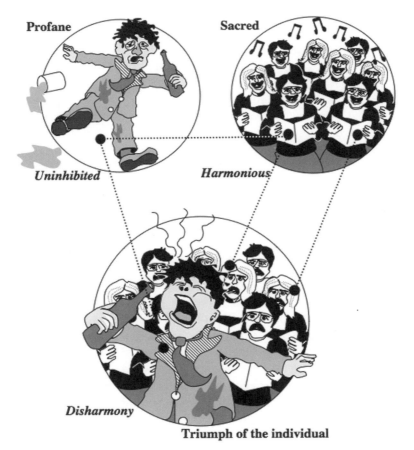

FIGURE 6.2 *The sacred and the profane in Leonard Cohen's lyric 'Like a drunk in a midnight choir'. Two familiar images are combined to yield a third that is less conventional, but which accurately evokes the author's desired meaning.*

much incongruous as mocking: it conveys its desired meaning – an inhibited striving for personal freedom from social expectations – using an image that is at once accurate but improper, and ridiculous but effective.

The effect of affect

With a little help – well, actually, a lot of help – from a computer, we can tag each property that is highlighted in our 'about' similes with a positive or negative tag, to indicate whether the property has a sentiment that is more flattering than critical. As we saw earlier, computers can now perform a decent, if unsophisticated, analysis of the gross sentiment of a text by considering the sentiment of the individual words it contains. To do this, computers use sentiment dictionaries that associate a positive or negative (or neutral) rating with a wide variety of words. One such resource is *SentiWordNet*,[36] a sentiment-tagged version of the WordNet[37] electronic dictionary. Another is Cynthia Whissell's *dictionary of affect*,[38] an inventory of over 8,000 English words with pleasantness scores that are statistically aligned from human ratings. We would like to separate the question of whether the apparent sentiment of the property in an 'about' simile is grossly positive or negative from the question of whether the simile is ironic or not, since our answer to the latter can colour our views on the former. Some adjectives, such as *dull, unattractive* and *stupid*, are uniformly critical in any context, but others, such as *fragile, tough* and *menacing*, occupy a usage-sensitive middle ground between clearly positive and clearly negative. Any sentiment analysis of these similes will yield debatable results, and so we may as well have an unbiased computer perform the analysis for us.[39]

The pleasantness ratings range in Whissell's *dictionary of affect* range from 1.0 (most unpleasant, such as *ugly*) to 3.0 (most pleasant, such as *genuine*), with a mean rating of 1.84 and a standard deviation of 0.44. A computer can simply assume that the property of a simile is conventionally *negative* if it possesses a pleasantness score less than one standard deviation below the mean (1.36) and is conventionally *positive* if it possesses a pleasantness score greater than one standard deviation above the mean (2.28). Whissell's resource is by no means a perfect yardstick for measuring the sentiment of a property; indeed, as we have argued, there can be no such yardstick in principle, since most properties are complex chords, not simple notes, and reveal different shades of themselves in different contexts of use. Nonetheless, an imperfect yardstick is better than none at all if it is consistent and objective in how it works.

Figure 6.3 provides a breakdown of our corpus of simple 'as' similes by their ironic content (ironic or straight) and by the apparent pleasantness (positive or negative) of their highlighted properties. We can see in Figure 6.3 that the

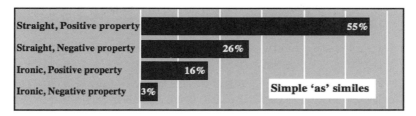

FIGURE 6.3 *Distribution of simple 'as'-similes by the pleasantness of their high-lighted properties (positive or negative) and the speaker's intention (ironic or straight).*

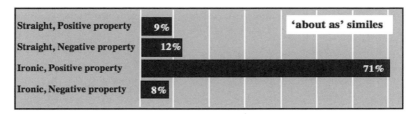

FIGURE 6.4 *Distribution of 'about'-similes by the pleasantness of their highlighted properties (positive or negative) and the speaker's intention (ironic or straight).*

avoidance of irony is the norm in these similes and that a positive attitude is conveyed twice as often as a negative attitude (55 vs 26 per cent) when irony is absent. In contrast, simple ironic similes are five times more likely to convey a negative attitude as they are a positive attitude (16 vs 3 per cent).

Figure 6.4 provides a comparable breakdown for 'about'-similes, which tend to use longer vehicles and exhibit a higher prevalence of irony.

Remember, of course, that an ironic simile that highlights an apparently positive property is actually conveying a critical and unflattering meaning, while an ironic simile that highlights an apparently negative property is actually conveying a positive and somewhat flattering meaning. Looking to the longer 'about' similes in Figure 6.4, we see that straight 'about' similes use a negative property to communicate a negative attitude a little more often than they use a positive property to communicate a positive attitude (12 vs 9 per cent), but that ironic 'about' similes use a positive property to communicate a negative attitude in almost 9 out of 10 cases (71 vs 8 per cent). Simple similes are thus more likely to impart a positive view of a topic, while longer similes that carry the 'about' marker are more likely overall (whether straight or ironic) to impart a negative view of a topic.

The property highlighted by a simile may have differing connotations from one context to another. When computers annotate the sentiment of similes in our Web-corpus, they tend to smooth over this context-sensitivity with a gross average of a property's pleasantness in all contexts. As shown in Figure 6.3, just 3 per cent of simple 'as'-similes are ironic *and* highlight an apparently negative property, while Figure 6.4 shows that this percentage rises to 8 per cent for 'about'-similes. Some of these properties are ambivalent, as when *menacing, bad, dangerous* and *wicked* are considered positive by a self-described tough guy (think of Michael Jackson singing '*You know I'm Bad, I'm Bad*'[40]), or when *fragile* is used to describe a dainty loved one or a delicate piece of art or when *tame* is used to positively describe a friendly pet but to negatively describe a street thug. Yet, for most intents and purposes, and with some obvious exceptions (ranging from 3 to 8 per cent of cases), the average pleasantness rating of a property seems to be a very good indicator of the pleasantness of that property when highlighted in a simile,[41] ironically or otherwise.

As shown in Figure 6.4, four fifths of 'about' similes are used to achieve a sardonic effect, either by directly describing a topic in negative terms (12 per cent) or by indirectly implying a critical perspective via irony (71 per cent). In contrast, Figure 6.3 shows that simple 'as'-similes are used for sardonic purposes in just two fifths of cases (16 per cent ironically highlight a positive property and 26 per cent non-ironically highlight a negative property). Negativity is under-represented in simple similes, since straight conventional similes communicate a positive description more than twice as often as a negative description (55 vs 26 per cent). Irony appears to provide a necessary corrective to this imbalance, allowing negative descriptions to be crafted from positive properties. In simple similes, the balance is almost restored, with positive outweighing negative by 58 vs 42 per cent. Figure 6.4 shows that 'about' similes more than correct the remaining imbalance by employing increased length and ingenuity in the service of negativity and ridicule.

The lessons of irony

Creative language makes willing bedfellows of the logical and the ridiculous. But if logic presents us with the clear distinctions of soundness, contradiction and fallacy, then the ridiculous is an altogether fuzzier and ill-defined notion. It does not rely on the breaking of rules or the crossing of clear, well-defined boundaries. The ridiculous is not a semantic notion,[42] hardwired into the meanings of words and proscribed by definitions of how they should sensibly be used. Rather, the ridiculous is a fluid pragmatic notion, one that crucially depends on an unstable mixture of commonsense, culture, psychological insight and social expectation. Dividing by zero? That's illogical. Jogging in high-heels? That's ridiculous. Writing an *un*authorized *auto*biography or making a black café-au-lait? That's illogical. Making a fish smoothie or putting a cat in the blender? That's disgusting, and of course, ridiculous. Describing an elephant seal as a bear in a wet suit? That's perceptually accurate, and improper (indeed, a crime against the dignity of a proud animal), and laughably ridiculous. Losing a match and declaring yourself the winner? That's illogical. Winning the 17th match after 16 straight losses? That verges on the pathetic, but with a touch of the inspirational. Displaying hubris at this 1-out-of-17 achievement? That's ridiculous. Illogical behaviour is often denounced as ridiculous, but the ridiculous is a far bigger and more amorphous notion than simple illogicality.

The world is full of unlikely situations that are improbable but real, and made logically possible by their very existence, yet our well-tuned nonsense detectors scream '*ridiculous!*' The difference between the illogical and the ridiculous is akin to the difference between knowledge and wisdom, or fact and attitude or effect and affect. It emerges from the productive overlap between what is possible and what is pathetic, unwise, uncomfortable, ugly or dysfunctional. In *The Sign of the Four*, Sherlock Holmes famously asks of Dr Watson '*How often have I said to you that when you have eliminated the impossible, whatever remains, however improbable, must be the truth?*'[43] Perhaps not always the truth, but a potential for truth, certainly. Holmes, that master of logical reasoning, lectures Watson about our potential to find meaning and genuine insight into the improbable and the ridiculous. No aspect of creative language challenges our perception of the ridiculous – or hones this perception – quite like irony.

So, let's conclude this chapter with another sampling from our Web-corpus of creative 'about' similes, one that focuses on irony's love of what is possible but improbable and ridiculously unwise. The following is a list of the vehicles in 'about' similes that we find for the property *likely*. Once again, the ironic vehicles are starred with an asterisk:

about as likely *as . . .*

*Satan skating to work

*a quiet night in for Lindsay Lohan

*Santa Claus

*being hit by a meteor

*being accepted to Harvard

*a comic book about the Holocaust

*a low-flying pig

*a trip to the Death Star

*Elvis running for president

*aliens landing in New Jersey

the sun rising in the morning

*Jack Bauer saving the world on a daily basis

*a George Bush getting a third term

*Bigfoot

*a sobriety day at Lambeau Field

*lasting world peace

*a dog learning to play guitar

*Uma Thurman landing in my lap

*the parting of the Red Sea

*grass growing around a hog trough

*a magic fish

*turning lead into gold

*Madonna joining a nunnery

*flying cars

*Bridget Jones losing 10 pounds

*snow in the Sahara

*a neutered dog having puppies

*Bob Barker cutting a rap album

*my cat winning a Nobel prize

*Richard Nixon taking a second career as a hula dancer

*the Pope building minarets in Vatican City

*telepathy

*monkeys flying out of my ass

*snow in Los Angeles

*the sun rising in the west tomorrow

*a resumption of the Punic Wars

*flying pigs

*the Infernal Regions suffering a chilly spell

*Jenna Jameson becoming a plus-sized model

*racing Zambonis on the Sahara

*a blizzard in the Sahara Desert in July

*the Pope making a wine tour of Sonoma County

*Cristiano Ronaldo joining Swindon Town

*the marriage of Pamela Anderson to Richard Simmons

To quote astronaut Dave Bowman in *2001: A Space Odyssey*, 'My god, it's full of stars!'

7

Think like an investor

Buying low and selling high in the market for creative language

To use language creatively is to invest in language, either by adding new value to old forms and conventions, or by cheekily undermining those conventions to expose the limitations of received wisdom. Linguistic investments can be as simple as the refurbishment of a familiar phrase so that it can be 'flipped' for a quick profit, or as bold and iconoclastic as the breaking apart of a venerable linguistic institution when its perceived value becomes less than the sum of its individual parts. As we explore these parallels in this chapter, we'll see that the search for creative value among the familiar words and phrases of language has much in common with the search for monetary value in a business environment. Investors, in business or language, must have a keen eye for hidden value, and the agility to exploit this potential before others do it first.

Rembrandts in the attic

We all accumulate junk that we can't quite bring ourselves to throw away. We cram the stuff into closets and attics in the hope that it might once again prove useful some day. Our heads are full of the stuff too, from old wives' tales to the detritus of popular culture: half-remembered slogans, jingles, catchphrases, punchlines, lyrics, movie quotes and snatches of poetry. If we believe George Orwell, even our language is clotted with stale coagulations of words that have lost the power to vividly evoke their meanings. Recall how, in *Politics and the English Language*,[1] he fretted about the 'vast dump' of clichés and other jaded phrases that have accumulated within English, and how he fantasised about chucking many a clapped-out metaphor and threadbare idiom onto the bonfire. Yet there might be objects of genuine value hiding in these piles of seemingly old-fashioned rubbish, if only we would just take the time to re-assess their value in the new light of a fresh context. Indeed, given the inherently cyclical nature of fashion, a quick rummage in the attic or the flea market may well offer a more effective means of blazing a trail than a visit to the most fashionable boutiques.

This philosophy of the flea market resonates nicely with an intriguing theory that the psychologists Robert J. Sternberg and Todd I. Lubart call *the investment theory of creativity*.[2] This theory views every creative act as a conscious decision to thriftily exploit undervalued or unconventional ideas, in a way that can generate unexpected value in a new context. As Sternberg puts it, 'creative people *decide* to buy low and sell high in the world of ideas – that is, they generate ideas that tend to 'defy the crowd' (buy low), and then, when they have persuaded many people, they sell high, meaning they move on to the next unpopular idea'.[3] The investment metaphor nicely captures the prevailing intuition of creativity as an inherently risky business. For a producer commits resources to a creative act without knowing whether his desired goals will ever be realized, or whether his intended audience will recognize the value of the final result. Film studios, for example, invest obscene amounts of money and mobilize huge crews of skilled workers in the making of a movie that may yet fail spectacularly at the box office.[4] In linguistic creativity, one invests attitude and knowledge and one's credibility as a speaker in a creative expression, running the risk that witticisms will ring hollow, that jokes will fall flat, and more seriously, that ironic remarks will be taken at face value, perhaps causing the speaker to be associated with a repellent point of view. A creative investor is neither a 'value' investor like Warren Buffett, who looks for solid fundamentals on a balance sheet, nor a 'me too' investor who feeds on hype and follows the herd. More than money is invested, but time and energy and focus and trust. To be creative with words, as with anything else, one must be willing to occasionally look silly.

Sternberg and Lubart observe that 'evidence abounds that creative ideas are often rejected', noting that many works we now consider classics were initially rejected by publishers when first created. From an investment perspective, failed ideas are a thrifty place to look for surprising value, for failed ideas, like has-been actors,[5] sometimes catch a second wind. The 3M company's famous *Post-It* notes,[6] for instance, are a well-known application of a rather unsticky glue with an inferiority complex. This 90-pound weakling among adhesives was invented by 3M scientist Spencer Silver, who failed to interest his colleagues in a glue that was so weak it could be stuck and unstuck with ease. It was years before one such colleague, Art Fry, thought to use the glue to keep page markers from falling out of his hymn book. Yet even when pro-ductized, Fry's idea failed to take off, mainly because it solved a problem that consumers did not yet recognize as a problem worth solving. Only when free samples were given away did the public come to appreciate the many uses of sticky paper for themselves, and only then did it succeed.

In a world away from hymn books, Pfizer's anti-impotence drug *Viagra* started life as a rather unimpressive angina and hypertension medication,[7] whose active compound is called *Sildenafil*. Unfortunately, *Sildenafil* proved to be about as good at treating angina as Spencer Silver's glue was for build-ing model aircraft. However, Pfizer's chemists did observe that angina suf-ferers in clinical trials were coyly reluctant to return their unused pills. Inves-tigating further, Pfizer recognized *Sildenafil*'s potential as a new treatment for sexual dysfunction. Catching its second wind as the catchier *Viagra*, the new drug was a major success for Pfizer, both commercially and in terms of its impact on popular culture. Other drugs too have had a profitable second-life long after their original benefits have become a matter of conventional wisdom. Aspirin, for instance, is still used to treat aches and fevers, but it has also been creatively re-imagined and marketed as an effective means of reducing the risks and the effects of heart attacks and strokes. Even *Thalido-mide*, a drug associated with serious birth defects that is almost universally viewed with a mix of horror and contempt, has found a second life of sorts[8] as a treatment for the symptoms of leprosy and as a potential weapon in the fight against cancer.

Perhaps the most famous exponent of the investment theory is the Dadaist artist Marcel Duchamp.[9] In 1917, Duchamp submitted a signed urinal to an exhibit of the *Society of Independent Artists* in New York. Cheekily titled *Foun-tain* and adorned with the signature of the supposed maker, 'R. Mutt 1917', Duchamp's contribution is what artists call a *readymade*,[10] a found object with perceived merit that an artist chooses and presents as a work of art. While the Society initially rejected Duchamp's *Fountain*, denying that it was any kind of art at all, Dada or otherwise, it has since found notoriety and lasting fame as one of the most influential artworks of the twentieth century.[11] Duchamp had a much larger goal than the artistic rehabiliation of the much maligned urinal: his goal was to challenge cozy conceptions of what does and does not constitute art. Duchamp's creative investment in *Fountain*, though meagre from a craftsman's perspective, requires a corresponding investment from the viewer, for the work asks us to view a piece of porcelain toilet-ware not just as an object with its own aesthetic value but as a signifier for something larger: the artist's power to decide on what constitutes art.

As shown by its initial rejection, Duchamp's investment was clearly a risky one, since producers often clash with consumers – even consumers that are themselves producers – about what constitutes the most salient properties of a creative product. While consumers are normally guided by conventional wisdom, creative producers focus on secondary properties that are less obvious but just as valuable. A producer may thus need to persuade consumers that a product should be evaluated in a very different light. In most cases, the obvious quality or utility of a product is its own best argument, but in others, a producer may have to vigorously defend a creative choice. Duchamp (or an anonymous champion[12]) defended *Fountain* in an unsigned article for the magazine *Blind Man*,[13] arguing that: 'Whether Mr Mutt made the fountain or not has no importance. He CHOSE it. He took an ordinary article of life, placed it so its useful significance disappeared under the new title and point of view – created a new thought for that object'. Duchamp re-imagined the artist as primarily a creator of ideas, and in readymades like *Fountain* he found a daring means of expressing new ideas by reusing some very familiar forms.

In the words of computer scientist Bipin Indurkhya, innovators like Duchamp re-conceptualize a familiar object.[14] Not only do they change the way they themselves think of, and mentally represent, an object, they may also encourage others to adopt this new conceptual representation as well. Doubters will look at Duchamp's *Fountain* and see just a urinal, while proponents who look at it will see a piece of art. The reality is that each camp is looking at exactly the same object, but each is conceptualizing this object in very different ways. Viewers who bring different expectations to the work will appreciate different aspects of it, and different features will be foregrounded by each as the most salient. Creative re-conceptualization, then, is a process of selectively moving features from the conceptual background to the foreground, and vice versa. Duchamp wasn't selling a urinal in 1917 but a fresh new way of thinking about art and everyday objects.

Mind the salience gap

Experience shapes our expectations of the world. When faced with a familiar stimulus, the associations that come most rapidly to mind are generally those that have proven most salient to the interpretation of similar stimuli in the past. But these unbidden associations can also work against us, to produce confusion and surprise in situations that merely seem familiar, as in the case of Duchamp's mischievous *Fountain*. To use the terminology of Victor Raskin and Salvatore Attardo, Duchamp's *Fountain* forces the viewer to switch scripts, and to vacillate between scripts, from the museum script to the restroom script and back again to the museum script. Duchamp knew that his sculpture would always carry the whiff of the men's room, for the salience of *urine* to *urinal* is wired into our mental lexicons: we cannot help but think of the former, however fleetingly, when we encounter the latter, whether in a gallery or in a toilet. In contrast, James Joyce forces this association to the fore in *Ulysses*, when he tells us that Mr Leopold Bloom enjoys the 'fine tang of faintly scented urine'[15] in his breakfast kidneys.

Suppose, at Halloween, you see a child draped in a white sheet, peering through specially cut holes while toting a Jack-o'-Lantern in one hand and a sack of candy in the other. This familiar stimulus is not a word in our mental lexicons, but it does match a cliché-archetype with some very salient associations, so we effortlessly assume that the child is dressed as a *ghost*. After a moment's reflection, other potentially relevant facts might also come to mind: for instance, that white sheets are often used for wrapping corpses, wherein lies their connection to ghosts, as well as the more practical observation that this sheet has likely come from someone's bed. As postulated in Rachel Giora's aptly named *Graded Salience hypothesis*,[16] salience is not an all-or-nothing distinction. Rather, salience admits gradations or degrees, and the factors influencing the perceived degree of salience include 'conventionality, frequency, familiarity or prototypicality'.[17] The mental associations that one can bring to bear on the interpretation of a familiar stimulus will thus occupy different positions along a salience gradient, with those that appear most salient (such as those associated with words in our mental lexicons) being activated first, to exercise the greatest influence, initially at least, on the interpretative process.

The existence of a salience gradient provides ample opportunity for a creative speaker to manipulate the expectations of an audience, especially where clichés and other familiar forms are concerned. With just a hint of pragmatic insincerity, the comedian George Carlin has thus asked us to ponder the following possibility: 'Could it be that all those trick-or-treaters wearing sheets aren't going as ghosts but as mattresses?'.[18] Carlin's joke, which exploits the cultural associations shown in Figure 7.1, demonstrates that our conventional knowledge of an object – in this case, that bed-sheets are typically used to cover mattresses – is not always the most salient for understanding its use in a familiar context. The salience gradient allows a creative writer to exploit a gap between the highly predictable associations of an audience and the far less predictable associations that are required to understand the writer's own perspective, which may be wittily incongruous.

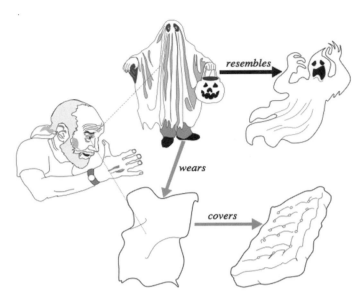

FIGURE 7.1 *Re-conceptualization as Arbitrage: creative comedians exploit gaps in the perceived salience of different pieces of cultural knowledge in familiar-seeming contexts. A child wearing a bed-sheet at Halloween might be dressed as a ghost (figurative association, strong salience) or as a mattress (literal association, weak salience).*

Crafty comics are masters at playing the gradient of using high-salience associations to establish audience expectations before then using lower-salience associations to undercut these expectations. Salience offers us time-tested inferential short-cuts for understanding familiar situations, yet there are creative insights to be had – often more profitable than that of a throwaway quip – when we choose to re-conceptualize the familiar, to view it afresh as something alien and unfamiliar. In the language of the *buy-low-sell-high* philosophy, high-salience associations are for 'me-too' investors; a creative individual must be willing to explore the whole gradient if one wants to identify profitable exceptions to conventional wisdom.

Short-selling in a complacent market

Stock market investors can exploit the herding effect of salience in different ways. Some use financial analysis to identify stocks that the rest of the market has overlooked and undervalued, while others do the opposite, and profit from an anticipated decline in the fortunes of an *over*valued company. Investors who are willing, for instance, to scour the foreign press or trawl certain internet forums may acquire facts pertaining to the health of a company that do not appear salient to others. Thus, shrewd investors in 2008 would have seen a chance to profit from the soon-to-drop stock price of a company like GM, with its (then) single-minded reliance on gas-guzzling, ecology-smashing behemoths, or Toyota, with its initially sluggish reaction to claims of malfunctioning accelerators. This kind of financial re-conceptualization is called *short-selling*, or *shorting the market*, or more simply, *going short*. A short-seller does not buy-low and sell-high, but sells high and *then* buys low. Technically speaking, a short-seller borrows a quantity of stock from a broker, sells the stock while it is still trading at a high price, and then waits for the price to fall. After the anticipated fall, the investor then buys back the stock at a lower value, returns the stock to the broker and keeps the surplus profit. Short selling is a creative way of preserving the liquidity of a market, and allows companies to hedge against events that they would prefer not to happen. Nonetheless, excessive short-selling has been blamed for the worst crashes of the stock market, in 1929 and 2008. If short-selling is creative, it is a distinctly insolent form of creativity. So, ripe pickings for humour, then.

Creative speakers often invest in commoditized language, to derive a profitable return by emphasizing an unexpected meaning from the lower reaches of the salience gradient. These speakers achieve their return on investment through what Hanks calls an *exploitation* and what Giora calls *optimal innovation*. For clichés and stereotypes can always be bought low, and once a novel twist has improved their communicative value, sold high (or at least a little higher). The literary critic Christopher Ricks put it thus: '*Instead of banishing or shunning clichés as malign, haven't we got to meet them, to create benign possibilities for and with them?*'[19] One benign investment strategy is the simultaneous use of a cliché in two different frames of reference, a meaning-maximization strategy that humor theorists call *double-grounding*.[20] *The Economist*, an otherwise sober publication on business topics, has an obvious weakness for this particular strategy, and its weekly articles on current affairs are frequently topped with a frothy and disposable wit. For instance, double-grounding is evident in *The Economist*'s title for an article on government efforts to curb price fixing, 'Cartels: Fixing for a fight'[21] while an article on SABMiller's attempt to buy the brewer Foster's deftly references Chaucer with the title 'SABMiller's Tale'.[22] This vein of benign possibility is easily exhausted, so to avoid repeating oneself it becomes necessary to move on, to new clichés and variations, just as Sternberg and Lubart would predict.

Conversely, if speakers refuse to meet their clichés head on, as Ricks advises, it can fall to listeners to explore not-so-benign possibilities of their own. We can view the lazy use of cliché by others as an opportunity for short-selling, and coin our own creative variations in response. In 1960, for instance, Hollywood released a cinematic love letter to German rocket scientist Wernher von Braun entitled '*I aim at the stars*'. As a key figure in the development of Nazi V-2 rockets in World War II, von Braun was spirited to America at war's end where he was to play an important role in the US space programme. But Hollywood might have given more thought to the title of its biopic, given that von Braun, a former member of the SS, had designed the missiles that rained down on London two decades earlier. The cliché of '*aiming at the stars*' was duly subverted by comedian Mort Sahl, who suggested the alternate title '*I aim at the stars (but sometimes I hit London)*'.[23] Short-selling another's complacent use of language doesn't just undermine an over-valued platitude, it yields a humorous return for the short-seller, who also gains the conversational upper hand. One can argue that Sahl wasn't just short-selling the grandiose idea that we can 'aim at the stars', but short-selling von Braun himself. Linguistic short-sellers punish weakness and simultaneously profit from it, by thwarting a victim's communicative goals while advancing their own.

This is adversarial creativity at another speaker's expense, with a result that is often humorous enough and insightful enough to justify the social cost. The Irish statesman Edmund Burke put it best when he said: 'He that wrestles with us strengthens our nerves, and sharpens our skill. Our antagonist is our helper. This amicable conflict with difficulty helps us to an intimate acquaintance with our object, and compels us to consider it in all its relations. *It will not suffer us to be superficial*'[24] (my italics). As shown in the following exchange, complacent speakers can indeed suffer for their superficiality.

S1: Well, everyone is entitled to their opinion.

S2: You mean, everyone is entitled to *your* opinion.

A cliché is a double-edged blade that can cut the one that wields it just as surely as it can cut an opponent. What better way to punish the superficial use of cliché than by showing, to very real effect, the dangerous opportunity one presents to an opponent when familiar phrases are used without sufficient regard to their 'object . . . in *all* its relations'?

On the night of his shock election defeat in 1945, Winston Churchill was in no mood for cheery platitudes. His wife's suggestion to '*look at this as a blessing in disguise*' was thus met with a withering put-down: '*Well, it's a bloody good disguise*'.[25] Humour researchers have given the name *trumping*[26] to this kind of linguistic short-selling, in which one speaker's lazy use of cliché is seen by another as an opportunity to subvert the unspoken assumptions that should properly, and thoughtfully, inform its use. By showing how these assumptions might not be valid in the current context of use, the cliché is turned against its user, often to humorous effect, as the user's lazy and superficial use of habitual language is exposed and devalued. Naturally, the subversive blow is sharpest if delivered quickly, providing ample evidence of the listener's quicker wit and deeper insights.[27] Conversely, the lazier the cliché or the meaner the stereotype, the sillier it can look when trumped. Consider this example attributed to the Irish philosopher John Scotus Eriugena, who served as court philosopher to emperor Charles the Bald in 845 A.D.[28]

> **S1 (Charles)**: *[sitting at dinner table]* What separates an Irishman from a drunken fool?
>
> **S2 (Scotus)**: *[from across the table]* Only this table.

The original exchange took place in Latin, not English, but the cliché – that close proximity is a sign of strong similarity – works just as well in both languages (Charles: *Quid distat inter sottum et Scottum?* Scotus: *Mensa tantum*). What makes clichés and stereotypes such a rich vein for humour is the unthinking way in which they are so often used. A speaker who lazily employs a cliché as a substitute for real insight is unlikely to properly plan for its use as a conversational gambit, and is easily caught off guard by an adversarial gambit in response. Trumping views conversation as a strategic game, rather like chess, in which each move aims to advance the goals of the speaker,[29] but at the risk of opening the speaker to an unanticipated attack. The irony of trumping is that the short-selling respondent effectively *agrees* with the speaker, for only by agreeing with what has been said can the speaker's utterance be turned into an instrument of self-harm. That is how short-selling works, after all: one must first borrow the stock that one believes to be over-valued. Consider this joke about an argumentative husband and wife:

> **S1 (wife)**:   *[pointing to monkey cage in zoo]* Your relatives, I suppose?
>
> **S2 (husband)**: *[nodding]* Yes, my in-laws.

So trumping uses superficial agreement to mask a deeper divergence of views. The 'yes' here is an implicit echo of S1's argument, which the respondent S2 borrows at face value and then short-sells. The argument returned to S1 is the same argument – the husband tacitly accepts that the monkeys are indeed his relatives – but it is an argument that has dramatically fallen in value. In the financial markets, short-sellers should avoid moral hazard by not actively causing a borrowed stock to fall in value, but this is precisely what a creative speaker does when trumping. The respondent S2 wants S1's argument to fall in value, and causes this collapse by inserting a clever variation (*relatives → in-laws*).

Clichés do not come with owner-manuals, but some consideration should always be given to their ideal conditions of use. One should not, for instance, describe a particular combination with the cliché '*a marriage of X and Y*' unless one sincerely believes that marriage is an idealized pairing. To describe an oddball combination like 'Frolf' as a '*marriage of Frisbee and Golf*' is to open yourself to trumpings of the form '*yeah, a shotgun marriage*', '*a broken marriage*', or depending on your politics, a '*gay marriage*'. Neither should you defend your social drinking with the cliché '*I only drink as much as the next guy*' since the next guy might well be an alcoholic.[30] Likewise, never tell your boss that '*I do the work of two people for this company*', since two idiots typically achieve much less than one competent worker, and you open yourself to the trump '*yes, Laurel and Hardy*'. Conversely, if you happen to be the boss, never say '*we are all in the same boat together*', since your peevish employees may well respond '*yes, you bang the drum while we man the oars*'.

How to think like an up-seller

Sternberg and Lubart's investment theory views creative individuals as *up-sellers*. In language, up-sellers create added value by injecting novelty and freshness into an all-too-conventional phrasing. Up-selling is efficient and creative whenever a variation yields a large improvement from a modest investment of effort. If you represent a sprawling chemical company like BASF, why say '*We make chemicals*' when you can evoke romance and magic with '*We create chemistry*' instead? As we have seen, up-selling typically occurs when a simple substitution in a well-known expression evokes both the conventional meaning of the form and yields an additional meaning besides, the producer's ROI (return on investment). In *Twelfth Night*, Shakespeare tells us that '*some are born great, some achieve greatness, and some have greatness thrust upon them*', while in *Catch-22*, Joseph Heller tells us that '*Some men are born mediocre, some men achieve mediocrity, and some men have mediocrity thrust upon them*'. The idea of striving to achieve mediocrity is pathetic enough, but the implied contrast with Shakespeare's original 'greatness' adds yet another layer of bathos to Heller's variation.

Investors obtain little or no ROI from lazy variations that exhibit just a superficial engagement with an original expression, for these are just another way of following the herd. Looking to the web, other frequent substitutions for 'greatness' in Shakespeare's line include 'weirdness', 'wickedness', 'excellence', 'leadership', 'power' and 'failure'. Some are near synonyms ('power', 'excellence' and 'leadership'), others are odd ('weirdness'), while some show just enough conceptual engagement with the original source material to be interesting ('failure'). The linguist Geoffrey Pullum has derided the use of these simple variations as 'phrases for lazy writers in kit form',[31] noting that one chestnut in particular – that Eskimos have an unfeasibly large number of words for snow – is commonly localized to whatever nationality a journalist wishes to lampoon. Pullum was especially exercised by a 2003 usage in *The Economist* which went 'If Eskimos have dozens of words for snow, Germans have as many for bureaucracy'.[32]

The economist Glen Whitman has minted the catchy label 'snowclone' to capture the potent mix of familiarity and virulent reproducibility that so annoyed Pullum, and the label has found favour with linguists and non-linguists alike.[33] Though obviously and only a metaphor, and a playful one at that, Whitman's evocation of cloning nicely captures our general ambivalence about replication without limits. Cloning is one of those technological possibilities that excites and worries in equal measure, and though many can see the benefits of thoughtful experimentation on a personal level, most are repulsed by the notion of mass commoditization on an industrial scale. Untrammelled replication, untroubled by thought, is rarely a good thing, for memes or for genes. But we should be careful not to deride all variations as snowclones, even if the underlying phrase has been over-used by others. In this spirit, the last variation on Shakespeare's line above, which substitutes 'failure' for 'greatness', is worth a closer look. This variation has been used to comic effect by journalist and film critic Joe Queenan in his long running campaign to simultaneously celebrate and castigate the actor Mickey Rourke: '*Some men have failure thrust upon them, but Rourke went out and seized failure by the throat*'.[34] While all snowclones are variations, not all variations are snowclones.

Orwell's contempt for over-used metaphors was especially pronounced in the case of journalists, since writers working in a jargon-rich domain are too-easily seduced by lazy tropes, especially those that come in the convenient 'kit form' deplored by Pullum. It can grate, for instance, when movie reviewers smugly refer to films as 'vehicles' and directors as 'helmers'. The newspaper of the entertainment industry, *Variety*, provides new readers with a glossary of its most frequently used metaphors,[35] which makes it all the more tempting for its writers to use them with abandon. Such clichés can seem cloying and pretentious to an outsider, who may feel that to use them is to endorse them. Yet because these clichés are grounded in metaphor, they are ripe for creative investment, allowing a writer to humorously subvert the surface meaning while exploiting the underlying literal meaning. The columnist Marina Hyde, who navigates two different cliché-silted domains for *The Guardian* – sports and movies – recently used this strategy to criticize the actor Kevin Costner on both flanks at once when, in an article on sports movies, she referred to '*the Kevin Costner vehicle – why can't the vehicle ever be a hearse? – that is Tin Cup*'.[36] This is no snowclone, for no other substitution could work as well here. Hyde was cannibalizing her own past writings with this quip, having taken the variation on a test-drive in the earlier headline '*Russell Crowe vehicle turns out to be a hearse*'.[37] We often try to wring as much value from a productive strategy as we possibly can, even at the risk of repeating ourselves.

How to think like a short-seller

Linguistic short-selling is often pointedly humorous, especially when it targets a strident speaker whose use of complacent language fosters a sense of pomposity and self-satisfaction. The reversal in these cases, what we have called a *trumping*, can cause the rapid de-pressurization of an over-inflated ego. The boxer Muhammad Ali relates one such story of what happened when he let his ego blind him to the obvious.[38] To his credit, Ali's own anecdote does not show him in a entirely favourable light. As he tells it, this exchange occurs soon after boarding an airplane, but let's omit the punchline for now:

> **Flight attendant**: Buckle your seat belt, Mr Ali, we're about to take off.
>
> **Muhammad Ali**: Superman don't need no seat belt!

Ali was undoubtedly a more thoughtful man than his braggadocio would suggest. This carefully nurtured up-selling of his own physical prowess, in and out of the boxing ring, was to produce some wonderful examples of witty bravado. It's not surprising then that he would describe himself as a superman – or indeed, as *the* Superman – and expect others to buy into this humorous delusion, in his presence at least. For Ali, the Superman mythos provided the perfect metaphor for this outsider who was now the hero of the mainstream, a peerless champion of unquestioned strength and rugged good lucks. So in the above exchange, Ali's ego leads him to profile just those parts of the *Superman* concept that emphasize his obvious strengths as a boxer. However, the *Superman* concept provides a rich base of knowledge that popular-culture has spread far and wide, and there are salient aspects of the concept that must be overlooked to make Ali's self-serving metaphor work in this context of airline travel. In financial terms, Ali's metaphor is weaker than it seems, and is ripe for a short-seller to step in and take a profit.

And profit she does. The full exchange in Ali's anecdote finishes with a resounding trump by the stewardess:

> **Flight attendant**: Buckle your seat belt, Mr Ali, we're about to take off.
>
> **Muhammad Ali**: Superman don't need no seat belt!
>
> **Flight attendant**: Superman don't need no airplane, neither.

Once again, we see that trumping requires a tacit acceptance of the victim's words at face value.[39] Note the use of 'neither' here, which suggests that the stewardess is adding to, rather than subtracting from, Ali's claim. A linguistic short-seller extracts the most profit when a victim's words are perceived to be trading at a high price. While short-sellers do not buy these words at their over-inflated price, a tacit acceptance of their meaning does allow the short-seller to borrow the words, before returning them in a much de-valued state. This borrowing is apparent in the echoic manner in which stewardess reuses most of Ali's own words.[40] But her borrowing adds an innocent-seeming variation that utterly demolishes the foundations of Ali's Superman metaphor. Ali profiles *Strength* and *Invulnerability* in his conceptualization of *Superman*, while the stewardess profiles *Flying-Ability* instead. In a boxing ring, Ali's perspective would surely triumph, but in an airplane, the stewardess scores a stunning knock-out. Is it a bird? Is it a plane? No, it's Muhammad Ali, made to look puny by a flight attendant bearing linguistic Kryptonite.

Clichés and stereotypes persist in a community because they capture useful generalizations. But this generality means they are rarely immune to exceptional cases. Much of their meaning is implied rather than explicitly stated, which enables a short-seller to safely reject these implications while remaining in overt agreement with what is actually said. To trump another speaker's cliché or stereotype, a short-seller must first identify the unstated assumptions that allow it to work as a successful generalization, and then respond with an exceptional case that makes it fall flat in the current context. The most apt exceptional cases become easier to identify with practice. For example, if an annoying acquaintance tells you that, despite your differences, he really does think that he and you *'are like brothers'*, a short-seller might agree by mentioning two well-known brothers who are famous for not getting along, such as *'Cain and Abel'*, or two brothers who are famous for being intellectually mismatched, such as *'Bill and Roger Clinton'*, or two who are famous for both of these reasons, such as *'Michael and Fredo Corleone'*.

This tendency of short-sellers to profitably exploit the hidden weakness of others is not limited to the domains of finance and communication. Tamar Gendler, a philosopher of science, argues that the exploitation of a conceptual weakness via the construction of an exceptional counter-example is key to the workings of *thought experiments*.[41] These are scientific and philosophical experiments that are performed not in the laboratory but in the confines of the mind itself. Yet the best thought experiments possess a logical force that makes them as convincing as any physical experiment that can be performed in the real world with the usual arsenal of gauges and stopwatches. The course of modern science has been deeply influenced by experiments that thinkers have performed in the comfort of an armchair and which need no physical confirmation. Perhaps the most famous of these is Galileo's proof that objects fall with a speed that is independent of their physical mass, and so, for instance, that Sumo wrestlers and supermodels fall at the same speed. This claim by Galileo contradicted conventional wisdom that scientists had held dear since antiquity. Aristotle, whose legacy seemed unshakeable, had claimed that heavy objects necessarily fall faster than light objects, and his claims do have a certain intuitive appeal: boulders should fall faster than pebbles, shouldn't they? But behind this appeal, Aristotle's theory was fatally flawed. Galileo was about to *go short* on Aristotle.

Popular history imagines Galileo climbing to the top of the tower of Pisa, to drop objects of different sizes and weights over the side. This quaint image misses the true essence of Galileo's contribution, which – like Duchamp's *Fountain* – was conceptual rather than physical. He didn't show that the sundry objects he is supposed to have dropped off the tower fall at the same speed. He showed that *all objects everywhere* must necessarily fall at the same speed, no matter where or how far they are dropped. Galileo used brains to trump Aristotle, not brawn, by identifying the unspoken assumption from which the Aristotelian theory derived its apparent value. Aristotle spoke of objects falling at different speeds, but he didn't feel the need to define precisely what he meant by an 'object'. Surely, you might think, we all know the meaning of 'object' in this context? Though the word is likely to bring a range of different objects to mind, Aristotle's theory assumes that all objects are stereotypically simple. His objects are rigid and uncomplicated, of a kind that few of us would find philosophically troubling, such as cannonballs, horseshoes, pots and pans. This stereotype was the weakness that Galileo would so ruthlessly undermine. He imagined an exceptional object that ran counter to Aristotle's expectations: two cannonballs of different sizes and weights, one heavy and one light, tied together by a flexible rope.[42] Each cannonball is clearly a different object, but the connecting rope turns the combination into a unified whole, a complex object. How would Aristotle's theory deal with this jerry-rigged oddity?

Not so well, as it turns out. Galileo showed that Aristotle's theory, like a flustered schoolboy, provides two contradictory answers to the question of which should fall faster, the heavy ball alone, or the rope-tied combination of heavy and light balls. According to the prevailing Aristotelian wisdom, the combination should fall *faster*, as shown in Figure 7.2(a), since the heavy and light ball together are clearly heavier than the heavy ball alone. But according to this wisdom, as the flexibly-tied combination plummets towards the ground, it should fall heavy-ball first, as in Figure 7.2(b). The rope would allow the light ball to trail behind at a fixed distance. Yet this also means that the light ball should act as a drag on its heavier companion. This drag should slow the

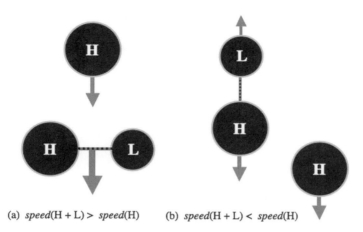

(a) *speed*(H + L) > *speed*(H)   (b) *speed*(H + L) < *speed*(H)

FIGURE 7.2 (a) *The combination falls faster than the heavy ball alone and* (b) *the light ball acts as a drag on the heavy ball, so the combination falls slower.*

heavier part of the duo, causing the combination of heavy and light balls to fall *slower* than the heavy ball alone.

No scientific theory can tolerate contradiction. A theory that contradicts itself is a madly-spinning compass that tells you *north* is anywhere you want it to be. Yet it's important to note that Galileo didn't sneak the contradiction into Aristotle's theory with some clever piece of scientific sophistry. The contradiction was there all along, lurking beneath the surface where blinkered scientists had simply failed to notice it.[43] The only way to resolve the contradiction is to abandon the link between mass and speed altogether and to adopt Galileo's position: all objects fall at the same speed, regardless of weight. As a theory. Aristotle's account was trading far above its true scientific value. It was only a matter of time before a shrewd short-seller like Galileo came along and knocked it down to size, reaping its unearned value for himself and his own theories.

This comparison of conceptual thought experiments and linguistic trumping has more than an abstract similarity to recommend it. In a very real sense, a thought experiment like Galileo's is truly a scientific joke of sorts,[44] a cruel logical prank at another theorist's expense. So it's worth nothing that when Galileo first presented this thought experiment in his book *Dialogue Concerning the Two Chief World Systems* – a controversial work that was to be a source of considerable friction with the church[45] – Galileo put the defence of Aristotle's theory into the mouth of a character named *Simplicio*. With a stroke, Galileo cruelly suggested that followers of Aristotle were not just naïve, but pedantic and simple-minded.[46] Galileo defeated his opponents with the cold logic of a short-seller, but couldn't resist one more rhetorical twist of the knife.

Investing in readymades:
Hand-made by robots

Though mostly remembered for his physical art, Marcel Duchamp was also noted for his linguistic creativity. For instance, the signature 'R. Mutt' which adorns his *Fountain* can be seen as a play on the name of a major urinal manufacturer ('Mott') blended with a reference to *Fountain*'s status as a readymade ('R. M'). The late palaeontologist and science writer Stephen Jay Gould, who was also a passionate scholar of Duchamp's work, wrote at length about the artist's ability to slice and dice words to yield new meanings. One particular example of the artist's playfulness – the enigmatic formula '*A Guest + A Host = A Ghost*' that was inscribed on candy wrappers at a Paris show in 1953 – has been described by Gould as 'a vital and central place in the totality of his life's work'.[47] Though clearly in awe of Duchamp, Gould thus saw an obvious continuity between the creativity of his readymades and his fascination with word play. The *ghost* pun and others do leverage our conventional associations with everyday words, but they seem too 'processed' to be genuine readymades. So what is the linguistic equivalent of a readymade? And if they exist at all, are these readymades an aspect of linguistic creativity in which humans (and perhaps even computers) can profitably invest?

Clichés and quotations seem to be the most obvious candidates for readymade status. Rather than express our own meanings in our own words, these pre-built forms allow us to reuse a combination of words and meanings that Shakespeare or Milton or Wilde or a legion of better writers have already built for us. Reference books are full of the things, and when reading the original texts, we sometimes memorize our own favourite lines for later use. However, these reusable forms lack the creative intent of readymade art, especially when we use them primarily as labour-saving shortcuts, or as a means to show off an expensive education. To use a cliché as a cliché is no more creative than Duchamp using his *Fountain* as a urinal. To be creative, the reuse must take the familiar form on vacation, to an incongruous new context where it raises as many questions as it answers. From this perspective, we must also deny readymade status to snowclones. While these variations on familiar forms do strive for a creative frisson of sorts, their real inspiration lies not in an interesting original phrase, but in someone else's exploitation of that phrase. Snowcloning is more akin to plagiarism than creativity; indeed, snowclones encourage mass-produced plagiarism on an almost industrial scale. Snowclones concern themselves with the appearance of creativity, but miss the whole point of creativity, somewhat like an artist who, on seeing Duchamp's *Fountain*, opens a factory for making novelty urinals.

A true linguistic readymade is any resonant phrase which speaks to the reader of broader possibilities in other contexts. Though not clichés as such, we encounter these phrases everywhere. The expression '*Chaos is a Greek word*' is found about 1,000 times on the web, most often as a simple statement of etymological fact. However, the phrase also makes an excellent title for a book about travelling or living in Greece. Not only does it suggest that *Chaos* is an inherently Greek concept,[48] it cheekily suggests that the Greeks invented *Chaos* and thus have a first-mover's advantage at being the most chaotic people on Earth. Robert Penn Warren took the title of his 1946 novel on political corruption, *All The King's Men*,[49] from a resonant line in the nursery rhyme *Humpty Dumpty*, inspiring Woodward and Bernstein to name their 1974 account of Nixon's downfall *All The President's Men*.[50] In 2010, the graffiti artist *Banksy* made a film named *Exit Through The Gift Shop*. The origins of this readymade title lie in signs that often adorn museums and galleries, none-too-subtly suggesting that you round off your visit with a little retail therapy. As a readymade, the phrase resonates with the fear that rampant consumerism has hijacked all aspects of modern society. Of course, different producers can be inspired by the same innocuous phrase, and a London band had already taken *Exit Through The Gift Shop* as their name a year earlier. The band subsequently renamed itself *Brace Yourself*, prompting Banksy to thank its members with an original painting with the readymade title *Brace Yourself*. That Sotheby's valued the painting at £200,000[51] tells us something of the value the artist placed on his readymade film title.

In a practice that became the norm for college students in the seventeenth century, students were encouraged to maintain a book of commonplaces – a recording of interesting thoughts, observations and phrases that they might encounter in the course of their day. The practice, called *commonplacing*, is even referenced in Shakespeare's *Hamlet*.[52] Imagine if modern students were likewise encouraged to keep a commonplace book too, to record any resonant phrases that caught their eye. One need not know how the phrase is to be used in some future creative setting, only that it has some concise, descriptive utility that might make it useful in some other, perhaps incongruous, context. Different phrases will make a subjective appeal to the wit and the whimsy of different readers. For instance, the title of every chapter in this book is a linguistic readymade, or a variation thereof, a pre-existing phrase with a specific relevance to the contents of the chapter.

A book of linguistic commonplaces would be quickly filled, and most of its phrases might never enjoy a creative afterlife. Nonetheless, even a casual flick through a book of disorganized jottings can be inspirational in itself, as disjointed phrases – when shorn of their original contexts of use – are all the more likely to suggest surprising new uses. Intriguingly, this is just the kind of activity that a computer can perform with aplomb. Imagine a computer that scanned all of the daily newspapers, all of the weekly and monthly magazines, and whole libraries of digitized books, keeping a hopeful record of any phrase that was both concise and dense with evocative imagery. Later, when asked to suggest a pithy way of conveying a given meaning, our computer of commonplaces could trawl through its vast collection of phrases to pull out the most useful readymades. A phrase would earn its readymade status, in the creative sense of Duchamp, whenever the new purpose it is retrieved to serve differs from that for which it was originally crafted. Suppose you are reading a research article about *robotic fish*. (Bizarrely, the web contains many articles on these mechanical oddities and their scientific uses.[53]) The idea, and the phrase, might strike you as such an odd one that you record it in your book of commonplaces, without any explanatory notes. Remember, we want to completely free these phrases from their contexts, like a kidnapper cutting out words for a ransom note. Later, when looking for an evocative simile for emotional coldness, we may come across the phrase again in our book. Since both robots and fish are stereotypically cold (recall our discussion of stereotypes in Chapter 4), we can appreciate the phrase as an especially resonant vehicle for coldness, and state our target to be '*as cold as a robotic fish*'.

Orwell dreaded the idea of a human writer acting like a machine, mechanically assembling prefabricated strips of language into colourless prose. By recognizing the potential value of linguistic readymades, we can turn the standard automation scenario on its head, by training our computers to reuse prefabricated phrases that have already been composed by humans. In the search for reusable readymades, a computer can work much more efficiently than a human, to quickly scan, snip, store, index and retrieve millions of phrases that might one day prove useful as readymades. To demonstrate the feasibility of such a system on a large scale, we construct a virtual warehouse of readymades, each waiting to be called into action. As raw material, we exploit a large database of frequent text sequences on the web known as the *Google n-grams*.[54] It goes without saying that computers still lack the necessary experience of the real world to see the creative resonances in phrases like '*exit through the gift shop*' and '*do not adjust your set*'. But when it comes to using the knowledge it does possess, and exploiting it on a large scale, a computer is an information processor without peer.

We showed in Chapters 4 and 6 how a computer can acquire large amounts of commonplace information about the world from the similes that are used on the web. From these similes a computer can learn that statues and libraries are commonplace images for quietness and stillness. So when a computer comes across '*the statue in the library*' in a sample of web-text, it can easily recognize this phrase as a more resonant description of quietness than either 'statue' or 'library' alone. The original creator of the phrase may well have been describing a real statue in a real library, and had no figurative intent whatsoever. However, when the phrase is cut loose from its original context, it becomes a pitch-perfect vehicle for our later figurative purposes. Though it's no *Fountain*, it's no urinal either, and coinages like '*as quiet as a statue in a library*' capture the true essence of a Duchampian readymade: pre-constructed forms with a context-transcending elegance, they mean what our new context takes them to mean, and not what they were first made for.

A screenshot of this finder of readymades, named *The Jigsaw Bard*,[55] is shown in Figure 7.3. Readers are encouraged to visit *www.educatedinsolence. com* to use the *Bard* for themselves. Figure 7.3 shows the readymades that our computational Bard dredges up from the depths of the Google n-grams when presented with the property 'cold'. In the column headed *Simple Elaborations*, we see a list of stereotypes for coldness, modified by adjectives which help to draw out the unpleasantness of this particular state. All of the descriptions in this column are true readymades, simple phrases uttered in one context but put to new uses in another. So, if you want to describe something as cold, why not follow the Bard's advice and compare it to '*a wet haddock*', '*a wet January*', '*a heartless robot*' or '*a bitter storm*'? The *Bard* has acquired each of these reinforcing properties from the web, using the query '*as cold and * as*' to seek out the adjectives that are most commonly used to reinforce the idea of coldness.

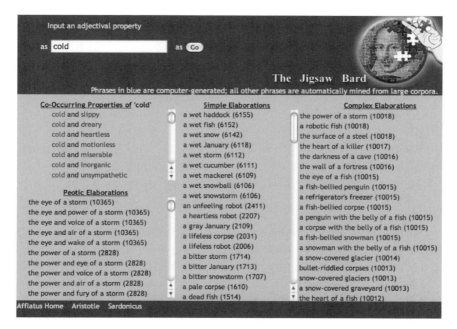

FIGURE 7.3 *Screenshot of The Jigsaw Bard, retrieving linguistic readymades on demand.*

In the column headed *Complex Elaborations*, we see readymade phrases that contain two mutually-supportive stereotypes for the same property. So for 'cold' we see not just our *'robotic fish'* from earlier, but *'a refrigerator freezer'*, *'snow-covered glaciers'*, *'bullet-riddled corpses'* and *'a snow-covered graveyard'*, Phrases like *'a fish-bellied corpse'* and *'the heart of a fish'* are composed by the *Bard* itself, jigsaw-style, from the recurring text fragments it has collected in its analysis of the Google n-grams. The *Bard* is clearly on firmer ground when dealing with true readymades, but some of its own compositions show promise: *'the heart of a killer'* has the ring of familiarity, and *'the wall of a fortress'* is oddly evocative, and even *'a fish-bellied penguin'* is naïve but apt, if a little comical too. When it comes to linguistic creativity, computers are still no better than *idiom savants*, capable of collecting and manipulating texts with great speed and efficiency, but lacking a nuanced sense of the world to really leverage what they know. But all of this will change, gradually, as computers acquire increasing amounts of tacit world knowledge. Since the bulk of this common-sense will come from language itself, and from the myriad perspectives and expressions that can be found on the web, our speed-reading savants may yet surprise us all. Meanwhile, applications like *The Jigsaw Bard* show that a computer can even now serve as a useful, if scattershot, muse.

Concluding thoughts: Investing in language

When Britain set up the Bletchley Park code-breaking unit during World War II, Winston Churchill insisted that it recruit the most able code-breakers from all walks of British life. After meeting the oddball academics and crossword fanatics that were recruited to crack the German U-Boat codes, Churchill quipped *'I know I told you to leave no stone unturned, but I didn't expect you to take me quite so literally'*.[56] Yet by looking further than the usual suspects, Bletchley recruited a remarkable team that was to yield dramatic results in the war at sea. In a simple but memorable variation of an old cliché, Churchill later described Bletchley as *'the goose that laid the golden egg, but never cackled'*.[57]

Creative speakers must turn over some very unlikely stones to reap a surprising reward. The less promising the stone, the more surprising the reward. So a creative producer invests in metaphor when literal expression is in abundant supply, and re-invests in literal meanings when the market becomes flooded with overused metaphors. It is tempting to think of convention and creativity as sworn enemies, each locked in a constant struggle to banish the other from our language. But the truth is more prosaic, and altogether more useful than this conflict metaphor might suggest. Wherever we see convention, we also see the potential for creativity, for convention breeds complacency, and complacency is a productive pre-condition for novelty and surprise. Investors can profit in the stock market when a good company is trading below its fair market value, and when a poor company is trading above its fair value. To reap this profit, a savvy investor must overturn the prevailing complacency of the marketplace. Successfully overturning preconceptions, like overturning stones, requires that we know where best to apply leverage. It's not enough to break with convention for its own sake. The use of rare synonyms or unusual jargon is no substitute for genuine linguistic creativity, just as the arbitrary or petulant use of negation is no substitute for real irony. Every act of linguistic creativity is a calculated investment, in which the relationship between the effort we put in, and the profit we take out, is understood (if not always understood *fully*) in advance.

Linguistic creativity can take many forms, and its results are found on all points of the continuum between original insight and clever expression. In this book we have primarily focussed on the creativity that emerges from the variation of familiar linguistic forms and ideas. Though not the whole story, creative variation does account for a significant chunk of our everyday innovation in language, especially as it happens on the web. Not only is this a form of linguistic creativity that is amenable to large-scale analysis by a computer, it is a skill that is easily honed by a human speaker. For there is no divine mystery in the workings of creative variation, and one does not need to be blessed by God or by Nature to see the creative potential of the most commonplace structures in language. Everything we need to understand an optimal variation is right there, in the linguistic record. Neither does one need to be wired differently, or to have a brain that runs at a higher clock-speed. One simply needs to foster a conscious engagement with language, to appreciate that the most valuable resources are often those that are hidden in plain sight. If language is an instinct[58] – and the automatic urge to habitually use familiar words and phrases in specific circumstances does seem to be an instinctive reaction of sorts – it is an instinct that the creative producer must learn to consciously subdue and control. The key here is *control*, for the goal of creative variation is not to deactivate our instincts and denature our language, but to channel our habitual and often unthinking reactions through an intermediate level of analysis and experimentation. As we gain insight from the creative variations of others, we can re-invest these insights into our own creative efforts, and thus experience the thrill of creation for ourselves. Creative variation is an investment not just in our own language, but in language overall, for the best variations enrich the language for everyone else too.

Many times in this book, we have appealed to the web to provide evidence for particular linguistic forms and creative strategies. Search engines such as Google, and databases of web-content such as the Google n-grams, have been used to demonstrate the productivity of certain patterns, or the viability of acquiring certain kinds of stereotypical knowledge from the web. These resources have thus indirectly provided the knowledge base for the various software applications we have described here, from the *Aristotle* and *Metaphorize* systems for generating metaphors to *The Jigsaw Bard* (each of which, and more besides, can be accessed at *www.educatedinsolence. com*). In some respects then, search engines like Google or Yahoo or Bing already provide some useful services for the creative writer. For instance, the Google * wildcard allows us to turn familiar phrases into structured templates, so that we might go fishing on the web for creative variations of our favourite clichés and metaphors. But these search engines are fine-tuned for commonality at the expense of rarity and diversity. It is still difficult to use an engine like Google, say, to find a wide range of variations for a given phrase, since the cleverest engines often favour the most authoritative results. In Churchillian terms, they prefer to look under the biggest and most obvious stones, while a seeker of novelty would prefer them to look under the smallest and most obscure. Google's * wildcard is a minor feature for expert users, but ranking pages on authoritativeness is its biggest selling point.

Nonetheless, the best providers are adept at spotting new search trends and quickly adapting to the needs of their users. If increasing numbers of people use popular search engines to seek out creative uses of language, these engines may well respond with new features to aid in the *creative information retrieval*[59] of linguistic innovations on the web. These developments will allow users to search for more than superficial textual matches to their queries, but for resonant alternatives that have the same deep meaning. Creative users will increasingly view the web as a vast and growing treasury of readymade expressions that can serve fresh creative purposes for those who retrieve them. The web would thus become the ultimate thesaurus and Duchampian companion, always on, always responsive, and always changing. For lovers of creative language, this would certainly be a golden egg worth cackling about.

Notes

Chapter 1

1 A good introduction to this topic is offered by Jim Steinmeyer's book *Hiding the Elephant: How Magicians Invented the Impossible*.

2 I refer here to the Vintage collected edition; see Conan Doyle (2009).

3 Conan Doyle (2009:177).

4 In this vein, Colton (2008) considers how our (mis)perceptions guide our appreciation of creativity.

5 Conan Doyle (2009:176). Giora *et al.* (2005) view this as 'ironic over-statement', noting that negation merely tones down the irony. We consider irony in Chapter 6.

6 Boden (1990/2004, 1999).

7 Sawyer (2006) takes a pin to a variety of romantic conceptions. See also Sawyer (2003) for an exploration of the collective creativity that emerges from group interactions.

8 Conan Doyle (2009:190).

9 Csíkszentmihályi (1990, 1996).

10 Orwell (1946). The essay is freely downloadable from many websites.

11 Bowdle and Gentner (2005). See also Veale and Hao (2007c) for a discussion of how some metaphors may begin their careers as similes.

12 Quoted in *The Guardian* on April 24, 2011 by Hitchens' friend, Martin Amis.

13 The court's decision, and the growing role of corpus linguistics in legal cases, is discussed by Ben Zimmer in the March 2011 edition of *The Atlantic* magazine.

14 Justice Roberts' opinion in *FCC v. AT&T INC. (No. 09-1279) 582 F. 3d 490*, reversed, can be read online at: http://www.law.cornell.edu/supct/html/09-1279.ZO.html.

15 Quoted in G. K. Chesterton (1933:85). Chesterton makes play of Shaw's dictum here, by noting 'Mr. Bernard Shaw said that the only golden rule is that there is no golden rule. He prefers an iron rule; as in Russia'. Much sport can be had by taking the second-hand metaphors of others at face value, as Chesterton does here to Shaw, for in playfully dismantling their metaphors we can also dismantle their arguments.

16 Kreuz and Glucksberg (1989), Kumon-Nakamura, Glucksberg and Brown (1995).

17 Sternberg and Lubart (1995, 1996), Sternberg (2003:106–23).

18 Harry Houdini, born Erik Weisz (later Ehrich Weiss), is such a remarkable subject that almost any book on the man is worth reading. I refer throughout this chapter to the 1997 biography by Kenneth Silverman, *Houdini!!! The Career of Ehrich Weiss.*

19 Silverman (1997:259).

20 Ibid.

21 Ibid.

22 Orwell's *Nineteen Eighty Four: A Novel* echoes many of the themes of his 1946 essay, and imagines how a totalitarian regime might use linguistic inventiveness to creatively disguise the insidious levers of state control.

23 Harry Houdini was the stage name of Ehrich Weiss. In a minor act of linguistic creativity, he chose the name to honour his hero, the French magician Robert-Houdin.

24 Silverman (1997:111).

25 Ibid.

Chapter 2

1 L. Frank Baum's *The Wonderful Wizard of Oz* was first published in 1900.

2 Wittgenstein (1969) notes 'One is often bewitched by a word. For instance, by the word "know" '. Wittgenstein (1953, para 29) declares: 'Philosophy is a battle against the bewitchment of our intelligence by means of language'.

3 Wittgenstein (1953, Section 38).

4 The designer, affectionately dubbed 'Kaiser Karl', was quoted on VOGUE. com on 9 February 2009: '[my sunglasses] They're my burka . . . I'm a little shortsighted, and people, when they're shortsighted, they remove their glasses and then they look like cute little dogs who want to be adopted'.

5 Aristotle's *Poetics.* S. H. Butcher's 1895 English translation of the original can be read online at MIT's *Internet Classics Archive*: http://classics.mit.edu/Aristotle/poetics.html.

6 *De Oratore* ('On the Orator'), book III. This passage is translated in McCall (1969).

7 Ortony (1979).

8 See Richard Ellmann's 1988 biography for a discussion of Wilde's work ethic.

9 Dennett (1991).

10 For example, this waggish retort occurs in Carruthers (2005:247).

11 Google's founders describe the workings of their search engine in Brin and Page (1998).

12 Lady Ada Byron's notes on Babbage's proposal for an analytical engine were published in *Taylor's Scientific Memoirs* in 1843, under the pseudonym A. A. L.

13 Amabile (1983).

14 Amabile (1996:35). Teresa Amabile's 1996 book, *Creativity in Context: Update to the Social Psychology of Creativity.* Westview Press, Colorado/Oxford.

15 In one episode of Star Trek titled *Return of the Archons* (season one), Kirk persuades a nefarious computer to commit suicide, citing the computer's lack of appreciation for creativity as a reason for its failure.

16 Penrose (1989, 1994).

17 The researcher Rosalind W. Picard popularized the term *Affective Computing* in her 1997 book of the same name.

18 This research area within Computer Science goes by the name *Sentiment Analysis*. See Pang and Lee (2008) for a survey.

19 Quoted in the *San Francisco Chronicle*, 14 May 2003.

20 In Aristotle's *Rhetoric*, book II. See also Morreall (1983:5).

21 Sawyer (2006).

22 Hennessy and Amabile (1988:13).

23 From *Odes* 1.11 by Quintus Horatius Flaccus, better known as 'Horace'.

24 Hanks' definitive book on TNE, *Lexical Analysis: Norms and Exploitations*, is forthcoming. For now, the key references are Hanks (1994) and Hanks (2004).

25 Giora (2003), Giora *et al.* (2004).

26 Maxson (1997:55).

27 Frost (1995:304).

28 From the Central Internal Affairs Directorate in Kemerovo. The thief was armed with an awl. The English is creative in parts and unintentionally hilarious in others. See http://eng.mvdrf.ru/news/13827/?print.

29 Gottlieb and Kimball (2000).

30 Hitchens (2010:165).

31 We can trace Hitchens' development process by comparing different drafts of his text. Curiously, the phrase 'paintbubbling hangover' was used in the *Sunday Times* extract of his book on 28 February 2010, prior to its official publication, but this was then changed to 'paint-stripping hangover' when the book was subsequently published.

32 Okakura (1964:15).

33 Chabon (2008:7).

34 Quoted in Behan (1965:159). The play in question was *The Hostage*. Behan's outburst serves as a forceful renunciation of what Michael Reddy (1979) has called the *conduit metaphor of language*.

35 Kavanagh (1972).

Chapter 3

1 For example, Bruner (1962) suggests that creativity often produces both an 'effective surprise' and the 'shock of recognition'.

2 The verdict from the *West-End Whingers* blog was 'Dull. Like watching paint dry, and as we all know, paint never dries'. http://westendwhingers. wordpress.com/2010/03/02/review-love-never-dies-Adelphi-theatre/.

3 Newell *et al.* (1963).

4 For a technical analysis of IBM's *Deep Blue* system, see Campbell *et al.* (2002).

5 Perkins (2001:46–96).

6 Everdell (1997:265).

7 Boden (1990, 1999). For a more formal treatment, see Wiggins (2006).

8 Ritchie (2006) offers a probing critique of Boden's transformational hypothesis.

9 See Douglas Hofstadter *et al.* (1995) for a good cross-section of Hofstadter's research.

10 Quoted in *Newsweek*, January 30, 1956, p. 56.

11 Quoted in Squire (2004:54).

12 See Douglas Hofstadter (1997) for an entertaining tour through the constraint-laden processes of creative translation.

13 Guilford (1950) gave renewed impetus to the field of creativity research with a paper simply titled 'Creativity'. Coincidentally, Alan Turing also published his seminal paper on AI in 1950. Guilford (1967) outlines the structure-of-intellect (SI) theory, in which divergent production is identified as 1 of 6 key intellectual processes.

14 Turner and Fauconnier (2002).

15 Ann Richards, July 18, 1988. Keynote address to the Democratic National Convention.

16 See Hofstadter and Mitchell (1995) for a description of the *CopyCat* project.

17 The March 2008 issue showed a picture of the governor with the caption *What Obama, McCain, Clinton and the rest can learn from Arnold Schwarzenegger*.

18 'The Governator' was the title of an article about Schwarzenegger in *The Guardian* newspaper, on August 8, 2003.

19 Crevier (1993).

20 McCarthy (1999).

21 See Koestler's masterful 1964 book *The Act of Creation*.

22 Attardo & Raskin (1991).

23 Schank & Abelson (1977).

24 Chafe (2007).

25 Raskin (1985).

26 For a skeptical view of the explanatory power of script conflict, see Veale (2004a).

27 Norrick (1986).

28 Suls (1972).

29 Attardo and Raskin (1991).

30 Oring (2003).

31 Goffman (1961) notes that 'As every psychotic and comic ought to know, any accurately improper move can poke through the thin sleeve of immediate reality'.

32 Ritchie (1999).

33 Attardo (1994:144) is careful to point out that 'the "resolution" of a joke is not supposed to get rid of the incongruity, but to co-exist and accompany it'. So resolution does not explain away incongruities, rather it enriches them with meaning.

34 The comedian Stewart Lee (2010:197) describes this means of joke production as *The Pull Back and Reveal*: 'the first part of a sentence creates a certain set of expectations . . . which is then reversed in the second half of the sentence as the frame of the picture, so to speak, widens to include details that, had they been evident initially, would have clarified the situation immediately'.

35 Hofstadter (1997), Hofstadter and Gabora (1989).

36 Though see Ritchie (2003) for a counter-balanced, critical view of the GTVH.

37 Attardo *et al.* (2002).

38 This is an anecdote widely told about Wolfit. For instance, see the Daily Telegraph on 12 April, 1993: 'The too, too divine days of Sir Donald.'

39 *The Economist* letters page, 25 March, 2010. See www.economist.com/node/15767227.

40 See Paulos (1982:97) for a less 'graphic' graphical interpretation.

41 For an introduction, see Saunders (1980).

42 Paulos (1982:75–97).

43 Quoted in Simon Hoggart's column in *The Guardian* newspaper, November 28, 2009.

44 Rozin *et al.* (2006).

45 See http://www.lyricstime.com/tab-benoit-garbage-man-lyrics.html.

46 The full text of the October 5, 1988 debate is available online from the *Commission on Presidential Debates* at http://www.debates.org.

47 Loewenstein and Heath (2009).

48 Thomas Scheff (2009:185–98).

49 Ricks (1980:54).

Chapter 4

1 *The Independent* newspaper ran an article by Andy Kershaw on September 23, 2005 titled *Bob Dylan: How I found the man who shouted 'Judas'*.

2 Used on page 62 of Matt Skinner's *Thirsty Work*. Octopus Publishing Group.

3 The term *vehicle* was popularized by the metaphor scholar Ivor A. Richards (see Richards, 1936). The term seems especially apt when you consider that *metaphor* literally means 'to carry over'.

4 Fauconnier and Turner (2002, chapter 8), and Turner (1993, chapter 9). [*Reading Minds*. Princeton University Press].

5 Glucksberg (1998, 2008).

6 Glucksberg and Keysar (1990) and Glucksberg and McGlone (2001).

7 See http://www.vegansoapbox.com/red-meat-is-the-donald-trump-of-cancer/.

8 In the work that first introduced the word-concept 'stereotype', Lippmann (1922:12) notes that 'Great men, even during their lifetime, are usually known to the public only through a fictitious personality'.

9 In a 1962 commencement address to Yale University.

10 A history of the Encyclopédie can be found in Blom (2005).

11 H. T. Price (1919).

12 Outlined in Montesquieu's monumental *De l'Esprit des lois* ('The Spirit of the Laws'), published in Geneva in 1748.

13 This hypothesis is advanced in Collins (2004).

14 Reissued by Filiquarian Publishing in 2007. The text of Lippmann's book is accessible via Project Gutenberg at http://www.gutenberg.org/cache/epub/6456/pg6456.html.

15 Lippmann (1922/2007:88).

16 Putnam (1975:256) argues 'Communication . . . does not presuppose that any particular stereotype be *correct*, or that the majority of our stereotypes remain correct forever.'

17 Putnam (1975:256).

18 The idea of 'inference-rich categories' as containers of social knowledge comes from Harvey Sacks (1995:41).

19 Pinker (2008:418).

20 Svennevig (1999:59–60).

21 Jung (1978:57).

22 Rosch (1975), Lakoff (1987:79–114) and Geeraerts (2006:146–65).

23 Tarantino (1994).

24 Lakoff (1987:79–114).

25 McLuhan and Watson (1970:20).

26 Ibid. and (p. 21)

27 Dickens (1845:1).

28 Ibid. (p. 153).

29 Norrick (1986).

30 Moon (2008).

31 Taylor (1954).

32 This computational work is described in Veale and Hao (2007a, 2007b, 2008). A multilingual version for Chinese similes is described in Veale, Hao and Li (2008).

33 Peacock (1816:154). Online at http://www.thomaslovepeacock.net/Headlong.html.

34 In line with the *salience-imbalance* view of Ortony (1979).

35 Adam Kilgarriff (2007).

36 Nonetheless, Keller and Lapata (2003) have shown that the web can be used as a reliable source for the general frequencies of simple phrases that do not occur in a local corpus.

37 The *Aristotle* system is described in Veale and Hao (2007b).

38 Orwell (1949).

39 Quoted in Ricks (1995:356).

40 Ricks (1995:357).

41 For example, Ricks (1995:356) admires William Empson's 'audacious compacting of clichés'.

Chapter 5

1 Ford and Crowther (1922).

2 Brown (2003).

3 Lee (2010).

4 Reported in an article in *The London Times* by Andrew Collins on August 15, 2009.

5 Afterword to King (1982).

6 *The Observer*, Sunday, September 20, 2009.

7 The Orwellian idea that some language is 'junk' is the guiding conceit of *Junk English* by Smith (2001).

8 Lakoff and Johnson (1980) and Lakoff (1987).

9 Johnson (1987).

10 Gibbs (1994).

11 Barnden (2006).

12 Lakoff and Johnson (1980:44).

13 Clarke (1997). The song is called 'Daisy Bell', and it contains the telling line 'I'm half crazy, all for the love of you'. HAL, of course, goes half crazy too.

14 Crouse and Trusheim (1988) provide a sceptical take on the SAT.

15 The analogies component of the SAT test has now been dropped. Adam Cohen's Op-Ed in the *New York Times* on March 13, 2005 ('An SAT Without Analogies Is Like: (A) A Confused Citizenry. . .') offers an interesting response to the decision.

16 Boryslawski (2004:191–4).

17 See, for example, the translation by Seamus Heaney (2001).

18 Freud (1905:93), Attardo (2001a:25), Veale (2007:191).

19 WordNet is described at length in Fellbaum (1998).

20 Veale (2004b) uses the lightweight lexical ontology *WordNet* (Fellbaum, 1998) to solve the SAT analogy set in Turney (2006), achieving approximately 40 per cent performance.

21 Turney (2006).

22 Quoted in *That's Shanghai* magazine, January 5, 2010.

23 *The Independent* newspaper, October 2, 2004. The article, by James Sherwood, is titled 'Orient express'.

24 Gentner (1983).

25 *BBC News*, November 4, 2002. See http://news.bbc.co.uk/2/hi/europe/2270642.stm.

26 For example, Gentner and Toupin (1986).

27 Glucksberg (2001), with a contribution from his colleague Mathew McGlone.

28 Glucksberg (2001:46).

29 Bowdle and Gentner (2005). See also Veale and Hao (2007c) for a discussion of how some metaphors may begin their careers as similes.

30 The 1950 film *Sunset Boulevard* was directed and co-written by Billy Wilder.

31 *Rolling Stone*, issue 1076, April 3, 2009.

32 Sadly, Amy Winehouse passed away in 2011, two years after Hawke offered this implied comparison to Janis Joplin, adding yet another layer of resonance to his blend.

33 Robert Mankoff (2002:88).

34 Obvious 'blend' movies are crossovers such as 2004's *Alien vs Predator*.

35 See, for example, Seth Grahame-Smith's 2009 parody mashup *Pride and Prejudice and Zombies*.

36 The Twitter hashtag #KanyeNew-YorkerTweets is used to mark tweets in which users pair cartoon images from the *New Yorker* with gnomic tweets from rapper Kanye West.

37 Fauconnier and Turner (1998, 2002).

38 Fauconnier (1994, 1997:42).

39 Veale (2006c) and Veale and Butnariu (2010:399) describe how blended word forms on the Web can be automatically harvested and interpreted.

40 Pass notes No 2,707: Sam Mendes. *The Guardian*, January 6, 2010.

41 Fauconnier and Turner (2002:332–3).

42 Wilde (1890/1988).

43 This is also the conceit at the heart of Irvine Welsh's 2006 novel, *The Bedroom Secrets of the Master Chefs*.

44 Fauconnier and Turner (1994).

45 See Geeraerts (2006) for a selection of basic readings.

46 Veale (2006a) and Veale *et al.* (1999).

47 For example, see Wilks (1978), Martin (1990), Fass (1991), Way (1991), Veale and Keane (1992), Veale & Hao (2008) and Shutova (2010).

48 For example, see Falkenhainer *et al.* (1989), Holyoak and Thagard (1989), Hofstadter *et al.* (1995), French (1995) and Veale and Keane (1997).

49 Veale and Hao (2007a, 2007b, 2008) and Veale *et al.* (2008).

50 Veale and O'Donoghue (2000) and Pereira (2007).

51 *Metaphorize* is described in algorithmic detail in Veale and Li (2011).

52 Lenat and Guha (1990).

53 This manual coding effort is described in Veale (2006b).

54 Quoted in Preston (1997:223).

Chapter 6

1 Carroll (1871/1992:198).

2 Martin (1990) provides good coverage on conventional metaphors.

3 Engel (1982:90).

4 Ibid. (1982:84).

5 Ibid. (pp. 104–42).

6 Ibid. (p. 105).

7 Ibid. (p. 108).

8 Ibid. (p. 128).

9 Ibid. (p. 132).

10 Ibid. (p. 137).

11 This quip is widely attributed to the late George Carlin; see Kessler (2007:188).

12 John Donne (1624) *Devotion XVII, Devotions upon Emergent Occasions*.

13 The song, by the band Lazlo Bane, is called 'Superman' and can be found on their 2002 album *All the Time in the World*.

14 Reddy (1979).

15 The notion that speakers must constantly take account of what they believe to be the intentions and beliefs of those they are communicating with, so that they can achieve successful communication by aligning their interpretation of each utterance to this inter-speaker model, is often called *intersubjectivity* (e.g. Verhagan, 2005). Intersubjectivity thus assumes that speakers can construct a good working theory of what is in the mind of others (e.g. Tomasello, 1999).

16 Though it is tempting to think of interpretation as a process performed solely by the listener, successful communication needs the speaker and the listener to work jointly toward a shard meaning. An influential theory of joint action in language is outlined by Herbert Clark in his 1996 book, *Using Language*.

17 Goffman (1961).

18 Giora *et al.* (2010).

19 Glucksberg (2001:46).

20 Quoted in the *New York Times* Op-Ed by Roger Cohen, July 8, 2009.

21 Grice (1975).

22 Clark and Gerrig (1984).

23 Attardo (2001b).

24 Kumon-Nakamura *et al.* (1995).

25 Giora *et al.* (2005).

26 Kumon-Nakamura *et al.* (1995:4).

27 Speir's (1981) biography of Chandler discusses his often-parodied way with similes.

28 Raymond Chandler (1940).

29 Raymond Chandler (1954).

30 Moon (2008).

31 Taylor (1954).

32 Veale and Hao (2010) and Hao and Veale (2010) present a Web-based computational mechanism for automatically detecting irony in similes.

33 The document in question is accessible at www.dummocrats.com/archives/000928.php.

34 Fishelov (1992).

35 From his 1969 album *Songs from a Room*. See leonardcohenfiles.com/album2.html#10.

36 Esuli and Sebastiani (2006).

37 Fellbaum (1998).

38 Whissell (1989).

39 More computational detail is provided in Veale (2011).

40 From Michael Jackson's 1987 *Bad* album, on the *Epic* record label.

41 Veale and Hao (2007a, 2008) show that Whissell's dictionary gives consistent results when assessing the pleasantness of Web stereotypes and their properties.

42 Ritchie (1999, 2003:46–58) argues that the foundational notion of incongruity in humour corresponds to a range of different logical criteria.

43 Conan Doyle (2009:111).

Chapter 7

1 Orwell (1946).

2 Sternberg and Lubart (1995, 1996) and Sternberg (2003).

3 Sternberg (2003:106).

4 Any roster of the most famous super-bombs in cinema history will inevitably include films that are actually quite good, such as 1963's *Cleopatra* (which cost $250 million in today's money, but recouped just $150 million), or 1987's *Ishtar* (which cost over $50 million and recouped just a quarter of that).

5 Quentin Tarantino is perhaps the most famous exponent of the investment theory in Hollywood. Recall his timely and profitable investment in John Travolta in *Pulp Fiction*.

6 Obendorf (2009:202).

7 Trott (2008:275).

8 Stephens and Brynner (2001:123).

9 Kuenzliand Naumann (1989:73).

10 Taylor (2009).

11 As decided in a 2004 survey of 500 'art experts' in the run-up to that year's Turner Prize award. See the *BBC* report, http://news.bbc.co.uk/2/hi/entertainment/4059997.stm.

12 Writing in *The Independent* on December 3, 2004, Richard Cook assumes it was written by Duchamp himself, while others assume it was written by the magazine's editor, Beatrice Wood. See http://www.independent.co.uk/news/world/europe/how-duchamp-made-a-splash-and-changed-art-forever-675093.html.

13 The original half-page article, which is unsigned and uncredited, can be viewed here: http://sdrc.lib.uiowa.edu/dada/blindman/2/05.htm.

14 Indurkhya (1992:359).

15 Joyce (1922/1990:55)

16 Giora (1997).

17 Giora and Fein (1999:242).

18 Though widely attributed to George Carlin, the late comedian appears to disavow the quip on his official website: http://www.georgecarlin.com/home/not_carlin.txt.

19 Ricks (1980:54).

20 The *double-grounding* evident in newspaper headlines and cartoon captions is analysed in Brône and Feyaerts (2005) and Brône and Coulson (2010).

21 *The Economist*, April 18, 2002. http://www.economist.com/node/1087375.

22 *The Economist*, September 21, 2011. http://www.economist.com/node/21530163.

23 This mocking sub-title for the Von Braun film was attributed to Mort Sahl in an article in *Time Magazine*, August 3, 1998 by Lance Morrow. However, the waggish remark 'but sometimes I hit London' also appears in the film itself.

24 Burke (1987:444), 'Reflections on the Revolution in France'.

25 This anecdote is recalled in Haffner's 2003 biography of Churchill, p. 142.

26 See Veale *et al.* (2006) for the first use of the term *trumping* in this sense.

27 Trumping might be seen as a deliberate misunderstanding of a complacent speaker's use of formulaic language by a sharper and more insightful interlocutor. However, as argued in Brône (2008), the ability to delve deeper into the true meaning of a cliché is actually a form of hyper-understanding.

28 Recounted in Stanford (1984:174).

29 F or instance,Verhagen (2005) argues that the understanding of linguistic expressions primarily consists of 'making inferences that lead to adequate next (cognitive, conversational, behavioral) moves'.

30 Hosting the 2010 Golden Globes awards while holding a glass of beer in his hand, British comedian Ricky Gervais welcomed the next announcer on stage with the quip: '*I drink as much the next guy . . . unless the next guy is Mel Gibson*'.

31 Post on the *Language Log* site by contributor Geoffrey Pullum, October 27, 2003. See http://itre.cis.upenn.edu/~myl/languagelog/archives/000061.html.

32 *The Economist*, October 9, 2003, in an article on Germany's bureaucracy titled 'Breathe or be Strangled'. See http://www.economist.com/node/2127649.

33 *Language Log* post by Geoffrey Pullum, January 16, 2004. Online at http://itre.cis.upenn.edu/~myl/languagelog/archives/000350.html.

34 'The battle of Rourke's drift'. Article in *The Guardian* newspaper, January 2, 2009. See http://www.guardian.co.uk/film/2009/jan/02/drama-wrestler-mickey-rourke.

35 Variety calls it 'slanguage'. http://www.variety.com/static-pages/slanguage-dictionary/.

36 On *The Guardian* newspaper's Sports blog. Article by columnist Marina Hyde on January 29th, 2009 titled 'Wrestling with the boundaries of taste'.

37 Title of article in *The Guardian* newspaper's *Lost in Showbiz* blog by columnist Marina Hyde, published on July 30, 2008.

38 Recounted in Hauser (1992:479).

39 This Ali example is analysed as an instance of Figure-Ground-Reversal in Veale (2009).

40 The stewardess appears to agree with Ali here, by echoing his words, yet she ironically undermines him. See Kreuz and Glucksberg (1989) for a discussion of echoing in irony.

41 Mach (1976) and Gendler (2000).

42 Gendler (1998).

43 Koestler (1959/1990) puts this in stronger terms, and describes scientists prior to Kepler and Galileo as 'sleepwalkers'.

44 Incongruity resolution is argued to be a common feature of jokes and thought experiments in DeMey (2005).

45 Koestler (1959/1990:500).

46 Moss (1993:294).

47 Gould (2000). See http://www.toutfait.com.

48 The phrase is used resonantly in the *AAA Essential Guide: Greece*, p. 43.

49 Warren (1946).

50 Bernstein and Woodward (1974).

51 Reported in *The Observer* newspaper, April 25, 2010.

52 Stallybrass *et al.* (2004). Some scholars suggest that Hamlet's 'the table of my memory' is a reference to his book of commonplaces.

53 See, for example, http://www.robotic-fish.net/.

54 Brants and Franz (2006).

55 Veale and Hao (2011) describe the workings of the *Jigsaw Bard* in more detail.

56 Recounted in Clarke (1997).

57 Recounted in Hill (2004).

58 See, for instance, Pinker (1995). See also Sampson (1999) for the opposing view. However, I use the word 'instinct' here in a weaker sense than either of these authors.

59 To start the ball rolling, Veale (2011) synthesizes many of the concepts in this book into a computational framework for *Creative Language Retrieval*.

Bibliography

Amabile, Teresa M. (1983). The social psychology of creativity: A componential conceptualization. *Journal of Personality and Social Psychology*, 45(2):357–76.

—(1996). *Creativity in Context: Update to the Social Psychology of Creativity*. Westview, Colorado.

Aristotle. (335 B.C./1997). *Poetics*. Translated by Malcolm Heath. Penguin Classics.

Attardo, Salvatore. (1994). *Linguistic Theories of Humor*. Walter de Gruyter, Berlin.

—(2001a). *Humorous Texts: A Semantic and Pragmatic Analysis*. Walter de Gruyter, Berlin.

—(2001b). Irony as relevant inappropriateness. *Journal of Pragmatics*, 32:793–826.

Attardo, Salvatore and Raskin, Victor. (1991). Script theory revis(it)ed: joke similarity and joke representational model. *Humor: International Journal of Humor Research*, 4(3):293–347.

Attardo, Salvatore, Hempelmann, Christian F. and Di Maio, Sara. (2002). Script oppositions and logical mechanisms: Modeling incongruities and their resolutions. *Humor: International Journal of Humor Research*, 15(1):3–46.

Barnden, John. (2006). Artificial Intelligence, figurative language and cognitive linguistics. In G. Kristiansen, M. Achard, R. Dirven and F. J. Ruiz de Mendoza Ibanez (Eds), *Cognitive Linguistics: Current Application and Future Perspectives*, pp. 431–59. Mouton de Gruyter, Berlin.

Baum, L. Frank. (1900). *The Wonderful Wizard of Oz*. George M. Hill, Chicago.

Behan, Dominic. (1965). *My Brother Brendan*. Leslie Frewin, London.

Bernstein, Carl and Woodward, Bob. (1974). *All The President's Men*. Simon & Schuster, New York.

Blom, Philipp. (2005). *Enlightening the World: Encyclopédie, The Book That Changed the Course of History*. Palgrave Macmillan, New York.

Boden, Margaret. (1990/2004). *The Creative Mind: Myths and Mechanisms*, Second edition. Routledge, London, UK.

—(1999). Computational models of creativity. In Robert J. Sternberg (Ed.), *Handbook of Creativity*, pp. 351–73. Cambridge University Press, Cambridge.

Boryslawski, Rafat. (2004). *The Old English Riddles and the Riddlic Elements of Old English Poetry*. Peter Lang, New York.

Bowdle, Brian F. and Gentner, Dedre. (2005). The career of metaphor. *Psychological Review*, 112(1):193–216.

Brants, Thorsten and Franz, Alex. (2006). *Web 1T 5-gram Version 1*. Linguistic Data Consortium, Philadelphia.

Brin, Sergey and Page, Larry. (1998). The anatomy of a large-scale hypertextual Web Search Engine. *Proceedings of the 7th International Conference on the World Wide Web.*

Brône, Geert. (2008). Hyper- and mis-understanding in interactional humor. *Journal of Pragmatics*, 40(12):2027–61.

Brône, Geert and Coulson, Seana. (2010). Processing deliberate ambiguity in newspaper headlines: double grounding. *Discourse Processes*, 47(1):1–25.

Brône, Geert and Feyaerts, Kurt. (2005). Headlines and Cartoons in the Economic Press: Double Grounding as a Discourse Supportive Strategy. In G. Jacobs and G. Erreygers (Eds), *Discourse and Economics*. John Benjamins.

Brown, Dan. (2003). *The Da Vinci Code*. Doubleday, New York.

Bruner, Jerome. (1962). The conditions of creativity. In J. Bruner (Ed.), *On Knowing: Essays for the Left Hand*. Harvard University Press, Cambridge.

Burke, Edmund. (1837). *The Works of the Right Hon. Edmund Burke*, Volume I. Samuel Holdsworth, London.

Campbell, Murray, Hoane, Joe and Hsu, Feng-hsiung. (2002). Deep blue. *Artificial Intelligence*, 134(1–2):57–83.

Carroll, Lewis. (1871/1992). *Alice in Wonderland: Alice's adventures in Wonderland and Through the Looking-Glass*. J. G. Ferguson, Chicago, Illinois.

Carruthers, Peter (2005). *Consciousness: Essays from a Higher-order Perspective*. Oxford University Press, Oxford.

Chabon, Michael. (2008). *Wonder Boys*. Harper Perennial (reissue), New York.

Chafe, Wallace. (2007). *The Importance of Not Being Earnest: The Feeling Behind Laughter and Humor*. John Benjamins, Amsterdam.

Chandler, Raymond. (1940). *Farewell, My Lovely*. Alfred A. Knopf, New York.

—(1954). *The Long Goodbye*. Alfred A. Knopf, New York.

Chesterton, Gilbert Keith. (1974). *St. Thomas Aquinas: 'The Dumb Ox'*, Image.

Clark, Herbert H. (1996). *Using Language*. Cambridge University Press.

Clark, Herbert H. and Gerrig, Richard J. (1984). On the pretense theory of irony. *Journal of Experimental Psychology: General*, 113:121–6.

Clarke, Arthur C. (1997). Foreword. In David E. Stork (Ed.), *HAL's Legacy: 2001's Computer as Dream and Reality*. MIT Press, Cambridge.

Collins, Michael. (2004). *The Likes of Us: A Biography of the Working Class*. Granta Books, London, UK.

Colton, Simon. (2008). Creativity versus the perception of creativity in computational systems. *Proceedings of the AAAI Spring Symposium on Creative Systems*, Stanford University, California.

Conan Doyle, Arthur. (2009). *The Complete Sherlock Holmes*. Vintage Classics, London, UK.

Crevier, Daniel. (1993). *AI: The Tumultuous Search for Artificial Intelligence*. Basic Books, New York.

Crouse, James and Trusheim, Dale. (1988). *The case against the SAT*. University of Chicago Press.

Csíkszentmihályi, Mihály. (1990). *Flow: The Psychology of Optimal Experience*. Harper and Row, New York.

—(1996). *Creativity: Flow and The Psychology of Discovery and Invention*. Harper Collins, New York.

DeMey, Tim. (2005). Incongruity-resolution in humor comprehension, scientific discovery and thought experimentation. *Logical and Logical Philosophy*, 14:69–88.

Dennett, Daniel. (1991). *Consciousness Explained*. Penguin books, Harmondsworth.

Dickens, Charles. (1845). *A Christmas Carol*. Bradbury & Evans, London.

Ellmann, Richard. (1988). *Oscar Wilde*. Vintage Books, New York.

Engel, S. Morris. (1982). *With Good Reason. An Introduction to Informal Fallacies*. St. Martin's Press, New York.

Esuli, Andrea and Sebastiani, Fabrizio. (2006). SentiWordNet: A publicly available lexical resource for opinion mining. *Proceedings of LREC-2006, the 5th Conference on Language Resources and Evaluation*, 24:417–22.

Everdell, William. (1997). *The First Moderns: Profiles in the Origins of Twentieth Century Thought*. University of Chicago Press, Chicago.

Falkenhainer, Brian, Forbus, Kenneth D. and Gentner, Dedre. (1989). Structure-mapping engine: Algorithm and examples. *Artificial Intelligence*, 41:1–63.

Fass, Dan. (1991). Met*: a method for discriminating metonymy and metaphor by computer. *Computational Linguistics*, 17(1):49–90.

Fauconnier, Gilles. (1994). *Mental Spaces: Aspects of Meaning Construction in Natural Language*. Cambridge University Press, Cambridge.

—(1997). *Mappings in Thought and Language*. Cambridge University Press, Cambridge.

Fauconnier, Gilles and Turner, Mark. (1994). *Conceptual Projection and Middle Spaces*. University of California at San Diego, Department of Computer Science Technical Report 9401.

—(1998). Conceptual Integration Networks. *Cognitive Science*, 22(2):133–87.

—(2002). *The Way We Think. Conceptual Blending and the Mind's Hidden Complexities*. Basic Books, New York.

Fellbaum, Christiane (Ed.). (1998). *WordNet: An electronic lexical database*. MIT Press, Cambridge.

Fishelov, David. (1992). Poetic and Non-Poetic Simile: Structure, Semantics, Rhetoric. *Poetics Today*, 14(1):1–23.

Ford, Henry and Crowther, Samuel. (1922). *My Life and Work*. Doubleday, Page & Company, New York.

French, Robert M. (1995). *The Subtlety of Sameness*. MIT Press, Cambridge.

Freud, Sigmund. (1905). *Jokes and Their Relation to the Unconscious*. W. W. Norton, New York.

Frost, Robert. (1995). *Frost: Collected Poems, Prose & Plays*. The Library of America.

Geeraerts, Dirk (Ed.). (2006a). *Cognitive Linguistics: Basic Readings*. Walter de Gruyter, New York.

—(2006b). Prototype theory: Prospects and problems. In Dirk Geeraerts (Ed.), *Cognitive Linguistics: Basic Readings*. Walter de Gruyter, New York.

Gendler, Tamar Szabó. (1998). Galileo and the indispensability of scientific thought experiment. *The British Journal for the Philosophy of Science*, 49(3):397–424.

—(2000). *Thought Experiment: On the Powers and Limits of Imaginary Cases*. Garland, New York.

Gentner, Dedre. (1983). Structure-mapping: A theoretical framework. *Cognitive Science*, 7(2):155–70.

Gentner, Dedre and Toupin, Cecile. (1986). Systematicity and surface similarity in the development of analogy. *Cognitive Science*, 10(3):277–300.

Gibbs, Raymond W., Jr. (1994). *The Poetics of Mind*. Cambridge University Press, Cambridge.

Giora, Rachel. (1997). Understanding figurative and literal language. The Graded Salience Hypothesis. *Cognitive Linguistics*, 7:183–206.

—(2003). *On Our Mind: Salience, Context, and Figurative Language*. Oxford University Press, Oxford.

Giora, Rachel and Fein, Ofer. (1999). Irony: Context and salience. *Metaphor and Symbol*, 14(4):241–57.

Giora, Rachel, Fein, Ofer, Ganzi, Jonathan, Levi, Natalie Alkeslassy and Sabah, Hadas. (2005). On negation as mitigation: The case of negative irony. *Discourse Processes*, 39(1):81–100.

Giora, Rachel, Fein, Ofer, Kronrod, Ann, Elnatan, Idit, Shuval, Noa and Zur, Adi. (2004). Weapons of Mass Distraction: Optimal Innovation and Pleasure Ratings. *Metaphor and Symbol*, 19(2):115–41.

Giora, Rachel, Fein, Ofer, Metuki, Nili and Stern, Pnina. (2010). Negation as a metaphor-inducing operator. In L. R. Horn (Ed.), *The Expression of Negation*. Mouton de Gruyter, Berlin/New York.

Glucksberg, Sam. (1998). Understanding metaphors. *Current Directions in Psychological Science*, 7:39–43.

—(2008). How metaphor creates categories – quickly! In Raymond W. Gibbs, Jr. (Ed.), *The Cambridge Handbook of Metaphor and Thought* (chapter 4). Cambridge University Press, Cambridge.

Glucksberg, Sam and Keysar, Boaz. (1990). Understanding Metaphorical Comparisons: Beyond Similarity. *Psychological Review*, 97(1):3–18.

Glucksberg, Sam and McGlone, Matthew. (2001). *Understanding Figurative Language: From Metaphors to Idioms*. Oxford University Press, Oxford.

Goffman, Erving. (1961). *Encounters: Two Studies in the Sociology of Interaction*. Allyn & Bacon, Boston.

Gottlieb, Robert and Kimball, Robert. (2000). *Reading Lyrics*. Pantheon books, New York.

Gould, Stephen J. (2000). The substantial ghost: Towards a general exegesis of Duchamp's artful wordplays. *Tout-Fait, The Marcel Duchamp Studies Online Journal,* 1(2).

Grice, H. Paul. (1975). Logic and conversation. In P. Cole and J. Morgan (Eds), *Syntax and Semantics 3: Speech Acts*. Academic Press, New York.

Guilford, Joy Paul. (1950). Creativity. *American Psychologist*, 5(9):444–54.

—(1967). *The Nature of Human Intelligence*. McGraw-Hill, New York.

Haffner, Sebastian. (2003). *Churchill*. Haus, London.

Hanks, Patrick. (1994). Linguistic norms and pragmatic exploitations, or why lexicographers need prototype theory, and vice versa. In F. Kiefer, G. Kiss and J. Pajzs (Eds) *Papers in Computational Lexicography: Complex–1994*. Hungarian Academy of Sciences, Budapest.

—(2004). The syntagmatics of metaphor and idiom. *International Journal of Lexicography*, 17(3):245–74.

Hao, Yanfen and Veale, Tony. (2010). An ironic fist in a velvet glove: Creative misrepresentation in the construction of ironic similes. *Minds and Machines*, 20(4):483–8.

Hauser, Thomas. (1992). *Muhammad Ali: His Life and Times*. Simon & Schuster, New Jersey.

Heaney, Seamus. (2001). *Beowulf: A New Verse Translation*. W. W. Norton, New York.

Hennessy, Beth A. and Amabile, Teresa M. (1988). The conditions of creativity. In Robert J. Sternberg (Ed.), *The Nature of Creativity: Contemporary Psychological Perspectives*. Chicago University Press, Chicago.

Hill, Marion. (2004). *Bletchley People: Churchill's Geese That Never Cackled*. The History Press.

Hitchens, Christopher. (2010). *Hitch-22: A Memoir*. Atlantic Books, London.

Hofstadter, Douglas R. (1997). *Le Ton Beau De Marot: In Praise of the Music of Language*. Basic Books, New York.

Hofstadter, Douglas R. and Gabora, Liane. (1989). Synopsis of the Workshop on Humor and Cognition. *Humor: International Journal of Humor Research*, 2(4):417–40.

Hofstadter, Douglas R. and Mitchell, Melanie. (1995). The copycat project: A model of mental fluidity and analogy-making. In Douglas R. Hofstadter and the Fluid Analogies Research Group, *Fluid Concepts and Creative Analogies. Computer Models of the Fundamental Mechanisms of Thought*. Basic Books, New York.

Hofstadter, Douglas R. and the Fluid Analogies Research Group. (1995). *Fluid Concepts and Creative Analogies. Computer Models of the Fundamental Mechanisms of Thought*. Basic Books, New York.

Holyoak, Keith J. and Thagard, Paul. (1989). Analogical Mapping by Constraint Satisfaction, *Cognitive Science*, 13:295–355.

Indurkhya, Bipin. (1992). Studies in Cognitive Systems. *Metaphor and Cognition: An Interactionist Approach*. Kluwer Academic, Dordrecht.

Johnson, Mark. (1987). *The Body in the Mind: The Bodily Basis of Meaning, Imagination, and Reason*. University of Chicago Press, Chicago.

Joyce, James. (1922/1990). *Ulysses*. Vintage International, New York.

Jung, Carl G. (1978). Approaching the Unconscious. In C. G. Jung (Ed.), *Man and His Symbols*. Picador, London.

Kavanagh, Patrick. (1972). *The Complete Poems of Patrick Kavanagh*. Peter Kavanagh (Ed.). The Goldsmith Press, Newbridge, Ireland.

Keller, Frank and Lapata, Mirella. (2003). Using the Web to obtain frequencies for unseen bigrams. *Computational Linguistics*, 29(3):459–84.

Kessler, Greg S. (2007). *Internet Wisdom: The Best of Internet E-mail Wit and Wisdom*. Authorhouse, Bloomington.

Kilgarriff, Adam. (2007). Googleology is bad science. *Computational Linguistics*, 33(1):147–51.

King, Steven. (1982). *Different Seasons*. Viking Press, New York.

Koestler, Arthur. (1964). *The Act of Creation*. Penguin Books, New York.

— (1959/1990). *The Sleepwalkers: A History of Man's Changing Vision of the Universe*. Arkana.

Kreuz, Roger J. and Glucksberg, Sam. (1989). How to be sarcastic: The echoic reminder theory of verbal irony. *Journal of Experimental Psychology: General*, 118(4):374–86.

Kuenzli, Rudolf E. and Naumann, Francis M. (1989). *Marcel Duchamp: Artist of the Century*. MIT Press, Cambridge.

Kumon-Nakamura, Sachi, Glucksberg, Sam and Brown, Mary. (1995). How about another piece of pie: The Allusional Pretense Theory of Discourse Irony. *Journal of Experimental Psychology: General*, 124:3–21.

Lakoff, George. (1987). *Women, Fire and Dangerous Things*. University of Chicago Press, Chicago.

Lakoff, George and Johnson, Mark. (1980). *Metaphors We Live By*. University of Chicago Press, Chicago.

Lee, Stewart. (2010). *How I Escaped My Certain Fate*. Faber & Faber, London.

Lenat, Douglas B. and Guha, Ramanathan V. (1990). *Building Large Knowledge-Based Systems*. Addison Wesley, Reading, Massachusetts.

Lippmann, Walter. (1922). *Public Opinion*. Reissued by Filiquarian, 2007.

Loewenstein, Jeffrey and Heath, Chip. (2009). The Repetition-Break plot structure: A cognitive influence on selection in the marketplace of ideas. *Cognitive Science*, 33:1–19.

Mach, Ernst. (1976). On Though Experiments. In *Knowledge and Error*. D. Reidel, translated by Thomas J. McCormack and Paul Foulkes. Dordrecht, Holland.

Mankoff, Robert. (2002). *The Naked Cartoonist*. Black Dog and Leventhal, New York.

Martin, James H. (1990). *A Computational Model of Metaphor Interpretation*. Academic Press, Boston.

Maxson, H. A. (1997). *On the Sonnets of Robert Frost*. McFarland, New York.

McCall, Marsh H. (1969). Cicero, De Oratore, III, 39, 157. *The American Journal of Philology*, 90(2):215–19.

McCarthy, John. (1999). Creative Solutions to Problems. *Proceedings of the AISB'99 Symposium on AI and Scientific Creativity*. Edinburgh, Scotland.

McLuhan, Marshall and Watson, Wilfred. (1970). *From Cliché to Archetype*. Viking Press, New York.

Moon, Rosamund. (2008). Conventionalized as-similes in English: A problem case. *International Journal of Corpus Linguistics*, 13(1):3–37.

Morreall, John. (1983). *Taking Laughter Seriously*. State University of New York Press, Albany, New York.

Moss, Jean Dietz. (1993). *Novelties in the heavens: rhetoric and science in the Copernican controversy*. University of Chicago Press, Chicago.

Newell, Allen, Shaw, J. Clifford and Simon, Herbert A. (1963). The process of creative thinking. In H. E. Gruber, G. Terrell and M. Wertheimer (Eds), *Contemporary Approaches to Creative Thinking*, 63–119. Atherton, New York.

Norrick, Neal R. (1986a). A frame-theoretical analysis of verbal humor: Bisociation as Schema conflict. *Semiotica: Journal of the International Association for Semiotic Studies*, 60(3–4):225–45.

— (1986b). Stock Similes. *Journal of Literary Semantics*, XV(1):39–52.

Obendorf, Hartmut. (2009). *Minimalism: Designing Simplicity*. Springer, London.

Okakura, Kakuzo. (1964). *The Book of Tea*. Dover Publications.

Oring, Elliott. (2003). *Engaging Humor*. University of Illinois Press, Urbana.

Ortony, Andrew. (1979). The role of similarity in similes and metaphors. In Andrew Ortony (Ed.), *Metaphor and Thought*. Cambridge University Press, Cambridge.

Orwell, George. (1946). Politics and the English language. *Horizon,* 13(76), April issue.

— (1949). *Nineteen Eighty Four: A Novel*. Secker and Warburg, London.

Pang, Bo and Lee, Lillian. (2008). Opinion mining and sentiment analysis. *Foundations and Trends in Information Retrieval*, 2(1–2):1–135.

Paulos, John Allen. (1982). *Mathematics and Humor*. University of Chicago Press, Chicago.

Peacock, Thomas Love. (1816). *Headlong Hall*. T. Hookham, Jun & Co, London.

Penrose, Roger. (1989). *The Emperor's New Mind*. Oxford University Press, Oxford.

—(1994). *Shadows of the Mind*. Oxford University Press, Oxford.

Pereira, Francisco Câmara. (2007). *Creativity and artificial intelligence: a conceptual blending approach*. Walter de Gruyter, Berlin and New York.

Perkins, David. (2001). *The Eureka Effect: The Art and Logic of Breakthrough Thinking*. W. W. Norton & Co, Pennsylvania.

Picard, Rosalind W. (1997). *Affective Computing*. MIT Press, Cambridge.

Pinker, Steven. (1995). *The Language Instinct*. Penguin Books, London.

—(2008). *The Stuff of Thought*. Viking Penguin, New York.

Preston, John. (1997). *Thought and Language*. Cambridge University Press, Cambridge.

Price, Hereward Thimbleby. (1919). *Boche and Bolshevik: Experiences of an Englishman in the German Army and in Russian Prisons*. John Murray, London.

Putnam, Hilary. (1975). *Mind, Language and Reality: Philosophical Papers*, Volume 2. Cambridge University Press, Cambridge.

Raskin, Victor. (1985). *Semantic Mechanisms of Humor*. D. Reidel, Boston.

Reddy, Michael J. (1979). The conduit metaphor: A case of frame conflict in our language about language. In A. Ortony (Ed.), *Metaphor and Thought*, pp. 284–310. Cambridge University Press, Cambridge.

Richards, Ivor A. (1936). *The Philosophy of Rhetoric*. Oxford University Press, Oxford.

Ricks, Christopher B. (1980). Clichés. In Leonard Michaels and Christopher B. Ricks (Eds), *The State of the Language*. University of California Press, Berkeley.

—(1995). *The Force of Poetry*. Oxford University Press, Oxford.

Ritchie, Graeme. (1999). Developing the Incongruity-Resolution Theory. *Proceedings of the AISB Symposium on Creative Language: Stories and Humour*, Edinburgh, Scotland.

—(2003). *The Linguistic Analysis of Jokes. Routledge Studies in Linguistics*, 2. Routledge, Abingdon.

—(2006). The transformational creativity hypothesis. *New Generation Computing*, 24(3):241–66.

Rosch, Eleanor. (1975). Cognitive representations of semantic categories. *Journal of Experimental Psychology: General*, 104(3):192–233.

Rozin, Paul, Rozin, Alexander, Appel, Brian and Wachtel, Charles. (2006). Documenting and explaining the common AAB pattern in music and humor: Establishing and breaking expectations. *Emotion*, 6(3):349–55.

Sacks, Harvey. (1995). *Lectures on Conversation*, Volume 1. Wiley-Blackwell, Oxford.

Sampson, Geoffrey. (1999). *Educating Eve: The 'Language Instinct' Debate*. Cassell, London.

Saunders, Peter Timothy. (1980). *An Introduction to Catastrophe Theory*. Cambridge University Press, Cambridge.

Sawyer, Keith R. (2006). *Explaining Creativity: The Science of Human Innovation*. Oxford University Press, Oxford, UK.

—(2003). *Group Creativity: Music, Theater, Collaboration*. Psychology Press. Philadelphia, Pennsylvania, USA.

Schank, Roger and Abelson, Robert P. (1977). *Scripts, Plans, Goals and Understanding*. Psychology Press. Philadelphia, Pennsylvania, USA.

Scheff, Thomas. (2009). A New Goffman: Robert W. Fuller's 'Politics of Dignity', chapter 7. In Jacobsen, Michael (Ed.), *The Contemporary Goffman*. Routledge, New York.

Shutova, Ekaterina. (2010). Metaphor identification using verb and noun clustering. *Proceedings of the 23rd International Conference on Computational Linguistics*.

Silverman, Kenneth. (1997). *Houdini!!! The Career of Ehrich Weiss*. Harper Collins, New York.

Smith, Ken. (2001). *Junk English*. Blast Books, New York.

Speir, Jerry. (1981). *Raymond Chandler*. Frederick Ungar, New York.

Squire, Jason E. (2004). *The Movie Business Book*, 3rd Edition. Simon & Schuster.

Stallybrass, Peter, Chartier, Roger, Mowery, J. Franklin and Wolfe, Heather. (2004). Hamlet's tables and the technologies of writing in Renaissance England. *Shakespeare Quarterly*, 55:379–419.

Stanford, William Bedell. (1984). *Ireland and the Classical Tradition*. Irish Academic Press, Dublin.

Steinmeyer, Jim. (2003). *Hiding the Elephant: How Magicians Invented the Impossible*. Da Capo Press, Cambridge, Massachusetts.

Stephens, Trent D. and Brynner, Rock. (2001). *Dark Remedy: The Impact of Thalidomide and Its Revival As a Vital Medicine*. Basic Books, New York.

Sternberg, Robert J. (2003). *Wisdom, Intelligence and Creativity Synthesized*. Cambridge University Press, New York.

Sternberg, Robert J. and Lubart, Todd I. (1995). *Defying the Crowd: Cultivating Creativity in a Culture of Conformity*. Free Press, New York.

—(1996). Investing in creativity. *American Psychologist*, 51(7):677–88.

Suls, Jerry M. (1972). A Two-Stage Model for the Appreciation of Jokes and Cartoons: An information-processing analysis. In Jeffrey H. Goldstein and Paul E. McGhee (Eds), *The Psychology of Humor*, 81–100. Academic Press, New York.

Svennevig, Jan. (1999). *Getting Acquainted in Conversation: A Study of Initial Interactions*. John Benjamins, Amsterdam.

Tarantino, Quentin. (1994). *Reservoir Dogs*. Faber and Faber, London.

Taylor, Archer. (1954). Proverbial Comparisons and Similes from California. *Folklore Studies* 3. University of California Press, Berkeley.

Taylor, Michael R. (2009). *Marcel Duchamp: Étant donnés* (Philadelphia Museum of Art). Yale University Press, New Haven.

Tomasello, Michael. (1999). *The Cultural Origins of Human Cognition*. Harvard University Press, Cambridge.

Trott, Paul. (2008). *Innovation Management and New Product Development*. Pearson Education.

Turing, Alan M. (1950). Computing machinery and intelligence. *Mind*, 59:433–60.

Turner, Mark. (1993). *Reading Minds*. Princeton University Press, Princeton.

Turney, Peter D. (2006). Similarity of semantic relations. *Computational Linguistics*, 32(3):379–416.

Veale, Tony. (2004a). Incongruity in humor: Root-cause or epiphenomenon? *The International Journal of Humor*, 17(4):419–28, a Festschrift for Victor Raskin.

—(2004b). WordNet sits the S.A.T.: A Knowledge-based Approach to Lexical Analogy. *Proceedings of ECAI-2004, the 16th European Conference on Artificial Intelligence*.

—(2006a). Computability as a test on linguistic theories. In G. Kristiansen, M. Achard, R. Dirven and F. Ruiz de Mendoza Ibáñez (Eds). *Cognitive Linguistics: Current Applications and Future Perspectives. Applications of Cognitive Linguistics.* Mouton de Gruyter, Berlin.

—(2006b). An analogy-oriented type hierarchy for linguistic creativity. *Journal of Knowledge-Based Systems,* 19(7):471–9.

—(2006c). Tracking the Lexical Zeitgeist with Wikipedia and WordNet. *Proceedings of ECAI-2006, the 17th European Conference on Artificial Intelligence.*

—(2007). Dynamic creation of analogically-motivated terms and categories in lexical ontologies. In Judith Munat (Ed.), *Lexical Creativity, Texts and Contexts (Studies in Functional and Structural Linguistics),* pp. 189–212. John Benjamins, Amsterdam.

—(2009). Hiding in Plain Sight: Figure-Ground Reversals in Humour. In G. Brône and J. Vandaele (Eds), *Cognitive Poetics: Goals, Gains and Gaps.* Mouton de Gruyter, Berlin.

—(2011). Creative language retrieval. *Proceedings of ACL 2011, the 49th Annual Meeting of the Association for Computational Linguistics.*

Veale, Tony and Butnariu, Cristina. (2010). Harvesting and understanding on-line neologisms. In Alexander Onysko and Sascha Michel (Eds), *Cognitive Perspectives on Word Formation.* Walter de Gruyter, New York.

Veale, Tony, Feyaerts, Kurt and Brône, Geert. (2006). The cognitive mechanisms of adversarial humor. *Cognitive Linguistics,* 19(3):305–39.

Veale, Tony and Hao, Yanfen. (2007a). Making Lexical Ontologies Functional and Context-Sensitive. *Proceedings of ACL 2007, the 45th Annual Meeting of the Association of Computational Linguistics,* 31(1):57–64.

—(2007b). Comprehending and generating apt metaphors: A Web-driven, case-based approach to figurative language. *Proceedings of AAAI-2007, the 22nd AAAI conference on Artificial Intelligence.*

—(2007c). Learning to understand figurative language: From similes to metaphors to irony. *Proceedings of CogSci-2007, the 29th Annual Meeting of the Cognitive Science Society.*

—(2008). A context-sensitive framework for lexical ontologies. *The Knowledge Engineering Review,* 23(1):101–15.

—(2010). Detecting ironic intent in creative comparisons. *Proceedings of ECAI-2010, the 19th European Conference on Artificial Intelligence.*

—(2011). Exploiting readymades in linguistic creativity. A System Demonstration of the Jigsaw Bard. *Proceedings of ACL 2011, the 49th Annual Meeting of the Association for Computational Linguistics.*

Veale, Tony, Hao, Yanfen and Li, Guofu. (2008). Multilingual Harvesting of Cross-Cultural Stereotypes. *Proceedings of ACL 2008, the 46th Annual Meeting of the Association of Computational Linguistics.*

Veale, Tony and Keane, Mark T. (1992). Conceptual scaffolding: A spatially founded meaning representation for metaphor comprehension, *Computational Intelligence,* 8(3):494–519.

—(1997). The Competence of Sub-Optimal Structure Mapping on 'Hard' Analogies. *Proceedings of IJCAI'97, the 15th International Joint Conference on Artificial Intelligence.* Nagoya, Japan.

Veale, Tony and Li, Guofu. (2011). Creative Introspection and Knowledge Acquisition. *Proceedings of AAAI-11, The 25th AAAI Conference on Artificial Intelligence.*

Veale, Tony and O'Donoghue, Diarmuid. (2000). Computation and blending. *Cognitive Linguistics*, 11(3–4):253–81.

Veale, Tony, O'Donoghue, Diarmuid and Keane, Mark T. (1999). Computability as a limiting cognitive constraint: Complexity concerns in metaphor comprehension. In M. Hiraga, C. Sinha and S. Wilcox (Eds), *Cultural, Psychological and Typological Issues in Cognitive Linguistics*. John Benjamins, Amsterdam.

Verhagen, Arie. (2005). *Constructions of Intersubjectivity*. Oxford University Press, Oxford.

Warren, Robert Penn. (1946). *All the King's Men*. Harcourt and Brace, New York.

Way, Eileen Cornell. (1991). *Knowledge Representation and Metaphor. Studies in Cognitive systems*. Kluwer Academic, Dordrecht.

Whissell, Cynthia. (1989). The dictionary of affect in language. In R. Plutchik and H. Kellerman (Eds) *Emotion: Theory and Research*, pp. 113–31. Harcourt Brace, New York, NY, USA.

Wiggins, Geraint. (2006). Searching for computational creativity. *New Generation Computing*, 24(3):209–22.

Wilde, Oscar. (1890/1988). *The Picture of Dorian Gray*. Penguin Classics.

Wilks, Yorick. (1978). Making Preferences More Active. *Artificial Intelligence* 11(3):197–223.

Wittgenstein, Ludwig. (1953). *Philosophical Investigations (Philosophische Untersuchungen)*. Translated by G. E. M. Anscombe. Blackwell, Oxford.

—(1969). *On Certainty (Uber Gewissheit)*. G. E. M. Anscombe and G. H. von Wright (Eds), translated by Denis Paul and G. E. M. Anscombe. Basil Blackwell, Oxford.

Index